STUDIES ON THE AFRICAN ECONOMIES

General Editors: Paul Collier and Jan Willem Gunning
Published in association with the Centre for the Study of African
Economies, University of Oxford

Editorial Board:
Paul Collier, *Director, Development Research Group, World Bank*, and
Professor of Economics, University of Oxford; Jan Willem Gunning,
*Professor of Economics, University of Oxford, and Free University,
Amsterdam*, and *Director, Centre for the Study of African Economies,
University of Oxford*; Ibrahim Elbadawi, *World Bank*; John Hoddinott,
*Research Fellow, International Food Policy Research Institute,
Washington, DC*; Chris Udry, *Professor of Economics, Yale University*

This important new series provides authoritative analyses of Africa's
economies, their performance and future prospects. The focus will be on
applying recent advances in economic theory to African economies to
illuminate and analyse the recent processes of economic reform and
future challenges facing Africa. The books, published in association with
the Centre for the Study of African Economies, will bring together top
scholars from universities and international organizations across the
world.

Titles include:

Arne Bigsten and Steve Kayizzi-Mugerwa
CRISIS, ADJUSTMENT AND GROWTH IN UGANDA
A Study of Adaptation in an African Economy

Paul Collier and Cathy Pattillo (*editors*)
REDUCING THE RISK OF INVESTMENT IN AFRICA

Paul Glewwe
THE ECONOMICS OF SCHOOL QUALITY INVESTMENTS IN
DEVELOPING COUNTRIES
An Empirical Study of Ghana

John Knight and Carolyn Jenkins
ECONOMIC POLICIES AND OUTCOMES IN ZIMBABWE
Lessons for South Africa

Jo Ann Paulson (*editor*)
AFRICAN ECONOMIES IN TRANSITION
Volume 1: The Changing Role of the State

Jo Ann Paulson (*editor*)
AFRICAN ECONOMIES IN TRANSITION
Volume 2: The Reform Experience

African Economies in Transition

Volume 1: The Changing Role of the State

Edited by

Jo Ann Paulson

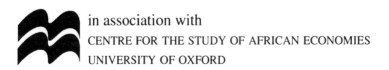

in association with
CENTRE FOR THE STUDY OF AFRICAN ECONOMIES
UNIVERSITY OF OXFORD

338.96
A2582
VOL. 1

First published in Great Britain 1999 by
MACMILLAN PRESS LTD
Houndmills, Basingstoke, Hampshire RG21 6XS and London
Companies and representatives throughout the world

A catalogue record for this book is available from the British Library.

ISBN 0–333–66545–7

First published in the United States of America 1999 by
ST. MARTIN'S PRESS, INC.,
Scholarly and Reference Division,
175 Fifth Avenue, New York, N.Y. 10010

ISBN 0–312–17751–8

Library of Congress Cataloging-in-Publication Data
African economies in transition / edited by Jo Ann Paulson.
p. cm.
Includes bibliographical references and index.
Contents: v. 1. The changing role of the state — v. 2. The reform
experience.
ISBN 0–312–17751–8 (v. 1). — ISBN 0–312–17752–6 (v. 2)
1. Africa—Economic policy. 2. Africa—Economic conditions—1960–
I. Paulson, Jo Ann.
HC800.A5674 1999
338.96—DC21   97–23323
                                                         CIP

© Centre for the Study of African Economies 1999

All rights reserved. No reproduction, copy or transmission of this publication may be made
without written permission.

No paragraph of this publication may be reproduced, copied or transmitted save with
written permission or in accordance with the provisions of the Copyright, Designs and
Patents Act 1988, or under the terms of any licence permitting limited copying issued by
the Copyright Licensing Agency, 90 Tottenham Court Road, London W1P 9HE.

Any person who does any unauthorised act in relation to this publication may be liable to
criminal prosecution and civil claims for damages.

The authors have asserted their rights to be identified as the authors of this work in
accordance with the Copyright, Designs and Patents Act 1988.

This book is printed on paper suitable for recycling and made from fully managed and
sustained forest sources.

10   9   8   7   6   5   4   3   2   1
08 07 06 05 04 03 02 01 00 99

Printed and bound in Great Britain by
Antony Rowe Ltd, Chippenham, Wiltshire

Contents

University Libraries
Carnegie Mellon University
Pittsburgh, PA 15213-3890

Notes on Contributors

CHRISTOPHER ADAM is University Lecturer in Development
Economics and a Research Associate at the Centre for the Study
of African Economies, University of Oxford. He received a
D.Phil. from Nuffield College, Oxford in 1992, and previously
worked as a macroeconomist in the Ministry of Finance of
Swaziland.

EDGARDO BARANDIARAN is Principal Economist at the World Bank
Resident Mission in Beijing, and was Principal Economist in the
Africa Region of the World Bank when this project was started.

ELLIOT BERG is a long-time consultant with a major role in past Africa
studies, and is presently with Development Alternatives Inc.

DAVID BEVAN is a Fellow of St John's College, Oxford, and a member
of the Centre for the Study of African Economies, University of
Oxford.

PAUL COLLIER is Director of the Development Research Group of the
World Bank, on leave as Professor of Economics, University of
Oxford, and a Fellow of St Antony's College, Oxford.

MICHAEL GAVIN is a Senior Economist in the Research Department at
the Inter-American Development Bank, and was Principal
Economist in the Africa Region of the World Bank when this
project was started.

JAN WILLEM GUNNING is Director of the Centre for the Study of
African Economies at the University of Oxford, on leave from
the Free University of Amsterdam.

JO ANN PAULSON is Senior Economist at the Financial Sector
Development Department of the World Bank, and was Senior
Economist in the Africa Region of the World Bank at the time
this project was started. She was formerly a faculty member of
the University of Minnesota.

Preface

The collected papers in these volumes are the outcome of a research programme initiated by Alan Gelb in the Transitional Economies Division of the World Bank and financed by Trust Funds from the Government of Japan. Staff support in the World Bank was arranged by Ishrat Husain.

The question for the project was whether there were lessons from African reform experience in the late 1980s and early 1990s that would ease the adjustment process in Mozambique. The search for lessons started with experience in countries with a similar background of strongly interventionist government and economic policy guided by socialism. This project turned out to be extremely difficult to execute. The African socialist countries are short of data, and lack a research community with time to undertake detailed investigation of past economic performance or to write scholarly papers. Many aspects of attempted reforms and economic management over the last decade have not been well documented, studied or debated. Furthermore the sample is limited because some of the African socialist countries are still mired in wars, making reforms impossible, while others have undertaken only mild reforms. Therefore over time the project shifted to a broader focus to look for lessons across a more diverse set of African countries.

The efforts of the authors of these studies to gather scarce information and data are gratefully acknowledged. There was also a dedicated pool of reviewers from the World Bank and academic institutions who kept the debates on the papers lively, and improved the quality of the work.

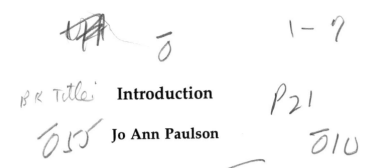

Introduction

Jo Ann Paulson

Economic performance in the majority of African countries has been disappointing since the 1970s. While there has been some improvement since the lows of the 1980s in reforming countries, the improvement has been short of what is needed to raise per capita income. The poor economic performance in Sub-Saharan Africa defies simple explanations, but there are some commonalities in past economic policies important for the discussions in this book. During the 1970s and part of the 1980s many governments on the African continent embraced state-led development strategies. Government efforts to use state institutions to compensate for the small base of indigenous capital and skill reflected the dominant development thinking at the time of independence.

The states that assumed a dominant role in the economy intervened in pricing and allocation, or monopolised the most important markets, e.g. foreign exchange, imports, credit, food staples for urban areas and primary commodity exports. Many states taxed agricultural or mineral exports heavily and invested in import-substituting industries operating as domestic monopolies protected through restrictive trade regimes. The vast majority of the population continued in smallholder agriculture, interacting with the broader economy through the state input and output marketing institutions. Cheap urban food policies were the rule, and production incentives and support services for smallholder agriculture were neglected. Throughout the economy, the private sector was at best ignored or at worst suppressed. This development strategy left undiversified economies with critical commercial functions assigned to the public sector and rigid economic policies, poorly equipped to respond to changing international economic conditions and terms-of-trade shocks. These policies exacerbated the other structural weaknesses inherited by many African countries.

There is a growing consensus that African countries need to moderate state-led development strategies, adjust the role of government in the economies, and reduce reliance on direct state production and control of markets. This means rethinking the mix of private and public activities and downsizing the state sector while strengthening the state functions needed to support markets; stressing efficiency of resource use for activities that remain in the public sector, and expanding the use of markets and allowing greater participation by the private sector. But reorientating the mix of state and private activities is not straightforward. The traumatic economic transition across the former Soviet Union has reinforced the pitfalls of liberalisation without clear property rights, laws and regulations, the difficulty of privatising into poorly developed markets, the possibility of perverse policy interactions, and the problems of establishing credibility for economic reforms.

This project was organised to examine the process, problems, and lessons learned as African countries attempted to recover from the economic decline of the 1980s by reorientating policies away from state dominance of the economy. The discussions draw from experiences across the continent, but emphasise the subset of African countries that strongly embraced statist economic policies in the 1970s and 1980s by declaring themselves Marxist. These countries have some of the most unfavourable initial conditions for reforms, and represent a convenient group to discuss early experience in trying to adjust the role of the state.[1]

Outline of the Volume

This collection of essays and studies was commissioned in 1992 and 1993. The authors were asked for their reflections on lessons learned from attempts to liberalise African economies, focusing on reforms needed to deal with the distortions and institutional structures from the period of state-led development policies. Some examples include administered allocation replacing markets; government bureaucracies that directly intervened in markets rather than developing the legal and regulatory framework for indirect control; fiscal budgets stretched across commercial activities as well as traditional public sector activities; capital-intensive parastatal industries, technologically outdated and starved of rehabilitation financing; and a suppressed and nervous private sector operating in an incomplete and frequently inconsistent framework of property rights, laws, regulations, and economic institutions. These issues loom large in the early stabilisation and structural adjustment efforts of not only the African Marxist states, but also other African countries of different political orientation that assigned an important economic role to the state.

The objectives of this project were modest. While the data and information were very spotty, the authors used the available evidence to discuss the process, problems and lessons from attempted reforms to lift some of the most distorting market restrictions. They tried to stimulate debate on the process of moving away from state control over critical activities in the economy. The work in this project was divided into four areas of inquiry and debate. The first set of papers deal with adjusting the role of the state in macroeconomic policy. The second section discusses moving away from direct government production through state enterprises. The third section (Part I of Volume II) includes studies on aspects of reforms in Mozambique, Angola, Congo, Madagascar, and Tanzania. The fourth section (Part II, Volume II) discusses government policy in the agricultural sector.

Part I: the Role of the State in Economic Reforms

The first set of papers focuses on the role of the state in setting policies that impact on macroeconomic performance, i.e. lifting price controls, trade reform, liberalising foreign exchange markets, and financial sector reforms. Another issue taken up in this section is the link between government policy and incentives for private investment during transition. This issue becomes crucial in setting transitional strategies in the search for investment to rehabilitate the economy or find new sources of growth.

The first paper, by Jo Ann Paulson and Michael Gavin, gives an overview of the economic performance of the countries covered in the study from 1980 to the mid-1990s. The aggregated data suggest that several of these countries suffered strong declines in economic performance during the early 1980s. After about five years of economic reforms, many of the countries had regained the ground lost during the period of weak economic performance. A brief review of the reform programmes in each country is given in the appendix to the chapter.

Edgardo Barandarian reviews the performance of African socialist economies with special emphasis on Angola, and concludes that while reforming countries appear to have made some progress in stabilising and liberalising prices, there has been little progress in reforming government or setting the legal foundation for private sector development. Barandarian attributes the lack of progress to the inability to reform government institutions.

Paul Collier and David Bevan review fiscal reforms; lessons from liberalising financial markets given the overhang of government indebtedness, decontrol of prices, and trade reforms with the potential interactions among these four types of reforms. On credit, price and trade liberalisation, they point out that removing micro-economic controls will have macroeconomic repercussions leading to potential incompatibility in the reform programme, i.e. an unsustainable balance of payments position or budget deficit. This plays into a very difficult problem in African reforms – lack of credibility.

Many African states made fixed exchange rates the central pillar of economic policy supported by government control, or heavy taxation of export markets and import rationing. Paul Collier and Jan Willem Gunning argue that governments which used fixed overvalued exchange rates as part of the control regime under socialism would find it difficult to gain credibility for their reforms unless moving to a flexible exchange rate determined by the market. Their paper focuses on the case found in most reforming socialist economies, few domestic banks and government control of the supply of foreign exchange. For this institutional arrangement they argue that use of *bureaux de change* with an interbank market is probably superior to an auction.

The legacy of state-led development includes dependence on public sector investment with severely constrained private sector activities and investment opportunities. For countries coming out of this situation, it is common to find that while parallel markets operate more openly and private agents enter activities requiring limited fixed investment such as trading and marketing, the first years of reform evidence limited private investment in the economy. This observation makes it tempting to opt for large public investment programmes that may rebuild the public sector. Investment issues are discussed by several authors, Collier and Gunning, Gavin, and Luiz Pereira da Silva and Andrés Solimano.

Collier and Gunning were asked to look at early investment behaviour by the private sector. They characterised the starting conditions for reforms in an African socialist economy as a significant, though concealed, part of the asset portfolio in foreign assets, a high level of inventories which is not recognised because firms appear to be input-constrained, a high proportion of fixed investment in imported capital but little non-tradeable capital, and neglect of the export sector. They argue that investment during the transition phase is likely to be sub-optimal. Relative price shifts, as well as the large inherited stock, discourage investment in imported capital. Investment in non-tradeable capital is seen as high risk since, even with liberalisation, there is uncertainty and lack of credibility in government policy. Also markets in capital goods are thin, reducing marketability and discouraging initial investment.

Collier and Gunning argue that there is little the government could or should do to increase investment during the transition. Cheap credit is not the answer since lack of credit is not one of the root causes of low investment and considerable savings may have been accumulated during the socialist period. But there are a few actions that may be beneficial, e.g. reducing the regulatory burdens on investment; easing constraints on the construction industry; undertaking policy actions that increase credibility of the reform programme to reduce the risk perceived by investors; government investment in non-tradeable capital that is then leased to the private sector; or temporarily undervaluing the exchange rate to attract repatriation of private resources held in foreign assets.

Part II: the Enterprises: Public and Private

The question of reforming public enterprises and/or privatisation has not had centre stage in the policy debates in Africa, although it is becoming more important over time. The first priority for most African governments has been to try and revive existing enterprises in the search for a supply response. Discussions on public enterprise reform or privatisation usually have been second or third round issues. There is, of course, variation in progress across the continent in commercialising parastatals and closing loss-making enterprises. However, it remains true that very few African countries have made privatisation a central focus of reforms, and efforts to commercialise public enterprises have been selective rather than systemic. This stands in contrast to the early stages of post-socialist transition in Eastern Europe and the former Soviet Union, where privatisation started early and was seen as central not only to improving efficiency of resource use, but also in political transformation.

The interested parties in the African dialogue on privatisation are far from a consensus. Instead, almost every aspect of this debate has been contentious, especially in the socialist countries targeted in this study. By their actions, many African governments have shown that financial discipline on the public enterprises and privatisation is not a priority, and there seems to be fear that the cost of enterprise reform will be deindustrialisation. In contrast, outside advisers and donors have pushed for privatisation, or at least more rigorous public enterprise reforms, and the closure of loss-making enterprises. The concern is that indirect budgetary leakages to the parastatals have undermined fiscal and monetary control, and a reduced government role in commercial activities may be necessary to gain credibility and build confidence for new private sector investment. The dialogue has led to much heat, many classification exercises and feasibility studies preparing for privatisation, but little action in many countries during the early years of reform. Now there is strong disagreement on whether lack of progress should be attributed to weak political will or to the inhospitable economic environment for privatisation. It is very difficult to bring data and analysis into this cloudy area. The financial and economic information available on the parastatal sectors is very spotty and unreliable in most African countries and incredibly weak in the sample countries for this study.

The lead paper in the public enterprise section focuses on whether African governments have changed their role as direct producers of goods and providers of services. Elliot Berg was asked to review the evidence available, survey what policy options had been tried, outline what seemed to have worked and what has failed, and focus on the operational lessons for the next stage of reforms. Berg found that privatisation had not made much headway in Africa at the time of the survey. Four constraints on privatisation were believed to be common: heavy aid inflows allowed governments to continue the soft budget constraint on parastatals; governments had failed to convince the private sector of a level playing field; there was uncertainty about the macroeconomic policy

environment and continuing controls on the private sector; and
there was weak state implementation capacity for complex
privatisation programmes. Berg argues that since traditional
privatisation efforts have been slow to show results, governments
should supplement these with non-traditional privatisation
programmes, e.g. leasing, management contracts, contracting-out,
internal divestiture, or fragmentation.

Christopher Adam, in his comment on Berg's paper, argues that
there are transitional problems in African countries that have
pursued state-led development policies, such as lack of a regulatory
framework and the potential for predation in the markets formerly
monopolised by state enterprises, so governments should be
cautious about accelerating privatisation efforts. Adam also
discusses constraints that slow privatisation, e.g. the nature of the
embodied capital stock, which he argues is likely to be unprofitable
at new relative prices once the economy is liberalised, and financial
markets are weak. While Adam believes it may be unwise to
privatise quickly, he argues that governments should move ahead
to privatise small enterprises, commercialise the parastatals, and
reform regulatory, trade and anti-monopoly policies at an earlier
stage. Like Berg, Adam thinks there is a role for non-divestiture
privatisation.

Note

1. The project does not attempt comprehensive evaluation of the
   reform experience of the Afro-Marxist states, but there is
   summary information given in Chapter 1 by Paulson and Gavin.
   There is little reliable information and data available on these
   countries. Instead, the effort was to pull lessons from experience
   of specific reform attempts from these economies, as well as
   other African countries.

Part I

The State in Macroeconomic Reforms

1 The Changing Role of the State in Formerly-Socialist Economies of Africa

Jo Ann Paulson and Michael Gavin[1]

Introduction

Beginning in the middle of the 1980s, a number of African economies redirected their development strategies away from the avowedly Marxist, state-dominated approach that they had adopted after independence, towards strategies that made better use of market mechanisms, and that strove to reorientate the role of the state in the economy. Many of the stages in these reform programme are similar to the steps taken by the formerly socialist economies of Asia, and East and Central Europe, and in the major liberalisations undertaken in many Latin American economies during the 1980s to introduce and strengthen capitalist structures. But while these other episodes have been the subject of much study, rather less is known about what happened in the African cases, and why.

The studies in this book attempt to improve our understanding of these reforms, through a number of approaches, including country studies and analyses of specific sectors. In this chapter we set the stage for those studies with a brief review of the economies, a sketch of the reform programmes that were implemented, and an overview of some key reform outcomes. The appendix to this chapter gives more details on the individual countries.

The information base upon which the chapter relies is limited; most of the countries are very poor, quite small, and as a result poorly documented. But some stylised facts emerge with sufficient clarity to pose important questions about the reforms. The data suggest that the reform programmes generally halted the marked deterioration of macroeconomic conditions that characterised the pre-reform period. In most cases production stopped declining, investment and output in the manufacturing sector stopped falling, and exports began to grow in real terms. But, while economic collapse was typically halted, the reform programmes have been able to recover lost ground, but have not triggered a strong recovery of income and output.

11

As we discuss in more detail below, the absence of a strong response of output, investment, and sectoral composition raises important questions about the course that the programmes have taken, and may shed light on reasons for the somewhat unspectacular results achieved so far. In the conclusion of the chapter, we raise an interpretation of the evidence, which raises the question whether the role of the state has really been transformed, or merely the mechanisms through which it seeks to achieve its ends.

The Sample Economies

This chapter, and the studies that follow, draw examples from across the African continent, but the emphasis is on countries that declared themselves Marxist in the late 1960s or early 1970s and therefore started economic liberalisation with a 15–20 year legacy of state domination of the economy: Angola, Benin, Congo, Ethiopia, Guinea, Madagascar, Mozambique, Somalia, and Tanzania.[2] These countries are related in this economic and political orientation, which we discuss below, and also in their poverty. The countries considered in this chapter include some of the poorest in the world; indeed, according to World Bank estimates, Mozambique, Ethiopia and Tanzania are ranked as the first, second, and third poorest countries in the world, respectively.

Of the nine countries in Table 1, only oil-producing Angola and Congo have incomes above the African average. Despite that oil income, in both countries many indicators of economic and social development, such as life expectancy and infant mortality, remain low, even by African standards. The formerly-socialist economies, in general, are below SSA averages on many social and health indicators. Average life expectancy at birth is 52 for Sub-Saharan Africa. While Madagascar, Benin, Congo, and Tanzania are close, or just slightly below that average, several of these countries are considerably worse, especially Angola at 47, Mozambique at 46, Guinea at 44, and presumably Somalia. In the indicators of education and literacy given here, Madagascar and Tanzania, are comparable to or better than the averages for Sub-Saharan Africa, despite much lower per capita incomes. Unfortunately, as is discussed below, the economic and political foundations for this progress proved inade-

Table 1: *Basic Indicators: African Socialist Economies*

	Population in mid-1994 (millions)	GDP (millions of US$, 1994)	GNP per capita		Adult Illiteracy (%) 1995	Urban Population % of Total 1995	Primary School Enrolment (%) 1991–93
			Atlas $ 1994	Average Annual % Growth 1985–94			
Average:							
Sub-Saharan Africa			451	-1.2	43	31	73
excl. South Africa			259	-1.0		29	69
excl. S. Africa and Nigeria			245	-1.5		27	69
Angola	10.7	7,238	..	-7.0		32	
Benin	5.2	1,927	370	-0.8	63	31	64
Congo	2.5	2,403	640	-2.7	25	59	..
Ethiopia	53.4	8,415	130	-0.7	65	13	23
Guinea	6.5	2,548	510	1.2	64	30	46
Madagascar	13.1	2,775	230	-1.7	..	27	73
Mozambique	16.6	2,060	80	3.5	60	34	60
Somalia	9.1	..	..	-1.2	..	26	..
Tanzania	28.8	4,412	140	0.8	32	24	70
Median SSA (47)	6.4	2,374.8	370	-0.6	44.0	31.3	71
excl. S. Africa and Nigeria	6.2	2,360.5	370	-0.6	45.0	31	70
Median AfSE (9)	10.7	2,661.4	230	-0.8	61.5	29.6	64

Source: World Bank, Africa Development Indicators. AfSE is formerly-socialist African economies.

quate to sustain itself, and social programmes suffered greatly as the economies declined in the 1980s.

African Socialism

This is not the place for an extended discussion of the nature of African socialism.[3] But a few details are relevant for setting the initial conditions. Between 1967 and 1975 a number of African countries adopted Marxism-Leninism as official doctrine and maintained that orientation at least through the early 1980s. As Young (1982) pointed out, between 1967 and 1975, nearly 20 per cent of African states had defined themselves as Afro-Marxist states. Tanzania was first, when in the 1967 Arusha declaration, six years after independence, its leadership proclaimed a shift toward an economic strategy based upon 'socialism and self-reliance'. In 1969, the new military regime of Marien Ngouabi in Congo-Brazzaville adopted Marxism-Leninism. The army rulers of Somalia followed the next year, as did the military regimes in Benin (1974), Madagascar (1975), and Ethiopia (1976). The newly independent countries that emerged from the disintegration of the Portuguese colonial empire, Mozambique, Angola, Guinea-Bissau, Cape Verde, and Sao Tome e Principe, moved towards Marxism-Leninism several years after independence. Few countries adopted Marxist-Leninism after 1975. We follow Young in accepting self-definition in political orientation and do not enter the debate on ideological depth or purity of commitment.[4] What is important is that these countries chose a strategy dependent on state-led economic growth, replaced markets with administered allocation and pricing in key sectors of the economy, and suppressed private sector activities.

While there was significant variation in the way that Afro-Marxist states controlled the economies, there were similarities that grew out of the structural characteristics of the economies and the time of adopting Marxism as well as the choice of economic strategy. These economies were called 'centrally planned', but the planning was not comprehensive. Instead the state attempted to control the economies through expansive fiscal policy, selective nationalisation, ownership of the 'commanding heights', and control over critical markets, e.g. pricing and allocation of scarce foreign exchange, imports, credit, urban food supplies, primary commodity exports, and skilled labour. Price controls were pervasive, as were monopoly state trading companies. These states nationalised or built parastatal industrial sectors, small in absolute size, but large relative to the formal economy. The industrial parastatals were protected from import and private domestic competition. The framework of price controls, implicit subsidies on imported inputs through overvalued exchange rates, credit at negative real interest rates, and access to public investment funds channelled from donors or extracted from state export monopolies, meant that the industrial parastatals were heavily subsidised from national resources. The lack of either trade or domestic competition robbed the economy of incentives to rationalise resource use.

Afro-Marxist governments either did not try or failed to collectivise agricultural production, although most nationalised all land and had a state-owned large farm sector. For a period, Tanzania attempted villagisation programmes, as did Ethiopia after land reforms (see Pryor, 1992). But the vast majority of the population continued in smallholder agriculture with the allocation of land still governed by traditional practices, with some input from the local party bureaucracy. State control of the agricultural sector was through input and output marketing channels, as well as the system of state distribution of consumer goods and price controls. Most of these states held monopolies on the marketing of the main food grains and all cash crop exports,[5] and the major agricultural inputs, especially fertiliser. Government heavily taxed cash crop exports through exchange rate appreciation of the late 1970s and early 1980s and the operation of inefficient monopoly export agencies. Cheap urban food policies were the rule and production incentives were neglected. Smallholder agriculture provided the bulk of employment but got very little from the government in support services or resources. Resources were channelled to the small but inefficient state or large farm sectors, especially in Ethiopia.

It would be artificial to claim a sharp distinction in structure or policy among the mixed, or even the market economies, and the socialist economies of Africa. In the development strategies adopted across the continent, the states heavily taxed agricultural or mineral exports through the state marketing institutions and channelled resources into state parastatals. Very few African countries gave sufficient attention to building infrastructure for private sector growth. However most mixed or market African economies had basic laws, regulations, property rights, tax systems, and support institutions for a private sector, albeit with less favourable treatment than given to state enterprises and activities. In the socialist economies, outside smallholder agricultural production, it was common to find that there was almost no infrastructure for a private sector, and state hostility had driven any private sector activities underground. There was a strong ideological and political bias against profits, commercial behaviour, and foreign investment. Therefore the Afro-Marxist states carried some of the patterns seen elsewhere on the continent to extremes, leaving a legacy of over-extended state structures, distorted and suppressed markets, undeveloped or missing legal and regulatory infrastructure for a private sector, and very nervous domestic entrepreneurs operating in parallel markets.

The macroeconomic repercussions of over-built industrial sectors operating under soft budget constraints, state monopoly banking systems, distorted pricing, and rewards for unproductive rent-seeking activities were devastating. These countries had dismal economic performance during the 1970s and 1980s. During the early 1980s, Young found that countries that professed African capitalism did better than the African populist-socialists or the Afro-Marxists (Young, 1982). There are of course exceptions, and some of these countries were able to exploit mineral and oil exports, e.g. oil in Congo, but in general the orientation of policy set the parameters for economic performance. In addition, the problems of distorting policies were compounded or dominated by proxy wars supported by outside interests in several of these countries, notably Mozambique, Angola, Ethiopia, and Somalia.

The Reforms

By the early 1990s most of the African socialist states were moving away from affiliation with Marxism. Those governments renounced Marxist-Leninism (Benin), distanced themselves from the doctrine (Angola and Mozambique) declared that for their economy Marxism-Leninism had failed (Ethiopia) or simply reached a state of ideological exhaustion (Guinea-Bissau, Madagascar, Sao Tome).

In other countries, including Angola and Congo, the regimes had moved quite far from their Marxist ideological roots.[6]

There are several important reasons for this reorientation of economic strategy, including disappointing economic performance in the early 1980s, which left many countries in a state of crisis; the shifting of political leadership to a younger generation more sympathetic to market structures; the easing of Cold War tensions allowing several of these countries to end civil wars; and, in the last few years, widespread political protests forcing the governments to move to multi-party elections.

The Economic Context

Economic performance deteriorated in many African countries in the late 1970s and early 1980s, and the economies we study here had some of the sharpest declines. Of course, generalisations about economic performance across Africa, even just the subset of countries discussed here, is a dangerous exercise. But despite local variation, there are important common patterns.[7]

The reasons for the economic decline are complex. External factors certainly played a role. The second oil price shock in 1979 adversely affected oil-importing economies, and recession in the industrialised countries pushed commodity prices lower. At the same time, foreign financing became scarce and expensive after late 1979. But the policy response to these external shocks often aggravated their effects, and in many cases even transformed favourable shocks into crises.

Many African countries had benefited from a temporary coffee price increase after the Brazilian crop was destroyed in 1976, and some of the worst economic performance was seen in the states that had used these higher commodity prices to finance hard-to-reverse expansions of the role of the state, and to launch massive public investment programmes. By the early 1980s, declining terms of trade and higher international interest rates revealed bloated and unsustainable levels of fiscal expenditure. The economies with large state sectors were among the hardest hit, as exemplified by the virtual economic collapse of Madagascar and Tanzania in the early 1980s.

In general, countries were slow to devalue and instead tightened rationing systems for foreign exchange and imports to deal with deteriorating balance of payments situations. In a vicious cycle, import compression led to lower capacity utilisation, inflation, soaring parallel exchange rate premia, and shortages of consumer goods, which in turn adversely affected incentives to produce the tradeables required to finance imports. Public investment budgets were overstretched and physical infrastructure was not maintained. In many countries, economic collapse began to undermine hard-won improvements in education, health and other social services.

The Political Context

The change in economic strategy in several of these countries was not associated with a major political upheaval or rejection of existing political structures. The typical pattern was for policy modification to start under ageing socialist leaders and be accelerated with change in leadership. Despite this, the process of economic reforms may have been eased by the generational change of leadership that started in the mid-1980s and the push for elections across the African continent in the early 1990s. For over a decade after independence, the political systems in Madagascar, Tanzania, Benin, Congo, and Guinea were under control of the first generation of post-independence leadership. The first 'changing of the guard' came with Sékou Touré's death in Guinea in 1984, followed quickly by a military take-over and a shift in economic policies. There was a change in leadership in Mozambique in November 1986 when Samora Moises Machel died in a plane crash and Joaquim Alberto Chissano became president. While Mozambique had started reforming the economy as early as 1984, the reforms accelerated in 1987. However, for years after the shift in economic policies started, the civil war intensified and overwhelmed announced economic reforms.

Julius Nyerere stepped aside as President of Tanzania in November 1985, but remained chairman of the sole political party, Chama Cha Mapinduzi (CCM). The Economic Reform Programme (ERP) was initiated in mid-1986 under the CCM president Ali Mwinyi within a socialist economic framework. By 1995 the country allowed multi-party election and Benjamin Mkapa was elected president as the third CCM government in Tanzania

The autocratic leaders of the socialist revolution in the 1960s and 1970s in Madagascar, Congo, and Benin were still in control when those countries started to loosen some controls on the economy, originally within a socialist power structure. But by the early 1990s, the old leadership of Madagascar, Congo, and Benin were forced by civil unrest into elections and then out of power. In those three countries internal political conflict is still evident, economic orientation is hotly contested, and continuation of pro-market policies is not assured.

Civil War

Several Afro-Marxist states spent the 1970s, the 1980s, and early 1990s mired in brutal internal conflict, partially fuelled and funded by outside interests intertwined with super-power conflicts. In recent years, with the decline in super-power tension there has been a weakening in outside military support and some of the most gruesome internal conflicts lost steam, e.g. Mozambique and Angola. Unfortunately, the legacy of proxy fights, including intense factional animosity and stockpiled weapons remains and contributes to on-going wars or very unstable peace arrangements in several countries. For example, factional fighting splintered Somalia in 1991 in a dramatic display of the tensions that had mounted in the country during the 19 years of 'scientific socialism' one-party rule under General Mohammed Siad Barre.

The conflicts in Mozambique and Angola started shortly after independence and lasted over fifteen years with a great deal of outside support. The peace agreement signed in 1992 in Mozambique allowed the country to start the tasks of resettling displaced persons, disarming the opposing armies, and rebuilding the economy. Chissano continued as president after the 1994 election and Frelimo still dominates the Parliament. Now Renamo is the legal opposition rather than the opposing side in a civil war, but the democratic peace may still be fragile. Peace is still not assured in Angola, although there have been several attempts to hold to peace agreements and disband the armies.

There was very little peace during the 17 years of socialism in Ethiopia, 14 of which were under autocratic Colonel Mengistu Haile Mariam. Mengistu was finally overthrown and a transitional government came to power in May 1991 under President Meles Zenawi and the Ethiopian People's Revolutionary Democratic Front, dominated by former guerrilla fighters from the north. Eritrea became independent from Ethiopia in April 1993 after a 30-year war for independence.

The Reform Programmes

Although the allegiance to Marxism and the ideological commitment to a major role for the state in the economy waned after the mid-1980s, for over a decade or more the influence of socialist ideas and political structures had shaped the institutional framework and created difficult initial conditions for reforms. In several countries no consensus has been reached that fundamental structural changes are needed, rather than modifications to the existing paradigm. It is not, therefore, surprising that none of these countries have attempted dramatic or quick reforms. Reforms have in all cases been gradual and incremental, partly by design and partly because of limited implementation capacity.

Starting from the economic devastation of the early 1980s, quite a few African countries gradually modified economic policies in the second half of the decade. By the early 1990s, many of the non-CFA Franc Zone countries had given up the grossly overvalued exchange rates common in the mid 1980s. With devaluations came less restrictive systems for allocating foreign exchange and therefore some import liberalisation. Donor funds also allowed the current account deficit to rise and import rationing to ease. Domestic monopolies were subject to more import competition. Most countries dismantled the system of state control of pricing and allocation of goods and liberalised many markets. The financing of fiscal deficits was eased by the greater availability of donor funds, so that dependence on the domestic banking system declined. A few years after initiating reforms most countries had liberalised trade somewhat and allowed foreign exchange markets to develop.

While there has been a shift on exchange rate, trade, and price control policies in some countries, change has been slow on other structural rigidities arising from state-led development strategies. Jobs with the government still are an important portion of formal employment. Civil services are still inefficient, but very difficult to reform. With few other options of formal employment, lay-offs from the public sector are politically difficult. The state banks still dominate financial markets, though most countries now allow private and foreign banks. The parastatal sector has survived, but may be a smaller portion of GDP. Only Guinea and Mozambique rank high in the number of privatisations by African standards. In Mozambique there has been considerable progress in privatising small ventures, and selling or using management contracts for the medium enterprises. There has been less progress with the larger enterprises. Guinea had a dramatic privatisation programme following the collapse of the state enterprises and state banks after the death of Sékou Touré. But the privatisation programme in Guinea has been criticised for lack of accountability and transparency.

Almost all of the countries have liberalised the markets for domestic food staples. In some cases this has meant dismantling marketing boards, and in others the private sector has been allowed to enter to compete with government agencies. Several of these countries kept pan-territorial pricing for producers and consumer subsidies on the main staple for several years after other domestic prices had been decontrolled, but those became incredibly expensive and eventually had to be abandoned. The state farms are mostly gone. There was not an important impact on production, but this freed up the credit and budget resources drained by the state farms before reforms. Government control of agricultural exports and mineral exports is still common, but some fringe commodities have been liberalised.

Reform Outcomes

Several years have passed since these economies began their reforms. In this section we attempt to construct stylised facts. Given the limitations of the data, we confine ourselves to 'before and after' comparisons of key macroeconomic outcomes and leave a more detailed discussion of timing and sequencing of reforms in each country to the appendix. The pre- and post-reform macroeconomic performance of these countries is compared to the year of initiating reforms. The base year is when major reforms were begun: 1986 for Guinea and Tanzania; 1987 for Madagascar and Mozambique; 1990 for Benin; and 1992 for Ethiopia and Congo. It was difficult to decide which dates should be used for Congo and Madagascar. Madagascar started a stabilisation programme as early as 1982, but did not start major structural reforms until 1987, so the comparisons use 1987 as the beginning of reforms. For all countries it was difficult to identify the lags between announcement and actual implementation of reforms. This was especially a problem for Congo. Congo had negotiated several structural adjustment programmes after 1986, but implementation was spotty and there was backtracking in the late 1980s. Therefore for this section, reforms in Congo are dated from the change in government in 1992.

External Factors: The Terms of Trade and Foreign Assistance

As noted above, most African economies faced harsh external conditions in the years leading up to reforms. Figure 1 shows that the decline in the terms of trade experienced in those years before reforms continued in the years immediately following the initiation of reforms.

Figure 1: *Terms of Trade, % Change (relative to reform year)*

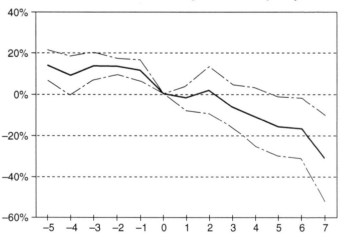

The solid line is the average across all countries for which data exist of the percentage difference between the terms of trade in a given year, and that recorded during the year that reforms were initiated. The dashed lines indicate the standard deviation of this average, to give some indication of the variability of country experience. The original data used to create the tables and figures in the body of the paper are presented in the appendix tables.

Table 2: *Foreign Aid as Per Cent of GNP*

	–5	–2	0	+2	+5	+7
Benin (1990)	8.42	9.51	15.67	12.87	na	na
Congo (1992)	7.18	9.57	4.10	na	na	na
Ethiopia (1992)	na	na	11.95	na	na	na
Guinea (1986)	na	na	7.42	11.21	13.49	13.07
Madagascar (1987)	6.72	6.24	10.86	12.32	12.60	na
Mozambique (1987)	10.41	69.74	32.78	64.14	117.20	na
Tanzania (1986)	12.20	9.06	11.27	23.43	38.67	37.83

Source: OECD. Includes grant and ODA loan support.

As the figure illustrates, the terms of trade declined, on average, by 20 per cent in the five years leading up to the reform programmes, and they continued to decline substantially in the years following the reforms. The post-reform declines were particularly large in Tanzania and Madagascar.

The effect of these declines was at least partially offset by the substantial increase in foreign assistance that was typically observed under reforms. As Figure 2 illustrates, after a reform programme was implemented foreign assistance increased,[8] on average, by about 20 percentage points of GDP.

There is substantial variation in country experience with foreign aid, with Mozambique and Tanzania experiencing particularly large increases. In Mozambique, foreign transfers rose from about 18 per cent of GNP in 1986 to about 90 per cent in 1990–93. This extremely high level of support was for resettling refugees and demilitarising the armies. In Tanzania, transfers rose from about 11 per cent of

GNP in 1986 to roughly 40 per cent of GNP in 1989–93. Guinea also received substantial support for its reform efforts, with foreign assistance of roughly 10 percentage points of GNP.

Figure 2: *Foreign Aid, % of GNP*
(difference between observed value and value when reforms were initiated)

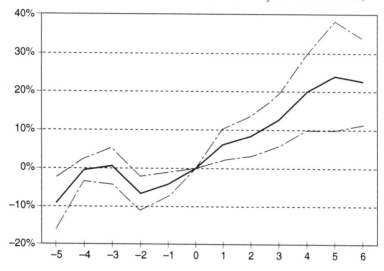

Economic Growth and Investment

An overriding objective of the reforms was to end the pre-reform stagnation and, in several cases, declines in production and real incomes. Figure 3, which illustrates the course of real GDP over the reform period, suggests that the reforms were partially successful in doing so. That figure presents the simple average across countries of real GDP per capita, expressed in each year as a proportion of output in the first year of reforms.

The typical experience is one of substantial declines in production in the years preceding the initiation of reform. By the time reforms were initiated, real output per capita had fallen, on average, by about 13 per cent from the level attained five years previously. After the reforms were initiated, the decline in production was halted, but the subsequent recovery has tended to be sluggish, with per capita production remaining for several years below the level reached five years before the reforms were initiated.

Figure 3: *Real GDP Per Capita*
(ratio real value in reform years to real value when reforms were initiated)

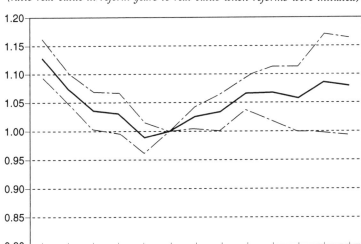

Most countries fit this pattern of pre-reform decline and slow post-reform recovery, though there are two major exceptions. Congo continued to decline two years into reforms. Madagascar had a prolonged period of stabilisation in the early 1980s and started structural change in 1987/88. Real GDP growth was low in 1987 and 1988, which translated into declining per capita GDP. Per capita GDP growth did not show a strong response until 1990. This was followed by civil unrest to force out the socialist government and a 6 per cent decline in GDP in 1991, a transitional government in 1992, and multi-party elections in 1993.

But in the other countries the pattern of pre-reform decline and slow post-reform recovery is fairly clear. The declines were most pronounced in Ethiopia and Mozambique, where output per capita fell by roughly 25 per cent in the five years leading up to reform. While less catastrophic than this, the declines were also very substantial in the other countries.

Though most countries recovered after reforms were initiated, the recovery was relatively sluggish. During the first five years of recovery, per capita growth averaged one per cent per year, although Mozambique and Tanzania, with pronounced pre-reform declines, experienced somewhat more rapid growth. And after five years of recovery, only Mozambique, and Tanzania had recovered the per capita output recorded a decade before. This may also be true for Guinea, but there are no GDP estimates for the pre-reform period. This growth experience differs from the experience with Latin American and formerly-socialist economies of Europe and central Asia in ways which are discussed in the conclusion.

Table 3: *Real GDP Per Capita in Reforming Socialist Economies (year when reform begins = 1.00)*

	–5	–2	0	+2	+5	+7
Benin (1990)	1.109	1.055	1.000	1.026	na	na
Congo (1992)	1.043	1.010	1.000	0.884	na	na
Ethiopia (1992)	1.234	1.175	1.000	1.072	na	na
Guinea (1986)	na	na	1.000	1.029	1.040	1.055
Madagascar (1987)	1.079	1.030	1.000	1.010	0.903	0.880
Mozambique (1987)	1.235	0.908	1.000	1.163	1.156	1.294
Tanzania (1986)	1.076	1.009	1.000	1.052	1.131	1.091
Average	1.129	1.031	1.000	1.034	1.057	1.080

Source: World Bank, World Tables 1995.

Corresponding to this slow recovery of output was a relatively sluggish response of investment to the reform programmes. Figure 4 illustrates the typical response. There is no clear pattern in the years leading up to reforms. The investment booms of the late 1970s and early 1980s seen in many of these countries had been followed by worse economic performance and lower investment in the five years before reforms. There is a slight tendency for investment to increase, on average, after initiation of reforms. However, these averages mask important differences in country experience, as can be seen in Table 4.

After reforms were implemented, real investment rose as a share of real GDP in Guinea, Madagascar, and Tanzania, and declined, from very high levels, in Mozambique. Investment also rose slightly in Benin, an increase which gathered strength in years three and four of the reform process, during which investment rose by nearly

4 percentage points above the very low rate recorded during 1990 when reforms were initiated.

Figure 4: *Real Investment as Per Cent of Real GDP*
(difference between observed value and value when reforms were initiated)

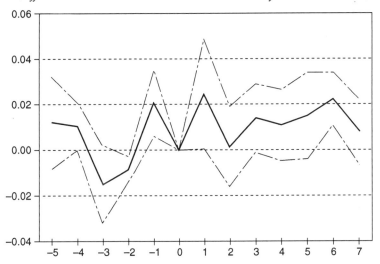

Table 4: *Ratio of Real Investment to Real GDP in Reforming Socialist Economies*

	–5	–2	0	+2	+5	+7
Benin (1990)	8.94	12.42	11.95	12.52	na	na
Congo (1992)	17.51	12.10	11.65	na	na	na
Ethiopia (1992)	na	na	na	na	na	na
Guinea (1986)	na	na	14.07	15.88	15.71	16.95
Madagascar (1987)	8.51	8.63	10.28	13.40	11.07	9.21
Mozambique (1987)	46.01	38.49	39.66	34.75	36.89	37.50
Tanzania (1986)	24.44	23.53	25.87	na*	32.29	29.43

Source: World Bank, *World Tables*, 1995.
*World Bank data indicate a one year decline to less than 7% of GDP. This decline does not appear in the country data, and appears to be a mistake.

Manufacturing: Did Reform 'Deindustrialise' Liberalising Economies?

A main concern of economic policy in the socialist economies of Africa was to promote (generally public) manufacturing enterprises. This was done through nationalisation of the large enterprises and public financed investment booms in the early 1980s, with the domestic manufactures then protected from international competition, and provided preferred and subsidised access to scarce foreign exchange and domestic credit. As a result of these policies, manufacturing sectors grew, though they were in many cases very inefficient.

The reforms all involved dismantling these policies, at least in large part, attempting to move economies toward market allocations of foreign exchange and credit under unified exchange rates and market-determined interest rates, reducing budgetary subsidies to manufacturing (and other) parastatal enterprises, and dramatically reducing rates of protection from international trade. In light of this, one might have expected a sharp decline in domestic manufacturing. In his study of Mozambique in the second volume of this study, Roberto Tibana reports that this was, in fact, the case, for Mozambique. On the other hand, Gavin reports that the Tanzanian manufacturing sector appears to have been remarkably little affected by the economic reforms undertaken in that country, despite the fact that terms of trade appear to have shifted against manufacturing as one would have expected.

What was the experience in other countries? Table 5 shows the average across the reforming countries of the share of manufacturing value added in gross domestic product, measured at constant prices.[9] Figure 5 shows the difference of the ratio between the year reform was initiated and the period before and after reforms.

In fact, not much appears to have happened; on average, the reforming economies experienced a slight decline in the share of manufacturing in total production *before* the reforms were initiated, and most had another very small decline in the first years of reforms.

There is substantial variation in the pre-reform experience, with Ethiopia and Tanzania experiencing declines in the manufacturing share of domestic production, Benin experiencing an increase, and Congo volatile. But the post-reform experience is more consistent;

the declines have been small, and several recovered to reform levels within a few years. Congo declined in the first two years. Madagascar experienced a decline that was still evident five years after the reforms. Benin and Ethiopia have each had small increases.

Table 5: *Ratio of Real Value Added in Manufacturing to Real GDP in Reforming Socialist Economies*

	−5	−2	0	+2	+5	+7
Benin (1990)	7.56	8.18	8.96	9.35	na	na
Congo (1992)	10.26	11.20	10.59	9.11	na	na
Ethiopia (1992)	4.53	4.35	2.67	3.81	na	na
Guinea (1986)	na	na	3.44	3.27	3.52	3.56
Madagascar (1987)	na	11.30	11.93	11.43	11.24	na
Mozambique (1987)	na	na	na	na	na	na
Tanzania (1986)	9.14	8.02	7.00	6.99	6.92	7.05

Source: World Bank, *World Tables*, 1995.

Figure 5: *Ratio of Manufacturing Value-Added to Real GDP*
(difference between observed value and value when reforms were initiated)

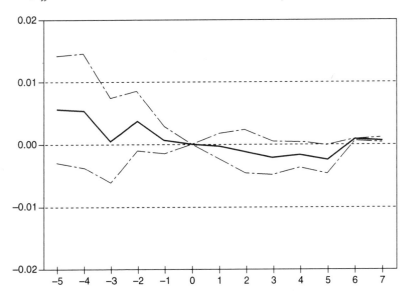

30   *Jo Ann Paulson and Michael Gavin*

These data suggest that the experience of Mozambique, where, as Tibana reports, manufacturing came under pressure in the aftermath of the liberalisation, was not typical.

International Trade and Payments

Protection of the manufacturing sector was but one manifestation of the largely inward-orientated development strategy pursued by the socialist African economies. A major objective of reform programmes was to promote a greater outward orientation, and rely upon exports as an engine of growth. Figure 6 shows that some progress was made in this respect, though the record is mixed.

Figure 6: *Ratio of Real Exports Relative to Real GDP*
(difference between observed value and value when reforms were initiated)

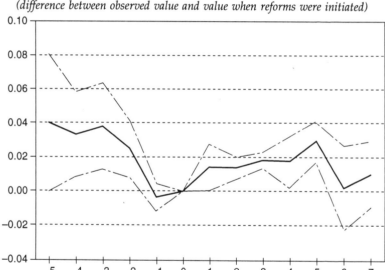

The figure shows the average across our countries of the ratio of real exports of goods and non-factor services to real GDP. The pre-reform period displays a striking decline in outward-orientation, as measured by a very sharp decline in the ratio of real exports to GDP. After reform is implemented, real exports return to the previously attained share of real GDP in about three years.

Table 6 shows that the decline in exports during the years leading up to the initiation of reform was a widespread phenomenon, with the exception of Congo. This decline in exports presumably reflects the anti-trade bias of the administrative measures – rationing of foreign exchange, licensing of imports, protection of import-competing domestic producers – undertaken to deal with chronic and intensifying foreign exchange shortages in the years of economic decline. In the post-reform period exports recovered significantly in Madagascar and Mozambique, and had a good start in the first two years of reforms in Benin, but the recovery was not sustained in Guinea.

Table 6: *Ratio of Real exports of Goods and Non-factor Services to Real GDP*

	–5	–2	0	+2	+5	+7
Benin (1990)	34.38	21.59	21.59	23.99	na	na
Congo (1992)	39.45	46.14	45.58	na	na	na
Ethiopia (1992)	na	na	na	na	na	na
Guinea (1986)	na	31.19	31.19	33.70	32.20	30.28
Madagascar (1987)	14.62	12.60	12.56	12.52	15.32	na
Mozambique (1987)	20.36	14.81	12.94	13.46	18.01	15.89
Tanzania (1986)	na	na	na	na	na	na

Source: World Bank, *World Tables*, 1995.

Though there was some recovery of real exports, the current account nevertheless deteriorated, reflecting a decline in the terms of trade and an increase in imports. Figure 7 shows that, on average, the current account deficit (before official transfers) declined by nearly 6 percentage points in the years just before reforms, and by about ten percentage points in the years following the reform.

These current account deficits were in large part financed by a surge in official transfers, and indeed it is in Mozambique and Tanzania, the countries where the increase in foreign transfers was most pronounced, where the current account deteriorated most strongly.

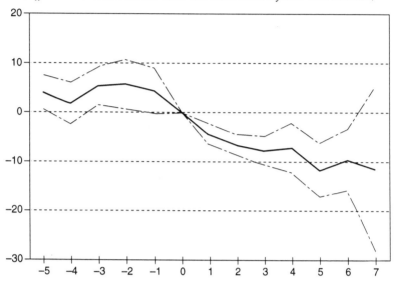

Figure 7: *Current Account Surplus before Official Transfers, % of GDP (difference between observed value and value when reforms were initiated)*

The Sample Countries and SSA Averages

Before reforms, the formerly-socialist economies of Africa usually performed below average for the African continent. In the pre-reform periods, growth was slower than the (unweighted) Sub-Saharan average about 80 per cent of the time. After reforms, growth was slower than the Sub-Saharan average only about a quarter of the time. The countries discussed in this chapter thus went from quite consistent underperformance, to performance on par with, or perhaps slightly better than average, for the continent as a whole. The notable exception is Congo, where per capita incomes continued to decline sharply in the 1990s, due to a combination of economic and political factors.

Table 7: *Current Account Surplus before Transfers, as a Fraction of GDP*

	−5	−2	0	+2	+5	+7
Benin (1990)	−6.45	−12.30	−6.17	−8.16		
Congo (1992)	−12.65	−11.33	−12.82	−21.97		
Ethiopia (1992)	−5.34	−2.82	−1.83	−7.36		
Guinea (1986)			−7.80	−12.85	−13.51	−2.12
Madagascar (1987)	−10.99	−9.02	−10.12	−9.33	−9.46	−16.63
Mozambique (1987)	−27.71	−17.17	−51.23	−63.74	−68.54	−59.30
Tanzania (1986)	−8.67	−7.83	−11.15	−22.94	−35.19	−39.40

Source: World Bank, *World Tables*, 1995.

Table 8: *SSA Growth Rates of Per Capita GDP*

	1985	1986	1987	1988	1989	1990	1991	1992	1993	1994
Benin	4.5	−0.8	−4.4	0.4	−5.7	**0.5**	1.5	1.0	0.1	1.0
Congo	−3.9	−9.6	−2.8	−1.2	−0.2	−1.8	−0.6	**−0.4**	−4.5	−7.4
Ethiopia	−11.0	6.4	10.6	−2.7	−2.6	0.5	−9.4	**−6.0**	9.0	−1.7
Guinea	na	**na**	0.0	2.9	0.3	1.3	−0.6	0.1	1.3	1.3
Madagascar	−1.7	−1.1	**−1.9**	0.2	0.8	−0.1	−9.0	−1.7	−0.5	−1.8
Mozambique	−1.6	−4.3	**15.1**	9.5	6.2	−0.2	2.9	−3.3	13.2	−1.1
Tanzania	−2.5	**1.6**	1.4	3.7	5.0	3.0	−0.6	−3.0	−0.6	na
Average growth:										
Sample	−2.8	−1.3	2.6	1.8	0.5	0.5	−2.3	−1.9	2.6	−1.6
SSA	0.9	0.5	−0.2	1.9	0.8	−0.7	−0.7	−1.9	−1.0	−0.9

Source: World Bank *World Tables*, 1995. Underlined growth rates indicate the year in which implementation of major economic reform began.

Conclusions

The other papers in this study discuss the reform experience from different perspectives: macro, micro, and sectoral. The authors have a host of hypotheses and evidence to help interpret the aggregate information presented here. The purpose of this chapter was to briefly outline the economic and political context for the reform programmes and review the aggregate information available to frame the discussion.

We end with some of the questions that the data suggest to us. As the data above show, these countries have made some progress in reversing the pre-reform decline in economic performance. But there has not been much action in the aggregate figures, especially with respect to growth, investment, and the industrial composition of production during the reform period. Despite the apparent existence of excess capacity generated by the output decline that preceded the reforms and the increase in foreign aid, the reforms apparently have not triggered strong growth in output and in most countries investment has not increased much. In this, the African experience distinguishes itself from the Latin American, where major stabilisation and reform programmes have typically been followed by a strong, though temporary, output response. But Africa has also been spared the economic collapse and hyper-inflation seen in the first years of the break-up of the former Soviet Union when trade and currency relations among republics were severely disrupted.

It is puzzling that these African economies did not evidence more of the disruption that reforms might have been expected to generate. In particular, sectors that were formerly very heavily protected and in many instances extremely inefficient, such as manufacturing and the parastatal sector, have not downsized in a dramatic way. There is substantial evidence that, before the reforms, the manufacturing parastatals in the sample countries were frequently value-reducing at world prices. So the question becomes why, when the reforms exposed these inefficient enterprises to international prices and trade competition, was there apparently so little fallout?

Some part of the answer is likely to be data and information problems, which are particularly severe in these countries. But this cannot be the whole answer. Another possibility is that the formerly

Table 9: *The Samples Countries and SSA*

	1980	1981	1982	1983	1984	1985	1986	1987	1988	1989	1990	1991	1992	1993	1994
Growth, GDP/capita															
SSA	0.1	0.3	0.6	-2.6	-1.5	0.9	0.5	-0.2	1.9	0.8	-0.7	0.7	-1.9	-1.1	-0.9
Sample	4.9	1.6	-0.1	-3.3	-1.4	-2.8	-1.3	2.6	1.8	0.5	0.5	-2.3	-1.9	2.6	-1.6
Investment/GDP															
SSA	24.5	24.6	24.3	20.6	19.9	21.1	20.0	19.5	19.2	18.8	19.9	19.6	19.6	18.4	16.7
Sample	27.3	30.7	33.8	27.0	25.0	24.6	22.1	22.5	18.9	18.7	20.7	19.8	20.0	20.2	20.1
Manufacturing value added/GDP															
SSA	9.1	9.3	9.5	9.4	9.5	9.3	9.4	10.2	10.5	10.5	10.7	10.6	11.2	10.8	10.7
Sample	8.4	7.2	7.7	7.8	7.8	8.3	7.3	7.4	7.6	7.6	7.6	7.4	7.4	6.8	7.4
Terms of trade															
SSA	123.5	118.2	1111.9	112.4	117.4	115.4	111.0	100.0	102.8	100.4	101.6	98.6	92.0	9.17	na
Sample	132.7	127.2	119.4	118.3	129.2	123.4	119.7	100.0	104.1	101.6	96.1	95.6	93.8	9.39	na
Real exports/GDP															
SSA	29.3	28.0	26.3	26.2	27.2	26.9	28.9	28.0	27.5	27.9	28.1	28.2	28.5	27.2	28.3
Sample	31.4	28.9	25.1	23.3	24.6	24.9	25.5	26.0	26.2	25.6	25.8	26.1	26.4	27.3	26.7
CAS/GDP*															
SSA	-15.0	-17.8	-18.9	-16.1	-13.9	-15.0	-14.7	-14.1	-15.4	-15.1	-15.4	-16.8	-17.8	-17.2	-14.7
Sample	-14.0	-14.3	-17.9	-14.5	-8.6	-9.1	-14.3	-16.5	-21.6	-19.1	-20.3	-21.4	-21.9	-20.8	-19.3
Net foreign aid (% GNP)															
SSA	7.0	6.4	7.1	8.2	9.5	9.6	9.8	9.5	9.5	10.4	10.9	11.0	11.0	10.0	8.5
Sample	3.0	2.5	2.8	2.6	9.2	8.0	5.5	6.7	8.2	12.0	12.0	11.9	12.6	11.6	10.5

* current account surplus before official transfers.

protected enterprises and sectors suddenly became efficient enough to survive in the new environment. But this would have required highly visible measures, particularly large layoffs to address problems of overstaffing, and these have not been widely observed.

An alternative explanation is that the reforms focused on macro-economic measures, freeing up previously suppressed markets, and getting prices right, but the reform programmes have not systematically hardened budget constraints. In the absence of real budget constraints, market prices mean little. Evidence from later chapters of this book provide some support for the latter hypothesis. Elliot Berg's finding that privatisation or liquidation has proceeded very slowly suggests a political environment in which there is a certain reluctance to accept some of the painful outcomes ground out by the workings of a market economy. Gavin's paper on Tanzania suggests that, despite reforms on the macroeconomic side, important segments of the Tanzanian economy remained sheltered from market forces, in large part because the state-owned commercial bank continued to grant enterprises credit in the years following reform, despite the negligible prospects for repayment. The result was a very expensive recapitalisation of the state banks in 1992.

In all of these countries in this study the banks became insolvent during the first few years of reforms. The state banks in Guinea, Benin, and Congo were bankrupted very early in the reform programme suggesting that some of the problems were from the decline before reforms. Six state banks were liquidated in Guinea in 1986 and the three state banks in Benin were liquidated between 1989 and 1992. Both Guinea and Benin liquidated all state banks and invited in foreign banks, many as joint ventures with the government. In Congo the banking problems were obvious by 1988, even before there had been substantial economic reforms. Liquidation of one state bank started in 1992 and of another in 1994. The two remaining state banks are now being restructured to deal with the losses.

Madagascar, Tanzania, and Mozambique have recapitalised and kept the state banks. In all three countries the state banks have softened the budget constraints for state structures and parastatals during reforms. Very little information is available on the banks in Ethiopia and Angola, but in both countries the government has had to take over non-performing assets arising from lending to parastatals and state farms.

While state banks have softened the budget constraint in these countries, there have also been other means of subsidising the parastatals, including toleration of tax and import duty arrears, accepting delayed payment for foreign exchange, transfer of foreign debt servicing to the government, etc. The countries in the CFA Franc Zone had different constraints, and also used financing through arrears.

But the continuing drain of the parastatal sector is not the only possible explanation for the pattern of relatively slow recovery. There are other factors. First, the economic information is weak. Any private sector economic activities is likely to be under-reported, so it may be that recovery has been stronger than suggested by the official statistics. Second, several of these countries launched the reforms under ageing socialist dictators with a questionable degree of commitment to the new policies; undoubtedly discouraging fixed investment by the private sector. Third, several of these countries went through serious civil disturbances or fighting to force socialist/autocratic leaders out of power after nominally starting reforms. Fourth, the legal framework for private sector activities is slowly being erected, but property rights are not clear or secure yet. Fifth the labour forces are very short of market skills and experience. The list of other factors that have made economic reforms in these countries difficult could be expanded. But we will end here. Some of these issues are addressed in the chapters that follow, others are raised as important areas for further research.

Notes

1. The authors are economists at the World Bank and the Inter-American Development Bank respectively. This article reflects the views of the authors and does not represent the views of their institutions.
2. For reasons of data availability we are forced to work with a subset of these economies. Neither Angola nor Somalia will be included in the quantitative analysis, but descriptions of their reforms are given in the appendix.

3. Historical information on the birth and ideological focus of African socialism is given in a 1982 study by Crawford Young. Also see Pryor, 1992.
4. Young (1982), pp. 22–23. This project used as the sample most of the countries discussed by Young. There are several other classification systems that change the list of countries counted as Marxist slightly. These are discussed in Young (1982) and in Pryor (1992), pp. 361–66. In Pryor's classification, as of mid-1980, Angola, Benin, Congo, Ethiopia, Madagascar, Mozambique, Somalia, as well as the smaller nations of Cape Verde, Guinea-Bissau, Sao Tome, and Seychelles were considered Marxist. Zimbabwe was also classified as Marxist, while Guinea and Tanzania were not.
5. A majority of these economies is dependent on agricultural export performance, i.e. Benin, Ethiopia, Madagascar, Mozambique, Somalia, and Tanzania. Angola, Congo, and Guinea are dependent on mineral or oil exports.
6. Adapted from Pryor, 1992, pp. 22–23.
7. The appendix to this chapter briefly summarises country experiences.
8. This measure of net official transfers is the sum of grants and disbursement of ODA loans, i.e. all loans with a developmental purpose and grant element of at least 25 per cent. The data are from OECD. The denominator on this ratio is GNP rather than GDP. Using other data sources and GDP as the denominator does not change the trends shown here.
9. Since they are measured at constant prices, the data reflect changes in the volume of production only, not changes in the relative price of manufacturing.

References

Pryor, F. (1992) *The Red and the Green. The Rise and Fall of Collectivised Agriculture in Marxist Regimes*, Princeton NJ: Princeton University Press.

Young, C. (1982) *Ideology and Development in Africa*, Yale University Press.

Appendix A: Country Reviews

Angola

Angola has a strong natural resource base with oil, diamonds and fertile agricultural land, but the country has been at war for almost three decades, with devastating consequences for the population. Per capita GNP estimates fell from $715 in 1985 to $250 in 1994 with a population of just over 11 million. Absolute poverty is widespread and worsening. Much of the population have been forced off their land by war, with many living in squatter camps around the cities. Urban population, estimated at 15 per cent in 1970 rose to about 42 per cent in 1992 and to more than 50 per cent now. The war has been brutal with widespread use of land mines. Angola has the highest number of amputees of any country in the world, both in absolute and relative terms.

Even as the fight for independence in Angola was ending in 1975, the country plunged into domestic conflict. The People's Movement for the Liberation of Angola (MPLA) gained the upper hand in the conflict among rival domestic and foreign groups and declared the country socialist in 1977. But the conflict with UNITA continued.

Like Mozambique, the economy of Angola was thrown into disarray by the departure of many Portuguese settlers after independence, since the educational and economic opportunities for the indigenous population were severely limited during the colonial occupation. The government adopted central planning on a Soviet model and extended state control over hundreds of commercial farms, plantations, and small manufacturing businesses which had been abandoned, or relinquished by departing settlers. Large companies and the commercial banks were brought under state control and government administrators, with no training or experience, took over management. Non-Portuguese foreign capital and the oil industry were not affected.

The 400 state enterprises dominated the formal economy. In 1984, the public enterprises accounted for about three quarters of formal employment. Economic and financial information is scarce, but shows that state enterprises were dependent on subsidies even for working capital. Those enterprises, as well as all mixed and private businesses, were controlled with pervasive state administrative measures, including highly politicised allocation of grossly overvalued foreign exchange, price controls for most goods and services, rationed import licences, restrictions on operating margins, purchases by the public sector etc. Nominal wages were set centrally, though official wages were only a part of the total salary, the rest of the compensation being in the form of rationing coupons and consumption entitlements. Most of the population remained in rural areas engaged in peasant production or living in camps outside the urban areas, dependent on food aid.

Production in almost all sectors, except petroleum, was reduced to a fraction of the pre-independence years. The decline in diamond and coffee exports increased the dependence on oil as the only source of foreign exchange earnings. By 1994 oil accounted for 50 per cent of GDP, 97 per cent of exports, and 89 per cent of government revenue.

The large parallel markets, though technically illegal, were tolerated and played an important role in the economy. Controlled prices were rarely adjusted and with high inflation fuelled by excessive budgetary financing of the deficit, relative prices were very distorted, leading to shortages and rationing. As a result of the monetary overhang and shortages, parallel markets became extremely important. Even though very inefficient and distorted, parallel markets were the only source of goods and services not available in the official market. Smuggling, robbery, and corruption were endemic.

The Angolan authorities announced economic reform measures in 1985 but little happened. A few reforms were tried after 1987, but were poorly implemented. There was a currency reform, but only 5 per cent of the liquid balances with the public could be changed for the new currency, and receipts issued for the rest, with a vague promise that these receipts would be converted into interest bearing bonds in the future. Prices on the parallel markets soared as people tried to get out of holding currency and the economy turned to barter. Differences between parallel and official prices and exchange rates were, and are, enormous.

The economy continues to be chaotic. The economy suffers large chronic fiscal deficits from very large military expenditures, combined with inadequate control over government finances, large nominal wage increases to civil servants and subsidies to surviving parastatals. The estimated fiscal deficit for 1995 was $926 million, about 15 per cent of GDP. The deficits have been financed from the banking system, and it was estimated that hyperinflation reached 3,661 per cent in 1995.

With the end of the Cold War, the two sides to the Angolan war negotiated a settlement in May 1991. Unlike Mozambique, Angola tried to hold elections before demobilising the military. When dos Santos prevailed in the first presidential elections in September 1992, UNITA, led by Savimbi, refused to accept the outcome and the war resumed. Following two years of devastating conflict, another peace agreement was signed in Lusaka, Zambia, in November 1994. Attempts to implement the peace agreement, supported by the United Nations with 6,500 peacekeepers and 1,100 civilians, have been rocky and disarming the armies is behind schedule.

Benin

Per capita GNP in Benin is estimated at $370, and has been declining at about .8 per cent per year for the last ten years. With a population of 5 million, total GDP is about $2 billion. Agriculture accounts for 35 per cent of GDP, about two thirds of exports and employs about 63 per cent of the labour force. Cotton is the largest export. Official statistics report that 53 per cent of GDP is from the service sector and about 40 per cent of the population is in urban areas. Benin is usually close to the bottom of any list of countries based on social indicators of development.

From independence in 1960 to 1972, Benin was very unstable politically, and shuffled through a series of civilian and military regimes. Mathieu Kérékou took power in a military coup in 1972, imposed Marxism-Leninism in 1974 and nationalised major companies, banks and insurance companies. The state undertook an extensive public investment programme after 1974, much of it going into large industrial projects. Gross domestic investment averaged 18 per cent of GDP over the period 1974–83, but slowed after 1983. From the time they were built, these enterprises operated far below capacity and were a drain on the economy. Most of the investment was externally financed and by 1980 external debt stock equalled 80 per cent of GNP. The central government budget went from surplus in 1977–78, to deficit in 1980, averaging 13.8 per cent of GDP in the period 1980–85, due to the huge public investment programme, a

Benin

	1980	1981	1982	1983	1984	1985	1986	1987	1988	1989	1990	1991	1992	1993	1994	Averages 1980–85	Averages 1986–90	Averages 1991–94
Real GDP growth rate	6.78	9.95	2.24	-4.35	7.93	7.53	2.17	-1.50	3.41	-2.86	3.60	4.70	4.21	3.30	4.17	5.01	0.96	4.09
per capita	4.31	6.27	-0.81	-7.36	4.63	4.09	-1.00	-4.46	0.16	-6.02	0.76	1.48	0.91	-0.07	1.83	1.85	-2.11	1.04
Nom dom invest % of GDP	15.16	15.68	27.60	17.32	12.78	8.94	13.46	12.92	12.84	11.79	14.23	14.34	13.82	14.31	19.63	16.25	13.05	15.53
real invest % of GDP	21.81	22.57	31.59	19.34	13.23	8.94	12.96	12.20	12.42	10.49	11.95	11.34	12.52	13.72	15.79	19.58	12.00	13.34
Real VA manuf % of GDP	6.61	5.65	9.00	8.35	7.26	7.56	7.08	7.74	8.18	8.53	8.96	8.74	9.35	9.27	9.25	7.41	8.10	9.15
Budget deficit as % of GDP	na																	
Net for aid % of GDP	6.29	5.31	5.67	7.41	6.67	8.42	11.47	9.94	9.51	15.99	15.67	13.72	12.87	12.29		6.63	12.52	12.96
Current acc % of GDP	-7.94	-11.96	-35.44	-18.34	-11.18	-6.45	-12.19	-11.94	-12.30	-8.95	-6.17	-5.92	-8.16	-9.99	-3.15	-15.22	-10.31	-6.80
Real exports as % of GDP	41.73	41.44	30.03	22.78	28.95	34.38	30.67	32.78	28.98	22.11	21.59	22.15	23.99	22.72	19.27	33.22	27.23	22.03
Parallel exchange premium	0.99	1.01	1.01	1.05	1.04	0.99	0.99	1.01	1.01	1.02	1.04	0.94	1.02	1.01	1.05	1.02	1.01	1.01
Terms of trade	108	108	85	97	127	111	87	100	118	115	96	105	133	110		106.02	102.90	116.13
CPI inflation	na																	

Source: real GDP, gross domestic investments, value added manufactures, real export and current account, from *World Tables*; net foreign transfers from OECD; all other series, IMF IFS; parallel exchange premium = parallel rate (from Currency Alert)/official rate (IFS); budget deficit before grants.

narrow tax base, with extreme dependence on international trade taxes as a source of government revenue, and a rising wage bill.

The economy was under price controls, but these were difficult to enforce because of smuggled goods from Nigeria. Also membership in the CFA Franc Zone meant that the exchange rate did not become very distorted. The state created public monopolies in export and import commerce and controlled processing of cotton, the most important export. Food crop marketing and prices were regulated, though not as strictly as for export crops. There was some improvement with the cotton producer prices linked to world prices in 1981–82 and cotton output increased through the 1980s. The state maintained control of marketing and processing and distribution of inputs. Food crop marketing was liberalised in 1988–89.

After reasonable growth in the first half of the 1980s with per capita GDP increasing at about 2 per cent a year from 1980 to 1985, the economy declined in the second half of the 1980s. Per capita GDP growth fell, averaging losses of 3 per cent of GDP in the period 1986–89. The budget deficit averaged over 10 per cent of GDP over that period, mainly due to sharp declines in government revenues, rising debt service payments and a large wage bill. Facing declining terms of trade and substantial appreciation of the real effective exchange rate, export competitiveness was eroded, but Benin, as a member of the CFA Franc Zone could not devalue. Exports and imports both declined severely.

The public enterprises became an increasing drain on the economy in the 1980s with distorted pricing, overstaffing, undercapitalisation, and poor financial management. By 1985 parastatals employed about 51 per cent of the modern sector labour force and took well over half of domestic bank credit. The state banks, brought down by non-performing loans to the parastatals, collapsed in 1988–89 leading to a severe liquidity crisis, exacerbating the shortage of imports in the economy. Since the banks had served as the main source of public sector funding, the government fell into arrears on public sector salaries. Nationwide strikes followed in 1989.

The Socialist government of Mathieu Kérékou announced a change in economic policies in early 1989, but implementation was spotty, civil unrest accelerated and the economy continued to slide. In December 1989, with widespread political and civil unrest and large fiscal and external imbalances, Kérékou renounced Marxism-

Leninism and left office after 17 years in power. A transitional government was established in March 1990. A new constitution was approved by referendum in December 1990. Multi-party elections in March 1991 elected Nicéphore Soglo as Prime Minister. Pro-market reforms accelerated, but economic orientation and policies are still hotly contested.

The government turned to foreign banks to rebuild the banking system and by 1991 four private commercial banks were operating. Price controls were lifted in 1991 for most commodities and the state monopolies on domestic trade and imports of consumer goods ended. All quantitative restrictions on imports were replaced by tariffs and import licensing ended by March 1993. The number of public enterprises was reduced from 100 prior to 1984, to about 45 in 1989, with many liquidated. Under the new government the number of state enterprises was further reduced from 45 in 1989 to 32 by end-1993. The government converted the cotton sector processing and marketing company into a mixed company, allowing investment by cotton farmers. The state still has a monopoly on petroleum distribution.

Benin and the other countries of the CFA Franc Zone devalued the CFA franc from CFAF 50 to CFAF 100 to the French franc in January 1994. Real GDP growth was 4.2 per cent in 1994 and estimated at 5.8 per cent in 1995.

Congo

Congo used oil revenues to achieve one of the highest growth rates in SSA from 1977 to 1985, but after oil prices fell in 1985/86, the country went into a protracted economic decline. Per capita GDP in Congo declined at an average of 3.25 per cent per year over the last ten years falling to $620 in 1994. The economy remains undiversified. By 1995 oil accounted for 33 per cent of GDP, 85 per cent of merchandise exports, and over 50 per cent of government revenues.

At independence in 1960, the government of the Congo introduced a Socialist five year plan for 1964–68. After a coup in 1968, the military government formed a Marxist party, the Parti Congolais du Travail (PCT), in December 1969, that was the sole legal political party in the country until 1991. The military and the

Congo

	1980	1981	1982	1983	1984	1985	1986	1987	1988	1989	1990	1991	1992	1993	1994	Averages 1980–85	1986–90	1991–94
Real GDP growth rate	17.64	17.62	23.60	5.85	6.98	-1.19	-6.86	0.19	1.77	2.85	1.13	2.41	2.63	-1.50	-4.65	11.75	-0.18	-0.28
per capita	14.56	4.63	20.11	3.51	3.54	-3.76	-9.68	-2.76	-1.14	0.00	-2.04	-0.71	-0.40	-4.33	-7.67	7.10	-3.13	-3.28
Nom dom invest % of GDP	35.77	48.16	59.73	38.44	30.39	30.28	29.45	19.72	18.62	14.16	15.91	20.53	17.18	15.51		40.46	19.57	17.74
real invest % of GDP	33.85	52.08	57.66	46.04	38.27	36.79	25.48	17.51	14.68	11.62	12.10	15.18	11.65	10.04		44.12	16.28	12.29
Real VA manuf % of GDP	8.44	8.06	7.41	9.21	9.13	10.13	10.20	10.26	10.73	10.57	11.20	10.96	10.59	10.37	9.11	8.82	10.59	10.26
Budget deficit as % of GDP	na																	
Net for aid % of GDP	6.20	4.23	4.12	5.09	4.74	3.53	5.75	7.18	4.09	4.20	9.57	5.37	4.10	5.35		4.65	6.16	4.94
Current acc % of GDP	-13.48	-25.31	-16.69	-20.88	7.65	-9.33	-35.72	-12.65	-23.05	-7.47	-11.33	-18.97	-12.82	-21.39	-21.97	-13.01	-18.04	-18.79
Real exports as % of GDP	43.05	39.99	35.31	39.12	40.15	37.99	39.37	39.45	43.82	45.87	46.14	42.94	45.58	52.12		39.27	42.93	46.88
Parallel exchange premium	0.99	1.01	1.01	1.05	1.04	0.99	0.99	1.01	1.01	1.02	1.04			1.01	1.05	1.02	1.01	1.03
Terms of trade	142	172	165	149	149	150	91	100	84	92	108	99	98	93		154.40	94.90	96.50
CPI inflation	7.27	16.96	12.81	7.72	13.21	5.59	2.35	2.18	3.81	4.14	-4.79	9.16	1.99	2.00		10.59	1.54	4.38

Source: real GDP, gross domestic investments, value added manufactures, real export and current account, from *World Tables*; net foreign transfers from OECD; all other series, IMF IFS; parallel exchange premium = parallel rate (from Currency Alert)/official rate (IFS); budget deficit before grants.

labour unions also have significant power to influence policy in Congo.

Congo used oil revenues to built and support parastatals and a large civil service and became the dominant producer of goods and services, and the main employer. Over 50 per cent of the population moved to urban areas, dependent on public sector employment and heavily subsidised public services and utilities. By 1984 there were 51,000 civil servants in government employment, about 10 per cent of the active work force. The high investment rates of the early 1980s were financed with foreign debt as well as oil revenues, setting the stage for later debt servicing problems.

By the mid-1980s there were 90 public enterprises, of which over 70 were commercial and the state owned at least 50 per cent of all banks. The government state took a least part ownership in most major investments. But some important parts of the economy remained in private hands, e.g. the upstream enterprises for oil were always private and most of the smaller manufacturing companies. In the agricultural sector there were cash crop marketing boards and a few state farms but marketing for the major staple, manioc, was never controlled. Even though about half of labour force is engaged in agriculture, the sector was badly neglected. Markets were not as controlled or distorted as in some of the other African socialist economies. As a member of the CFA Franc Zone, imports were not restricted, the exchange rate did not become terribly distorted until the late 1980s, and price controls were never very effective.

When oil prices slumped in 1985–86, economic growth slowed, and the heavy international debt burden of the country forced the Central Committee of the PCT to adopt a structural adjustment programme in June 1985 and reached an agreement with the IMF in 1986. Implementation of the reforms was poor. The government fiscal deficit rose from 8.2 per cent of GDP in 1986 to 21.5 per cent in 1993. The government financed the deficit with increased domestic and external indebtedness and accumulating arrears. Real GDP growth was barely positive and per capita incomes were declining after 1985. There was not much structural change. The framework of controlled prices that had been set up in 1972 was slowly loosened. Further liberalisation in 1986 dropped the number of goods under controls from 38 to 9, but the framework for recontrol remained in place. Over the period from 1987 to 1989, a few commercial parastatals were liquidated and growth in parastatal staffing slowed. Prices were liberalised somewhat, but prices were not terribly distorted at the beginning of the reforms.

The pace of change accelerated in 1989 and 1990. In mid-1989, the party congress approved more liberal economic policies. However pressure for a multi-party system continued to grow backed by trade unions opposed to government austerity measures, students, and opposition groups. Labour unions, protesting job cuts and wage controls, organised strikes and slowed economic activities for the last six months of 1990 and forced the government to accept a multi-party system. The president convened a national conference on reform that ran from February to May of 1991. A transitional government was formed to assume power from the president.

Several economic reforms, such as restraining the public wage bill and size of the civil service were rolled back during the period of unrest. Even though per capita GDP was falling, the labour unions managed to get significant wage increases in 1990 and 1991. The budget was unable to cover the wage bill of the growing civil service, and government fell behind in paying salaries after 1992. By 1994 wage arrears were up to ten months of salary. But some progress was made on other measures. The government economic policy switched to support markets officially in late 1993 and the government abolished marketing monopolies for cocoa and coffee, timber, tobacco and import and distribution of meat, import of consumer goods, and food crops. Several of the remaining 42 parastatals were liquidated or privatised.

Elections were held in July 1992, electing Pascal Lissouba president. But disputes over the elections and actions of the President led to violent civil strife that lasted until January 1994. A compromise government took power under a negotiated arrangement. Per capita incomes continued to decline with a fall of almost 8 per cent in 1994. That year had brought the CFA franc devaluation and a sharp rise in prices. Congo is much more dependent on imported foods than the other CFA countries, importing almost 90 per cent of the food supply, so food prices rose sharply with the devaluation. Social indicators, health services, and education, have all deteriorated badly during the period of economic decline. The government continues to run arrears on salaries and pensions. Congo remains one of the most indebted nations in the world with a ratio of debt to GDP of 282 per cent at end-1995. Debt service in 1995 was 138 per cent of government receipts, 57 per cent of export earnings, and 36 per cent of GDP.

Ethiopia

Ethiopia is the second most populous country in Sub-Saharan Africa with an estimated population of almost 55 million, and one of the poorest countries in the world, with per capita GNP estimated at $100 in 1994 dollars. Agriculture is the backbone of the economy, accounting for over 50 per cent of GDP and over 75 per cent of exports, with coffee the most important export. About 90 per cent of the population is rural, with almost all engaged in traditional agricultural or livestock production.

Poverty is a chronic problem, worsened by periods of serious drought and a crippling civil war that ended only recently. It is estimated that about 52 per cent of the population live below the poverty line.

Ethiopia became socialist in 1974, when a military regime took power after civic opposition ousted the feudal regime of Haile Selassie. The Provisional Military Administrative Council adopted a Declaration of Socialism shortly after taking power and consolidated power under Mengistu Haile Mariam in 1977. The nationalisation programme after the revolution covered almost all large and medium-scale manufacturing industries, mines, commercial farms, banks, insurance companies, wholesale trade and a large share of construction companies. The private sector remained active in the small-scale manufacturing sector. In addition to the enterprises nationalised in 1975, the state increased public investment to begin new parastatals. Little information is available on the financial performance of the 300 state enterprises. The state introduced highly centralised resource allocation, including heavy trade and exchange rate controls on the overvalued currency. Exports fell leading to a shortage of foreign exchange, and decline in imports of spare parts and inputs. Parallel markets in foreign exchange were widespread and encouraged smuggling activity.

All land, rural and urban was nationalised in 1975. Under radical agrarian reforms, land was redistributed with a maximum individual limit of 10 hectares. Tenure was transferred to peasant associations. Private ownership in agriculture and hiring of rural labour were abolished, disrupting traditional production patterns.

Ethiopia

	1980	1981	1982	1983	1984	1985	1986	1987	1988	1989	1990	1991	1992	1993	1994	Averages		
																1980–85	1986–90	1991–94
Real GDP growth rate			0.71	10.39	-5.80	-9.60	9.50	13.80	0.10	0.20	3.40	-6.70	-3.20	12.30	1.30	-1.08	5.40	0.92
per capita			-1.34	8.33	-9.13	-12.79	5.93	10.31	-2.78	-2.96	0.36	-9.66	-6.26	8.79		-3.73	2.17	-2.38
Nom dom invest % of GDP		9.20	11.89	7.08	14.79	8.95	11.86	14.29	16.43	9.66	8.90	7.12	9.31	12.24	16.73		12.23	11.35
real invest % of GDP	na																	
Real VA manuf % of GDP		5.31	5.56	5.36	4.37	4.63	4.65	4.53	4.71	4.68	4.35	2.86	2.67	3.61	3.81	5.05	4.58	3.24
Budget deficit as % of GDP	-4.48	-3.83	-4.36	-10.77	-5.25	-6.21	-5.55	-4.45	-4.90	-6.09	-9.73	-8.50		-7.25	-8.46	-5.82	-6.15	-8.07
Net for aid % of GDP		-4.81										12.47	11.95	12.33				12.25
Current acc % of GDP			-6.81	-5.05	-6.59	-5.56	-3.76	-5.84	-6.63	-3.61	-2.82	-5.17	-1.83	-7.10	-7.36	-5.76	-4.53	-5.37
Real exports as % of GDP	na																	
Parallel exchange premium	1.35	1.50	1.59	1.69	1.93	2.32	1.84	2.22	3.19	2.85	2.90	2.97	3.40	2.42	2.19	1.73	2.60	2.75
Terms of trade	145	102	112	110	127	119	177	100	111	96	76	77	67	74		119.15	112.20	72.43
CPI inflation	4.48	6.14	5.89	-0.68	8.42	19.06	-9.81	-2.43	7.08	7.82	5.15	35.72	10.53	3.54	7.59	7.22	1.56	14.35

Source: real GDP, gross domestic investments, value added manufactures, real export and current account, from *World Tables*; net foreign transfers from OECD; all other series, IMF IFS; parallel exchange premium = parallel rate (from Currency Alert)/official rate (IFS); budget deficit before grants.

The agricultural sector was controlled through the marketing system and cooperatives. The Agricultural Marketing Corporation (AMC), established in 1976, purchased all agricultural products from state farms and producer cooperatives at low producer prices, and specified production quotas for individual smallholder farmers. Private traders were restricted, particularly on inter-regional trade. The Ethiopian Coffee Marketing Corporation established in 1975, became the principal exporter of coffee and restrictions reduced the private sector marketing share from 80 to 10 per cent. A large proportion of the public investment in agriculture was channelled to the unproductive state farms, producer cooperatives, and resettlement schemes. About 43 per cent of total government and banking resources allocated to agriculture, 94 per cent of seed distribution and 76 per cent of fertiliser distribution in the period 1983–87 went to the state farms which contributed only 5 per cent of production. This agricultural policy mix reduced output, exacerbated food shortages and came under severe criticism from donors. Variation in the growth rate in agriculture during the 1980s, with significant droughts in 1981, 1984 and 1987, and low production incentives translated into volatile performance of the economy.

During the 1980s, regional and ideological disputes intensified, and military expenditures absorbed a growing portion of national resources. Starting in 1988, Mengistu's government undertook limited reforms, including improving the environment for private investment and securing tenure for peasants, and increasing producer prices by 7.7 per cent for the first time after 8 years. Private trade in grain was partially liberalised, though a number of restrictions remained. The monopoly of the Ethiopian Coffee Marketing Corporation was abolished, and the export tax reduced to offset the fall in world prices. In 1990, all restrictions on private trade were removed and the system of fixed official prices abolished. But the reforms were late and overtaken by domestic conflict.

The domestic opposition, led by the Ethiopian People's Revolutionary Democratic Front (EPRDF), overthrew the socialist government of Mengistu in May 1991. Also the Eritrean People's Liberation Front (EPLF) gained support for a referendum on independence of Eritrea that finally came in April 1993. Producer cooperatives were completely abolished by 1992. Private sector trade increased. Exports increased in 1992, partially because of better production incentives, but also from a decrease in smuggling with the devaluation of the Birr by 58.6 per cent in October 1992. Taxes on all exports except coffee were removed. Foreign exchange allocation was liberalised through a foreign exchange auction, though import licences are still required for access to foreign exchange. Maximum import duties have been lowered from 230 per cent to 60 per cent. All retail prices, except petroleum, fertiliser and pharmaceuticals, have been decontrolled. A new land leasing policy has started, with an urban land auction conducted in January 1995. Agricultural marketing has been decontrolled and farmers can now hire farm labour. There have been several rounds of privatisations.

The country is still fragmented by considerable regional, political and ethnic tension. But defence expenditures have been reduced from 31 per cent of the budget before the reform period to 7 per cent in fiscal 1995. The Federal Democratic Republic of Ethiopia was formally proclaimed in August 1995.

Guinea

Guinea has an extremely rich natural resource base, with abundant land, significant gold, diamonds, and iron ore, and one third of world bauxite. Per capita GNP is estimated at $510 and has grown by about 1.3 per cent a year in the last ten years. Income distribution is highly skewed, poverty is widespread, and the country ranks very low by any measure of well-being of the population. While agriculture accounts for only about 24 per cent of GDP, it employs about 87 per cent of the labour force.

The country was under the totalitarian socialist rule of Sékou Touré from independence in 1958 to his death 1984. During that period the state attempted highly centralised control with administered prices and rationing for nearly all goods and services. The legal private sector was limited to agricultural production and minor services. Private industry and commerce were illegal, but some survived by smuggling and parallel market activities. The state used revenues from bauxite exports to finance a large civil service. The mining was done under concessions granted to foreign companies.

Guinea

	1980	1981	1982	1983	1984	1985	1986	1987	1988	1989	1990	1991	1992	1993	1994	Averages 1980–85	1986–90	1991–94
Real GDP growth rate	na							2.94	5.90	3.17	4.26	2.50	3.22	4.47	4.47		4.07	3.67
Per capita	na							0.01	2.98	-6.43	1.36	-0.61	0.01	1.32	1.42		-0.52	0.54
Nom dom invest % of GDP	na																	
Real invest % of GDP	na						14.07	15.58	15.88	15.37	17.40	15.71	16.47	16.95	17.98		15.66	16.78
Real VA manuf % of GDP	na						3.44	2.99	3.27	3.33	3.50	3.52	3.54	3.56			3.31	3.54
Budget deficit as % of GDP	na																	
Net for aid % of GNP	na						7.42	9.04	11.21	14.57	11.57	13.49	14.70	13.07			10.76	13.75
Current acc as % of GDP	na						-7.80	-3.60	-12.85	-10.81	-10.84	-13.51	-13.33	-2.12	-7.23		-9.18	-9.05
Real exports as % of GDP	na						31.19	32.33	33.70	34.28	32.65	32.20	28.96	30.28				
Parallel exchange premium	2.20	3.49	4.40	5.55	11.76	12.77	1.19	1.03	1.14	0.98	1.05	1.05	1.10	1.21	1.12	6.69	1.08	1.12
Terms of trade	150	152	140	131	126	120	100	100	100	97	105	97	84	91		136.50	100.50	90.33
CPI inflation	na																	

Source: real GDP, gross domestic investments, value added manufactures, real export and current account from *World Tables*, net foreign transfers, OECD; all other series, IMF, IFS; parallel exchange premium = parallel rate (from Currency Alert)/official rate (IFS).

The army seized power in a coup shortly after Touré's death in April 1984. The early reforms were a shock treatment to the economy after late 1985, allowing many state structures, including the banks, to collapse. Prices and agricultural marketing were decontrolled and the two state enterprises in charge of distribution of goods were liquidated. Much of the early growth came from smallholder farming and small-scale enterprises. The government undertook a rapid poorly-managed privatisation programme. By 1988, of the 131 public enterprises in existence when the programme began, the government had privatised 25, mostly industrial, and liquidated 68, mostly commercial. The privatisation programme was successful in moving enterprises out of the public sector, but drew sharp criticism for lack of transparency and mismanagement. Some of the investment was fraudulent, some depended heavily on financing from the domestic banking system with little equity, and many of the business ventures failed. The large enterprises stayed in the state sector and there has been little progress in restructuring or commercialising those enterprises. The government introduced a new currency in 1986. Access to foreign exchange was gradually allowed for the new private sector and foreign exchange bureaux were established in 1992. There has been an effort to improve fiscal management. The first formal government budget was prepared in 1989 and coverage is spotty. Employment in the civil service was cut from 90,000 in 1986 to 55,000 by late 1989 and less than 51,000 by the end of 1992. However, the remaining government employees still have considerable power to force higher salaries through civil disturbances.

A new constitution was approved in December 1990. President Lansana Conté has maintained power since 1984, winning the disputed presidential elections of December 5, 1993. The country has suffered sporadic civil and ethnic unrest during the 1990s and support for the government is uncertain. Corruption has been a terrible problem. There have been continued problems with the legal and judicial systems, and property rights and contract obligations are poorly or not enforced.

Madagascar

Per capita income in Madagascar is estimated at US $200 and over the last ten years has declined by about 1.7 per cent per year. With highly skewed income distribution, poverty is widespread. The island economy is dependent on agriculture as the main source of income for about 80 per cent of the population and 80 per cent of export earnings with just a few important cash crop exports, coffee, vanilla, and cloves. The small industrial sector is also dependent on agriculture, dominated by food processing, followed by textiles.

Madagascar had a period of very modest growth following independence in 1960 until 1970. The economy stagnated throughout the 1970s and the country adopted socialist economic policies in 1975. Foreign-owned land and assets, minerals, banks, and most internal and external distribution systems were nationalised. Government control over the agricultural sector was exercised through public marketing monopolies and state control of finance and external trade. Industrialisation was emphasised while agricultural incentives were neglected in favour of low food prices for the urban areas.

Between 1978 and 1980 the government undertook a massive public investment programme to expand import substitution manufacturing parastatals and strengthen public services, such as education. Many of the new industrial enterprises – funded by external borrowing on commercial terms, expansion of domestic credit and the coffee boom of 1976/77 – proved unviable. By the early 1980s, the decline in international commodity prices and higher international interest, revealed the unsustainable fiscal position. Real GDP declined 11 per cent between 1980 and 1982. The country attempted stabilisation measures throughout most of the 1980s, slowed inflation, and reduced the current account and fiscal deficits by rationing imports and investment and tighter controls rather than structural changes. Quantitative restrictions on trade increased, the currency remained overvalued, and most goods were still under price controls. The growth rate was modest, GDP growth was only 1.4 per cent per annum from 1983 to 1987 and per capita income continued to decline.

The country gave more attention to structural change after 1987. Price controls were eliminated during 1987/88 with the final controls on retail prices lifted in 1989. There was a 55 per cent devaluation of the real exchange rate in June 1987, protective import quotas were replaced by tariffs and an 'open general licence' system of foreign exchange allocation for merchandise imports was established in 1988. A new banking law in 1988 allowed for foreign

Madagascar

	1980	1981	1982	1983	1984	1985	1986	1987	1988	1989	1990	1991	1992	1993	1994	Averages 1980–85	1986–90	1991–94
Real GDP growth rate	0.81	-9.70	-1.81	0.90	1.70	1.15	1.96	1.18	3.40	4.08	3.13	-6.31	1.13	2.15	1.08	-1.16	2.75	-0.49
per capita	-2.75	-11.51	-5.81	0.26	-7.09	4.29	-7.41	-2.20	-0.02	0.65	11.97	-8.67	-13.41	-1.03	-2.10	-3.77	0.60	-6.30
Nom dom invest % of GDP	14.96	11.48	8.49	8.37	8.62	8.55	9.04	10.10	13.29	13.39	16.97	8.17	11.30	11.45	11.69	10.08	12.56	10.65
real invest % of GDP	13.22	10.20	8.51	8.35	8.62	8.63	8.92	10.28	13.31	13.40	16.62	7.70	11.07	11.77	9.21	9.59	12.50	9.94
Real VA manuf % of GDP					10.33	11.30	11.51	11.93	11.74	11.43	10.97	11.58	11.24			10.82	11.52	11.41
Budget deficit as % of GDP									-3.52	-4.14	-0.87	-5.11	-6.21	-4.78			-2.84	-5.36
Net for aid % of GDP	5.76	6.18	6.72	5.41	4.82	6.24	10.41	10.86	10.62	12.32	14.00	16.97	12.60	12.14	0.00	5.86	11.64	13.90
Current acc % of GDP	-15.43	-12.39	-10.99	-9.18	-9.24	-9.02	-8.37	-10.12	-12.58	-9.33	-14.26	-11.78	-9.46	-9.68	-16.63	-11.04	-10.93	-11.89
Real exports as % of GDP	18.95	15.49	14.62	12.70	13.16	12.60	12.35	12.56	11.14	12.52	13.59	15.20	15.32	15.72	16.65	14.59	12.43	15.72
Parallel exchange premium	1.25	1.41	2.00	2.05	1.53	1.04	1.21	0.79	1.19	1.02	1.0	1.07	1.20	1.16	1.02	1.55	1.05	1.11
Terms of trade	121	103	100	107	123	124	134	100	99	84	76	76	68	82		112.93	98.64	75.57
CPI inflation	18.22	30.54	31.79	19.33	9.86	10.56	14.50	14.99	26.85	9.01	11.78	8.59	14.51	10.01	38.94	20.05	15.43	18.01

Source: real GDP, gross domestic investments, value added manufactures, real export and current account, from World Tables; net foreign transfers from OECD; all other series, IMF IFS; parallel exchange premium = parallel rate (from Currency Alert)/official rate (IFS); budget deficit before grants.

and domestic private banks and the state banks were restructured in 1988/89. One state bank was sold to a French bank and a foreign bank took a minority position in another state bank in early 1991, but the largest state banks remained totally state owned. Agricultural markets were liberalised gradually crop by crop, e.g. internal trade in rice in 1986, with trade liberalised to allow private rice imports in 1990, and agricultural exports were liberalised over the period 1985 to 1992 as the country faced a 20 per cent decline in the terms of trade between 1988 and 1992. A few parastatals were liquidated, but there were not aggressive actions on commercialisation or privatisation. There is still little competition. The economy is dominated by large public enterprises and foreign firms, as well as a few 'favoured' private firms.

Positive but low real economic growth was not sufficient to stop the slide in per capita income, which continued to decline except in 1989 and 1990. The brief improvement in the economy faltered with unfavourable international export prices and political unrest by the early 1990s. The early stabilisation and modest structural reforms were undertaken under the same political elite who had presided over the socialist period. Popular unrest and a civil service strike disrupted the economy after June 1991, finally ending the 17 year rule of Didier Ratsiraka. A transition government was installed in January 1992 and Albert Zafy won multi-party elections in February 1993. There is still political opposition to economic reforms.

Mozambique

Mozambique is listed as the second poorest country in the world, with estimated per capita income of US $90. Over the last ten years, estimated GNP per capita growth has been about 3.8 per cent a year from a very small base. Mozambique is starting now to rebuild from over 15 years of brutal internal conflict. About 85 per cent of the labour force is engaged in agriculture, and almost all exports are agricultural. During the war, much of the rural area was subject to rural banditry that made normal economic activities impossible.

The socialist period began in 1975 when Frelimo assumed power after the collapse of the Portuguese colonial system. From independence in 1975 to 1990, Frelimo was the sole party and ran Mozambique along Marxist-Leninist lines. Almost from the beginning there was active military opposition operating in the country with considerable foreign support. Over 90 per cent of the population of Mozambique was illiterate at independence. Portuguese colonial policy had reserved all skilled jobs for the 200,000 Portuguese settlers. The economy was devastated by the abrupt departure of the Portuguese settlers, shutting down parts of the economy. The young, poorly prepared state sector expanded, partially by ideological design and partially by default to keep the economy running after the colonists left. The companies, farms and plantations abandoned/relinquished by departing Portuguese were 'intervened', merged into large units, and run by the state. Few industries were nationalised as a deliberate policy measure. All land was nationalised but the state recognised the tenure of those who occupied and worked it. The government developed a dominant state marketing agencies after the private colonial system collapsed. Prices were set centrally and pan-territorially, and were used to tax agriculture. Almost all funds allocated for agriculture went into the large state farms. During the early years resources were devoted to literacy campaigns and the illiteracy rate declined from 93 per cent of the population at independence to 68 per cent by 1989.

The economy slowly recovered from 1977 to 1981, but then deteriorated again after 1982 as the government faced active opposition from the Mozambique National Resistance (MNR or Renamo) operating with significant foreign support. Real GDP declined by an average of 6 per cent per year from 1982 to 1986. The war was brutal, targeting transportation, communication, health and education facilities with a terrible toll on civilians, especially in rural areas. Government economic policies exacerbated the problems with administrative controls on prices and allocation of goods and services with strong disincentives to production. Output in agriculture and industries fell by about 50 per cent from 1981 to 1985.

Mozambique began to reorient economic policy in 1983. Frelimo privatised the small shops and restaurants 'intervened' when the Portuguese left. More substantial reforms were tried after 1987 with the goal to restore production to the level of 1981 by 1990. Administrative controls were lifted slowly in stages, constrained by the shortage of skilled government employees capable of dealing with institutional reforms and the problems of a large vulnerable population displaced from their homes without an adequate safety net. Gradually, producer prices were raised closer to border prices

Mozambique

	1980	1981	1982	1983	1984	1985	1986	1987	1988	1989	1990	1991	1992	1993	1994	Averages 1980–85	1986–90	1991–94
Real GDP growth rate		6.01	-8.21	-15.59	-6.56	1.01	-2.31	14.70	8.21	6.48	1.02	4.89	-0.81	19.32	5.40	-4.67	5.62	7.20
per capita		3.28	-10.58	-17.72	-9.33	-1.61	-4.31	15.02	9.53	6.41	-0.34	2.93	-3.29	13.27	-1.13	-7.19	5.26	2.94
Nom dom invest % of GDP	22.48	22.84	22.80	12.17	13.89	16.99	18.79	39.66	47.53	42.50	45.87	48.49	53.20	59.71	60.21	18.53	38.87	55.40
real invest % of GDP	44.50	44.02	46.01	43.32	41.50	38.49	45.26	39.66	38.30	34.75	36.57	36.88	36.89	39.49	37.49	42.97	38.91	37.69
Real VA manuf % of GDP	na																	
Budget deficit as % of GDP	na																	
Net for aid % of GDP			10.41	4.97	63.40	69.74	17.97	32.78	56.04	64.14	81.41	79.73	117.20	85.56		37.13	50.47	94.16
Current acc % of GDP	-20.86	-22.87	-27.71	-27.12	-24.56	-17.17	-20.84	-51.23	-61.12	-63.74	-59.85	-59.02	-68.54	-56.19	-59.30	-23.38	-51.35	-60.76
Real exports as % of GDP	22.00	18.69	20.36	18.80	16.09	14.81	13.79	12.94	13.13	13.46	14.88	18.08	18.01	15.61	15.89	18.46	13.64	16.90
Parallel exchange premium	2.18	1.87	2.34	3.51	30.14	35.76	42.55	6.75		1.48	2.14	1.13	1.22	1.32	1.20	12.63	13.23	1.22
Terms of trade	121	125	101	107	122	113	109	100	109	123	120	122	122	124		115.77	112.24	122.77
CPI inflation									50.14	40.15	47.01	32.93	45.49	42.20			45.76	40.21

Source: real GDP, gross domestic investments, value added manufactures, real export and current account, from *World Tables*; net foreign transfers from OECD; all other series, IMF IFS; parallel exchange premium = parallel rate (from Currency Alert)/official rate (IFS); budget deficit before grants.

and consumer subsidies were reduced. Government freed a small part of the foreign exchange allocation and tariffs were reduced and harmonised to help liberalise trade. Smuggling from South Africa was common and tariff collection was spotty so the government was not able to enforce domestic price controls. The planning mechanism was downgraded and the role of state trading companies was reduced. The economy improved somewhat from 1987 to 1989 and inflation fell, but with much of the rural area disrupted by war and a severe shortage of foreign exchange and imported inputs, supply response was limited. Part of the improvement could be attributed to the massive inflows of foreign and humanitarian aid.

Enterprises, facing better quality imports smuggled in from neighbouring countries, were freed from the most restrictive practices of central planning after 1987. Budgetary subsidies were slashed, but the state banks still provided credit at negative real interest rates. Production patterns were largely determined by the availability of foreign exchange and donor-financed inputs. Privatisation expanded to include medium companies through management/worker buy-outs on credit or through joint ventures. The larger enterprises remained in the state sector, partially because of the difficulty of finding buyers. In agriculture, the number of state farms was reduced from 70 in 1986 to around 16 in 1989 with the assets transferred to the private sector.

The pace of exchange rate reform was accelerated from mid-1990 with the establishment of a secondary foreign exchange market and an increase in the rate of devaluation of the official exchange rate.

The ratio of the parallel to the official exchange rate fell from almost 7 in 1987 to 2 by 1990 and was only about 1.2 after 1991. However, the real growth rate was only 2 per cent from 1990 to 1992, due to renewed fighting and banditry, loss of Soviet aid, and a severe drought in 1992. Before 1992 the government discouraged labour shedding because the government was already dealing with large camps of displaced persons but as output fell labour policy became more flexible.

A new constitution came into force in November 1990 allowing for a multi-party system, but Frelimo was still the sole legal political party. A peace agreement was signed in October 1992. Unlike Angola, the peace process in Mozambique demobilised the military before the elections. National attention turned to efforts to negotiate a domestic peace agreement and prepare for elections. Joaquim

Alberto Chissano, who had become president in 1986 after the death of Samora Moises Machel, won the election in October 1994 and continued as president.

External aid was made available to help with the expensive task of demobilising the two combatant armies. The current account balance deficit was 78 per cent of GDP in 1993. The population has been returning from exile in neighbouring countries and settlement camps. But there are still unsettling episodes of unrest and banditry in rural areas.

Somalia

Factional fighting splintered Somalia in 1991 in a dramatic display of the tensions that had mounted in the country for many years. 'Scientific socialism' was adopted in 1969 after the military under General Mohammed Siad Barre seized the government and Barre's one-party rule lasted until 1991, when opposition groups united to drive him from power.

Livestock production, marketing and exports, are the most significant economic activities accounting for about 50 per cent of GDP and employment. Nearly 50 per cent of the population is nomadic and dependent on livestock herds. Livestock export marketing, controlled by 50 to 60 traders, was done by the private sector.

Barre's development strategy mobilised donor funds to start public industrial enterprises for food processing and basic consumer goods. Government control of the industrial sector was through the centralised distribution of critical inputs, e.g. foreign exchange and credit. Socialism was manifest through a major public sector role in the economy and the importance of domestic monopolies and prohibition of the private sector. When military alliances shifted from the USSR to the US during Barre's regime after the Soviet Union switched to support Ethiopia in the Ogaden war in 1977, there was little impact on economic policy.

Starting economic reforms in 1981, the remainder of the 1980s was characterised by on and off stabilisation efforts and two rounds of attempted liberalisation of the economy in 1986 and 1989. The period was characterised by recurrent breaks with the multilateral donors and mismanagement of foreign aid. Corruption, political instability, military expenditures and human rights abuses escalated and overwhelmed economic reforms.

The income situation slipped during the 1980s. Income was estimated at $280 in 1983, making Somalia the 18th poorest country in the world. The estimates and ranking were the same in 1988. By 1991, Somalia had fallen to the fourth poorest country in the world with income estimated at $170. More recent estimates are not available, but would undoubtedly place Somalia again as one of the poorest countries.

Civil unrest pushed Barre to agree to economic and political reforms by the late 1980s but the government had already lost control as the country and the economy disintegrated. A coalition of armed opposition intensified fighting and entered Mogadishu at the end of 1990. Inter-clan and inter-regional disputes broke out as the coalition collapsed. Somalia has been without national government since 1991.

Tanzania

Tanzania has a reported per capita income of $140, making it the fourth poorest country in the world. Over the last ten years, real per capita GNP growth has averaged about .8 per cent per year. Agriculture provides 60 per cent of GDP, 85 per cent of employment, and over half of export revenues.

In 1967, six years after independence, the Tanzanian leadership proclaimed a shift to economic policy based on 'socialism and self-reliance' in the Arusha Declaration. Banks, insurance institutions, private trading companies and large foreign-owned estates in sisal, tea, and coffee were nationalised. Most industrial ventures were nationalised or forced into joint ventures with the government. Import and export activities, as well as domestic wholesale trade in most commodities, were 'confined' to monopoly state trading companies.

The government also adopted a socialist rural development strategy. In the late 1960s the government encouraged relocation of scattered villages and homesteads into Ujamaa villages with the expectation that communal farming would replace private farming. The effort intensified with compulsory relocation programmes in the early 1970s. After severely disrupting the rural economy, the population was allowed to drift back to peasant farming, but the state controlled input and output marketing. The state dissolved the farmer-owned marketing cooperatives and introduced massively inefficient state marketing agencies that heavily taxed producers. Agricultural exports fell sharply.

The state successfully mobilised large inflows of foreign aid and captured the revenues from higher international coffee prices in the late 1970s to expand the parastatals. The 'Basic Industries' programme of 1981–83 was poorly conceived and implemented, consumed huge amounts of foreign aid and left the country with an unviable industrial base that operated at a fraction of capacity. Price controls were pervasive. The government controlled all foreign exchange and therefore all imports at the firm level.

The economy collapsed in the early 1980s. Real GDP declined from 1981 to 1983. With growing donor scepticism, foreign aid was no longer automatic. Imports fell by 40 per cent in nominal terms from 1980 to 1984. Price controls were maintained, but since few goods were available on official markets, the price controls only served to transfer significant rents to the bureaucrats with access to scarce goods. Goods disappeared into the parallel economy and parallel prices were many times official prices. Rural residents retreated into subsistence farming or resorted to smuggling to avoid the heavy taxation imposed on trade by the state. Earlier progress in extending literacy and basic health care lost ground.

Dr Julius Nyerere stepped aside as president and was replaced in November 1985 by Ali Hassan Mwinyi. Nyerere continued as CCM party chairman until 1990. While reforms were more substantial after 1986, the country remained socialist and reforms had to be presented as an adjustment rather than a rejection of past economic policy. The monopoly on foreign exchange had been a critical control mechanism for the government and that monopoly was relinquished only slowly. In an attempt to overcome the severe shortages of goods, the state allowed an 'own funds import' scheme in 1984 that gave import licences without question to importers with 'own funds'. This was followed with various schemes to distribute some donor foreign exchange outside direct government control and then allowing exporters to retain some earned exchange. Finally, in 1992 the government allowed foreign exchange bureaux. Even with very large nominal devaluation, inflation remained high and the real exchange rate was appreciated during several periods in the reforms. The institutional changes, as well as the move to more fre-

Tanzania

	1980	1981	1982	1983	1984	1985	1986	1987	1988	1989	1990	1991	1992	1993	1994	Averages 1980–85	1986–90	1991–94
Real GDP growth rate	2.66	-1.05	-0.41	-0.70	4.43	0.68	4.92	4.73	7.13	8.46	6.33	2.37	-0.09	2.57		0.93	6.32	1.62
per capita	-0.66	-4.10	-3.49	-3.76	1.20	-2.42	1.51	1.30	3.65	4.96	2.89	-0.62	-3.03	-0.43		-2.20	2.86	-1.36
Nom dom invest % of GDP	22.99	24.69	21.01	13.60	15.32	17.74	25.27	50.04	12.92	44.77	42.97	47.87	48.94	50.66		19.23	35.20	49.16
real invest % of GDP	23.17	24.44	25.29	17.98	23.53	30.01	25.87	39.74	6.61	26.53	29.57	32.29	31.18	29.43		24.07	25.66	30.97
Real VA manuf % of GDP	10.19	9.14	8.88	8.16	8.02	7.66	7.00	6.99	6.99	6.93	6.36	6.92	7.08	7.05		8.68	6.85	7.02
Budget deficit as % of GDP	-9.61	-10.24	-11.34	-7.86	-6.64	-7.51	-5.84	-7.55	-3.24	-2.52	-2.02	-5.06	-4.84	-8.14	-7.47	-8.86	-4.24	-6.38
Net for aid % of GDP	12.53	12.20	11.45	9.78	9.06	7.61	11.27	17.18	23.43	27.00	38.60	38.67	47.85	37.83		10.44	23.50	41.45
Current acc % of GDP	-12.22	-8.67	-9.83	-6.15	-7.83	-7.32	-11.15	-20.28	-22.94	-29.49	-37.07	-35.19	-38.96	-39.40		-8.67	-24.19	-37.85
Real exports as % of GDP	na	2.56	3.51	3.55	3.73	3.81	4.92	2.72	2.13	1.84	1.50	1.60	1.36	1.29	1.03	3.42	2.62	1.32
Parallel exchange premium	3.33																	
Terms of trade	142	129	127	128	131	126	141	100	107	103	93	94	85	83		130.53	108.70	87.23
CPI inflation	30.20	26.65	28.93	27.06	36.15	33.28	32.43	29.95	31.19	25.85	35.83	28.70	21.85	25.28	34.08	30.21	31.05	27.48

Source: real GDP, gross domestic investments, value added manufactures, real export and current account, from *World Tables*; net foreign transfers from OECD; all other series, IMF IFS; parallel exchange premium = parallel rate (from Currency Alert)/official rate (IFS); budget deficit before grants.

quent nominal devaluations, were reflected in the ratio of the parallel to the official exchange rate. The ratio climbed above 3 in 1981, reached 5 in 1986, and declined gradually to a ratio close to one by 1994. The system of pervasive price controls was dismantled from coverage of over 400 categories of goods in the early 1980s to 22 in 1987/88, and 12 in June 1988. The private sector was allowed to enter domestic trade to compete with parastatals, ending the government monopoly in wholesale trade.

Marketed agricultural production rose. Producer prices were not increased much through benefits dissipated by inefficiencies in the state agricultural marketing, but more incentive consumer goods were available in rural areas. The state monopoly on grain marketing was progressively loosened between 1985 and 1990 and the huge grain marketing parastatal, NMC, withered. Cooperatives were reconstituted to play a role in food marketing. Even though nominally private, these were creations of the state, closely linked to political interests, and many operated at a loss financed by the state banks. Liberalisation of export crop marketing was very slow and undertaken during a period of falling international prices on many export commodities. The state maintained monopoly control of exports and producer incentives remained low because of the inefficient marketing system throughout the early years of reform.

Foreign financing was important in ending the pre-reform import contraction and allowing the government to reduce reliance on the domestic banking system for deficit financing. But the banks continued as an important source of quasi-fiscal financing. Passive lending from the state banks and forbearance of arrears softened the budget constraint to agricultural marketing institutions, parastatals, and 'favoured' private enterprises leaving a huge stock of bad loans in the banks. This financing mechanism allowed the government to show a declining fiscal deficit, while still channelling resources to state structures. By 1988 the banks were in terrible shape and the government undertook an extremely expensive recapitalisation of the banks. While 'nominally' recapitalised, the state banks have not improved much and are still making losses. Monetary control has been a recurrent problem. Recorded inflation has been 22–35 per cent since the beginning of the 1980s. The more than 300 parastatals survived with a host of mechanisms used to soften the budget constraint. In addition to financing from state banks, there were arrears on counterpart funds, taxes, import duties, etc. The

Tanzanian approach had been to allow private sector entry to compete with the parastatals, but privatisation was very low on the policy agenda during the first years of reform. By 1995 the country allowed multi-party election and Benjamin Mkapa was elected president as the third CCM government in Tanzania.

2 Government in Africa's Emerging Market Economies

Edgardo Barandiaran[1]

There is a consensus of opinion across the political spectrum that the boundaries of state intervention and management in Africa should be more circumscribed than they have been. Sometimes it is said that the need is not so much for less government as for better government. Extensive state interventions in, and management of, economic life might be desirable, if only their quality were assured. This point glosses the argument only slightly, if, as seems usually the case, the quality of government deteriorates the more there is of it. The consensus to which I referred seems to be present even in official circles of Africa. But that would surely not be so if African economic growth had not been checked in the 1980s, if external debts had not become onerous, and if the real resources available to governments had not consequently diminished. Ideas of what tasks may fittingly be undertaken by governments in Africa have long depended on current financial prospects; governments have been unambitious only so long as they were not becoming richer. (Rimmer, 1989, p. 175)

Several African[2] countries are making a radical break with the quasi-socialist systems that emerged after their independence. They are in the midst of a historical transformation towards democracy and markets. Among many challenges, these countries face the long-term task of reforming their governments: what functions should government perform? how should government redeploy human and physical resources to private activities and to new public activities? how should government secure enough revenue to finance its activities? how should government manage its revenue to maximise social benefit over time?

This chapter addresses these and other questions posed by government reform in Africa. Instead of providing a thorough description and assessment of this reform, which would have required the systematic application of some analytical framework to particular country experiences, the chapter only outlines such a framework and argues its relevance to Africa's emerging market economies. The basic premise is that reform should be judged by its progress to achieve an ideal institutional structure and its expected outcomes, rather than by particular outcomes that compare favourably with past performance. The benchmark should be absolute and normative, not relative and positive.

1. The Collapse of African Quasi-Socialist Economies

The economic systems that emerged in Africa after independence had some resemblance to the classical socialist economy as defined by Kornai (1992). They possessed some attributes of the economies that had completed the transition from capitalism to socialism in the 1950s. But there were important differences. According to Kornai's account, in 1987 only seven African countries (Angola, Benin, Congo, Ethiopia, Mozambique, Somalia, and Zimbabwe) could be regarded as socialist, although five others (Cape Verde, Guinea Bissau, Madagascar, São Tomé, and Seychelles) could have fitted his definition. A few others had started their political and economic reform before 1987 but would have qualified as socialist before embarking on reform. Others attempted to develop socialist institutions in the 1960s and 1970s but failed to implement them, and ended up with economies that resembled the mercantilist systems of many Latin American countries in the nineteenth century, in turn a natural continuation of the colonial economy.

Africa's quasi-socialist economies, founded on the mercantilist systems of colonial times rather than on the (primitive) capitalist systems that preceded socialism elsewhere, failed to make the transition to the classical socialist economy. Once the revolutionary, pro-independence forces that facilitated the mobilisation of resources to provide goods and services to a majority of the population faded, and once redistribution of existing wealth became a conflict mainly among domestic groups, the ruling party failed to set an effective central organisation for production and trade. The central organisation of the classical socialist economy eventually collapsed everywhere, but in Africa, this central organisation failed even to emerge.

This failure does not deny the important role played by other economic forces, both internal and external, in the collapse of Africa's economies. In particular, the changing external environment posed a heavy burden on Africa's limited capacity for designing and executing appropriate policy responses. Some countries did not have the capacity to manage the windfall gains from main exports wisely or to use large flows of foreign aid efficiently, while others failed to finance temporary losses properly or to adjust promptly to permanent losses.

Indeed, the initial conditions of the ongoing process of political and economic reform differed sharply across countries. In addition to the extent to which each country deviated from the classical socialist economy and the extent to which each one had been able to respond to the external environment, the political circumstances were different. For example, in some countries, reform followed long civil wars with substantial losses of human and physical capital. This has been the case of Angola.

Angola's Experience[3]

By the time of its independence in 1975, Angola was a divided country in which the rapidly increasing Portuguese population had managed to attain a relatively high standard of living.[4] In the post-war period Portuguese settlers were attracted to Angola mainly because of the potential of mining and plantation agriculture. Indigenous Angolans benefited very little from that expansion, however. They were not able to acquire or develop skills and had to choose between working in the growing activities controlled by the Portuguese and farming in the areas where they were forced to relocate. Not surprisingly, the departure of 85–90 per cent of the Portuguese settlers in 1975–76, aggravated by the loss of physical capital destroyed during the war of independence or taken out by settlers, seriously disrupted the economy. Thus, the drastic reduction in the country's human and physical capital means that the output level before independence is useless as a benchmark for assessing the economy's potential and performance after 1976.

Since independence, Angola's economy has performed poorly. Despite the rapid expansion of oil production at a time in which prices have been higher than ever before, living standards have hardly improved and poverty remains a formidable problem. Until

1990, this performance was largely explained by the Government's attempts to impose a socialist system, and by a violent civil war in which opposing sides were backed by large numbers of foreign troops. In late 1992, the civil war restarted without foreign intervention and since then economic performance and living conditions have deteriorated further.

According to our gross estimates of Angola's GDP (Table 1), it appears that oil output increased 180 per cent between 1976–80 and 1986–90 while non-oil output increased only 7 per cent between those two five-year periods. In 1991, oil output accounted for between one third (at current prices) and one half (at constant 1976–80 prices) of the country's GDP compared with 25 per cent in 1976–80. The dismal performance of the large public sector explains most of Angola's poor GDP growth in 1976–90.

Notwithstanding the increase in GDP, national disposable income increased little, if at all, between 1976 and 1990. In addition to lower oil prices, national income was affected by the rapid growth of factor payments to the rest of the world because of the expansion of oil produced by foreign companies, the services of foreign troops and the interest bill on the growing foreign debt. Factor payments amounted to around 15 per cent of GDP in 1986–90 compared with no more than 5 per cent in 1976–80 (Table 2). In that period Angola did not receive any foreign aid that could have offset, at least partly, the increasing factor payments.

Declining living standards resulted from allocating an increasing share of the constant national income to finance the civil war, and from a rapidly growing population (2.7 per cent per year in the 1980s). Consumption, excluding military expenditures, declined from over 90 per cent of national income in 1976–80 to no more than 85 per cent in 1986–90, while population increased around 50 per cent in the same period (Table 2). Thus, real per capita consumption declined around 20 per cent between the two five-year periods.

Despite a per capita GDP much higher than the average of US$275 for the group of Africa's low-income countries, in 1991 Angola's indicators of nutrition, health, life expectancy, infant mortality and education were worse than the average for this group of countries. In addition, social conditions deteriorated in the 1980s, especially education. According to the 1990 Luanda household budget and nutritional survey, 36 per cent of the population of

Luanda were below the poverty line and 6 per cent of the same
population were below the extreme poverty line.

Table 1: *Angola: Gross Estimates of GDP and its Composition*
(US$ billions)

	1976–80	1981–85	1986–90	1991
At current prices				
Total GDP	4.25	6.00	6.55	7.50
– Oil	1.10	1.50	2.15	2.55
– Non-oil				
Public sector	2.35	3.20	3.00	3.00
Private sector	0.80	1.30	1.40	1.95
At constant 1976–80 prices				
Total GDP	4.25	5.10	6.40	7.00
– Oil	1.10	1.50	3.00	3.60
– Non-oil				
Public sector	2.35	2.55	2.35	2.15
Private sector	0.80	1.05	1.05	1.25

Source: author's estimates. The estimates are based on official estimates of
national accounts for a few years in the late 1980s and oil production in the
past 16 years, as well as on information on prices.

Note: the oil sector includes crude oil, gas and petroleum products. The
public sector includes all levels of government and all public enterprises.
The private sector includes subsistence agriculture and a few other
activities, mainly services.

Since independence, oil has been the main source of foreign
exchange and government revenue, as well as an important
determinant of living standards. By 1975, oil production had already
become an enclave in Angola's economy, but the Government

moved quickly to exercise ownership and control over it through the establishment of SONANGOL, a public enterprise which in 1978 became the sole concessionaire for oil exploration and production in the country. At the time, the conditions were right for SONANGOL to attract numerous international oil companies to explore and produce, and the success of the incentives given to these companies is reflected in the large increase in production and exports during the 1980s.

Table 2: *Angola: National Disposable Income and Consumption*
(at current prices in US$ billions)

	1976–80	1981–85	1986–90	1991
GDP	4.25	6.00	6.55	7.50
National income	4.00	5.30	5.50	6.40
Consumption*	3.60	4.70	4.70	5.25
Consumption* (constant prices 1976–80)	3.60	3.75	3.60	3.90
Per capita consumption* (constant prices, US$)	480	445	385	380

Source: author's estimates, see Table 1.
* Excluding military spending.

Oil has affected the rest of the economy mainly through the Government and foreign exchange budgets. Even without taking full account of oil companies' payments to SONANGOL, by 1990 tax revenue from oil began to account for more than 90 per cent of both government's current revenue and the foreign exchange allocated through the so-called foreign exchange budget. Thus, the allocation of oil revenue became a critical issue in the Government's economic management. It is no exaggeration to say that the allocation of oil revenue overshadowed the management of other public resources which were quite considerable.

The significance of oil revenue was one of several reasons why Government was not able to implement the socialist system announced in 1976. After most enterprises had been nationalised or confiscated and state monopolies established in most activities, central planning and administrative controls became entrenched ideas in both the Party and the Government. Attempts to implement these ideas had to be revised frequently to accommodate and adjust to Angola's reality and peculiarities.[5] Although the Angolan system never settled, it developed all the weaknesses of the classical socialist economy, aggravated by the lack of managerial and technical skills and the absence of a few clear, well-defined objectives. Also, because of the challenge of managing and controlling the large and variable oil revenue, the central authorities did not have incentives to prepare plans or control the implementation of ill-prepared plans. Finally, the civil war outweighed the Government's pursuit of any economic objective, especially in 1985–88 when a military solution was likely.

In late 1985, a Party Congress acknowledged that the socialist system was working poorly. It was clear then that no plan was actually guiding the allocation of public resources – especially that the foreign exchange budget was ineffective as an allocative mechanism – and that the final distribution of consumption goods was increasingly determined by parallel markets rather than administrative control. In 1986–88 the failures become more notorious because of the decline in oil prices and the increase in military spending. The allocation of foreign exchange and other resources became occasionally an arbitrary, wilful political act, independent of economic consideration, but generally a result of opportunistic behaviour by subordinates. The distribution of consumption goods became largely determined by parallel markets, so most official prices, which had been fixed at the same level for years, became irrelevant.

In August 1987, the Government finally announced its intention of correcting the economy's pervasive imbalances and reforming the economic system. A Technical Secretariat was charged with the task of preparing policy and legal initiatives to correct the imbalances and enhance efficiency in resource allocation. Laws were passed in 1988 to improve both the planning system and the allocation of foreign exchange, to enlarge the role of the private sector, to increase the autonomy of public enterprises, and to encourage foreign investment. Later, in 1991, laws were passed to reform the central bank and to develop a financial system, to free prices and monetise wages. From 1989, serious but insufficient measures were implemented to correct the fiscal and external imbalances, but by the time of the presidential and congressional elections (September 1992) that precipitated the restart of the civil war, the imbalances were still significant.

2. Emerging Market Economies

From the experience of reforming socialist economies, it is well known that their systemic transformation involves four inter-dependent elements: insuring control of public finances (or stab-ilisation), changing to a price system, setting the legal order for private activities, and reforming government. All four elements are critical for a successful transformation: persistent imbalances in public finances generate uncertainty about economic policies and deny all other reforms a positive effect; continued reliance on administrative rationing encourages rent-seeking activities and aggravates pervasive distortions in resource allocation; reluctance to empower people to own real assets, to organise and to exchange severely limits the supply response to a price system; and continued undersupply of government services hinders investment in human and physical capital. The policy and legal reforms introduced in the past decade notwithstanding, Africa's reforming countries appear to have made some progress in stabilising the economy and changing to an effective price system, but little progress in setting the found-ations for private sector development and reforming government.

Stabilisation

Because of the large fiscal and balance of payments imbalances that precipitated the collapse of Africa's quasi-socialist economies, stabilisation became the immediate objective of economic reform. It has proved to be a complex problem indeed. Even where government could have restored control over its finances without major reforms in taxation and spending, stabilisation has been elusive. In most countries, reform was started after the accumulation of large public debts with domestic and foreign creditors which would be fully repaid only if governments were capable of taxing heavily a minority of the population or denying most government services to a majority of the population or getting access to new foreign aid. Not surprisingly, renegotiations for the existing debt with foreign creditors has been a critical component of stabilisation.[6,7]

In most reforming countries, correction of the flow imbalance in public finances – i.e. the generation of a primary surplus large enough to service the outstanding debt after it has been renegotiated – has demanded significant reforms in taxation and spending. The reduction of the flow imbalance notwithstanding, there is no indication that government's solvency has been restored. In most countries, the tax system has yet to be reformed to generate revenue efficiently and the budgetary process revamped to secure an efficient functional and intertemporal utilisation of this revenue. As long as government lacks the capacity to secure the control of public finances – as indicated by the persistence of fiscal imbalances that have to be financed by taxing monetary balances and financial intermediation, and by unsustainable levels of foreign grants and concessional credit – surveillance by IMF or other international organisations will continue to be the only alternative to maintain the credibility of the stabilisation programme.

Changing to a Price System

Many African countries used to rely on administrative systems for rationing foreign exchange, capital and a number of goods and services. A few countries attempted but failed to introduce a complex system for rationing all goods and services as in the classical socialist economy. The control of prices, wages and interest rates created large distortions, but parallel markets often mitigated the allocative effects of such controls at the cost of encouraging rent-seeking activities. Parallel markets flourished when governments attempted to repress the inflationary effects of their fiscal imbalances by controlling prices, wages and interest rates. Prices in parallel markets eventually reflected the relative use values or scarcities, and therefore when official prices were increased to parallel market levels, the adjustment had minor allocative effects.

A price system means unified prices for homogeneous foreign exchange, goods, services, labour and capital, as well as prices that respond freely to market forces. Reforming the rationing system requires both the unification and liberalisation of prices. The reforms, however, should take note of factors that may justify differences in policies about foreign exchange, goods and services, labour and capital.

a) Exchange rate unification is a key initial step in introducing a price system – even if Africa's quasi-socialist economies have been more open to international trade than suggested by trade statistics – and has to be implemented immediately to secure a rational allocation of foreign exchange. Thus unification assumes the convertibility of the national currency, at least for all current-account transactions. It has to be followed by a decision on the exchange rate regime which poses a serious dilemma because of the limited success so far in securing both fiscal discipline and flexibility in domestic prices.

b) The freeing of prices and the elimination of public sector employees' entitlements are major steps in unifying domestic markets for consumption goods and services. The domestic structure of relative prices may continue to be distorted, however, because of limited competition. Opening the economy to foreign trade, including the effective abolition of both the government monopoly on trade and the licensing system of imports and exports as well as a reduction in the level and dispersion of tariffs, is the best way to introduce competition immediately.

c) Since wage flexibility and labour mobility appear to have been a problem only in some urban centres where government has been the main source of employment, freeing up labour markets is closely linked to. government reform. In particular, the monetisation of public sector's wages and government's takeover of public enterprises' social responsibilities are prerequisites for developing labour markets.

d) The freeing of interest rates in the transition to a market economy requires balancing two competing objectives. On one hand, the banking system has to continue funding the existing public debt as well as the new public debt (even if the growth rate of this debt has declined as a result of fiscal adjustment). To secure the service of the public debt, interest rates should be as low as possible, which can be attained only by government control. On the other hand, to assure the expansion of financial intermediation (the banking system in particular) and to allow interest rates to play some role in the allocation of capital, the rates have to be set close to market-clearing levels. To get out of this dilemma, the existing debt with the financial system has to be re-financed (or even eliminated by an inflationary shot) and government borrowing from the financial system has to be legally constrained.

Setting a Legal System

The supply response to market-determined prices depends on how effectively and quickly the structure of incentives is reformed. The effectiveness of new structures will hinge on the relative roles of markets and governments, but except for a broad consensus among donors and an increasing number of African politicians on the impossibility of restoring any variant of the socialist economy, there is not yet much support for specific arrangements. Quickness in setting new structures will also depend on strong political support, but government's ability to implement them will be the critical determinant of lasting success.

The new structure of incentives should be based on the legal order of a market-friendly economy, i.e. on laws that create legal entitlement protected by government force.[8] By creating entitlements or individual rights, the legal order is supposed to establish well-defined limits on the discretionary power of government while imposing on government the function of enforcing the law. Also, by creating individual rights, the legal order conditions the opportunities for achieving individual aims, and incentives are then a question of expanding and contracting opportunities.

While reforming socialist economies in Eastern Europe have been advised to 'adopt' the well-tried legal structures of Western Europe, African countries will have to develop their own laws. Since most African countries cannot draw them from their past colonial and quasi-socialist systems, this development must rely on each country's own traditional standards of conduct, adjudication practices and enforcement mechanisms, but also on first principles as a reflection of the long-term experiences of many developed countries and a few developing ones. Whatever strategy is chosen to develop a legal system, first principles from the history of market economies will be important in the areas of property and contract, business and market organisation (including labour and finance), foreign trade and investment, and natural resources. Because Africa's growth potential still relies heavily on its vast natural resources, passing laws defining and assigning property rights over these resources should be a priority.

The laws on the books will have to be administered and enforced but most African countries lack such capacity. Building a capacity to administer and enforce the law means the set-up of cost-effective public institutions, in particular the judiciary system and a recording system of titles and transactions, as well as the development of the legal profession, especially lawyers, to whom the enforcement of the law is entrusted.

3. Less but Better Government

The market-friendly approach to development stresses the complementary and mutually supporting roles of markets and governments. In most countries which have done poorly over the past twenty years, the approach implies a much larger role for markets and a substantial improvement in the quality of government. Indeed, Africa's quasi-socialist economies are in this category, and the question arises as to how these countries should approach government reform.

Independent of the large fiscal imbalance that may have precipitated the process of economic reform, the relevant issue here is government's role in a market economy rather than the correction of that imbalance. In the short run, government reform is likely to aggravate the fiscal imbalance, and the high cost of financing it may even condition the pace of government reform. But the success of measures to reduce quickly the imbalance will depend on the effective implementation of reforms that support the complementarity of government and markets by reallocating government-controlled resources efficiently. Less government implies a transfer of some of these resources to the private sector, and better government implies a reallocation of the remaining resources to produce cost-effectively the outputs demanded by the policy.

The voluminous literature on the government's role in market economies notwithstanding, the proper division of labour between markets and governments will continue to be debatable. Theoretical argument cannot provide solid ground for such division because it necessarily oversimplifies the imperfections of both markets and government. For a long time that literature had been concerned about how the imperfections of markets could be overcome by perfect governments. Recently, the imperfections of government have suggested that governments may impose larger welfare losses than markets. Thus, the theoretical discussion of the cardinal choice between markets and governments is now based mainly on the shortcomings of both options, but theory can at best identify the imperfections but not the conditions under which they are likely to emerge or persist.

The experience of market economies appears to support an alternative approach to guide the division of labour between markets and governments. The basic idea is that, at least in the long run, the complementary and mutually supporting roles of markets and government assume a constitutional democracy, i.e. a political system in which a democratically elected government is effectively constrained by the rule of law and by well-defined institutions to avoid the concentration of power in a single body and to make authorities accountable. Within the broad institutional parameters of a constitutional democracy, and as long as the constitutional provisions to secure the rule of law and the accountability of government authorities are effective, government's economic role will vary (perhaps widely) depending on its comparative advantage to produce particular goods and services (alternatively, to intervene in the economy in a particular form). Because, in a constitutional democracy, government can claim an effective monopoly of very few goods and services, it must find out the productions in which it may have a comparative advantage by competing with other potential and/or actual suppliers. The experience of countries where market economies developed long ago may provide guidance about the sources of government's comparative advantage and the particular goods and services in which its advantage is likely to exist, but the possibility of other sources of comparative advantage and, more important, of factors that may strengthen or weaken this advantage elsewhere, cannot be excluded. In other words, government's comparative advantage depends on the particular conditions of each country.

A New Constitution for the Public Economy

Given the initial conditions of all socialist economies, expanding the role of markets means limiting and redefining the role of government. A first step is the setting of a legal order as outlined above. In particular, the rule of law means that government is constrained by society's dominant view of individual rights, and this constraint is essential to the constitution of government. In other words, constitutional government means government limited by a legal order embracing society's dominant view of individual rights. As social values evolve, the view of individual rights may change, and the legal order sooner or later will reflect the changes.

More important for the rule of law in Africa, the coexistence of alternative views of individual rights in a given territory is a source of conflict. Since national boundaries in Africa have been the legacy of historical circumstances and include several ethnic groups, each one with its own set of social values and therefore views of individual rights, their coexistence poses a serious problem. Indeed the accommodation of multiple legal orders into a single state appears always to be temporary and fragile. In most African countries, notwithstanding some success in the first years after independence, there has been little progress in achieving such coexistence of legal orders.

Although the rule of law implies that government's basic function is to enforce the law, it can also perform many other functions as shown by the experience of constitutional democracy everywhere. At the constitutional level, exceptionally government is prohibited to perform specific functions; usually the constitution determines which functions are to be monopolised by government. In addition to the monopoly of most services listed in the functional classification of government expenditure as general governmental services,[9] the constitution often grants government a monopoly of a few other services (e.g. the issue of the legal tender) and inalienable property rights on some natural resources. It also sets constraints on government powers to tax and borrow.

Those constitutional boundaries on government power are a necessary complement to the rule of law. They highlight the basic principle that government's role is first to enforce the law and second to perform the functions demanded by the polity. The boundaries, however, leave space to accommodate a broad range of views on government's role in the economy, from the non-interventionist American government of the last century to the welfare European states of the past fifty years. Not surprisingly, constitutional boundaries tend to change slowly, in response to fundamental changes in social values.[10]

In addition, the constitution conditions government's role in the economy through the institutions of governance (i.e. the institutions governing the relationships between the polity and elected and non-elected government officials). In a constitutional democracy the polity may be regarded properly as residual claimants of the net benefits or costs of government's actions, but with a limited interest in participating actively in government's decision process. Indeed, citizens are not exactly like shareholders of open corporations because citizens are expected to perform some role in the organisation of government (at least as voters) and their residual claims are not alienable. But models of corporate governance illustrate the need for constitutional provisions that allocate the steps of the decision process across related but autonomous bodies. The separation of powers, with at least two autonomous bodies participating in the decision process, reflects the concern for accountability, as well as the inherent difficulties of achieving a balance between authority and accountability.

Inasmuch as a constitutional democracy can be founded on alternative views on the substance of law and the boundaries of government, it can accommodate alternative models of governance. The effectiveness of each of these models appears to depend more on country-specific patterns of social interaction than on general principles. In particular, the dominance of congressional and parliamentary systems in developed countries does not mean that other models, such as a presidential structure, are ineffective elsewhere.[11]

The institutions of government in a constitutional democracy also reflect the distributive consequences of majority rule and representation. Since government's decisions reflect the position only of a majority, there is always a potential for redistributing income from a minority to a majority. Besides, since the direct participation of the polity in most decisions is very costly, elected officials must be entrusted with the responsibility of these decisions, at the cost of risking the misuse of resources. Thus, the constitutional constraints on government actions attempt to limit the potential for redistributing income and assets (independent of whether the recipient group is a majority or a minority), while the governance structure attempts to prevent the misuse of resources by elected and non-elected officials, even if they do not benefit personally from it.

In all constitutional democracies, the inherent difficulties of preventing undesirable redistributions of income and assets and the misuse of resources, including all forms of rent-seeking, have been a driving force in reforming the constitutional framework of the public economy. Most new institutions are initially very effective, but sooner or later they start to decay and have to be reinforced or even replaced. The increasing complexity of government institutions in constitutional democracies partly reflects this process of decay. The effectiveness of alternative institutions in preventing those phenomena appears also to be conditioned by country-specific forms of social interaction.[12]

Towards Competitive Government

We have observed that in constitutional democracies governments are granted the monopoly of a few services. In practice, notwith-standing the lack of specific constitutional provisions, they may have the monopoly of other services. More importantly, govern-ments appear to compete with a number of other organisations for meeting the demand for many other goods and services. Whatever the rationale for granting a few monopolies at the constitutional level, the important issues are why governments are able to monopolise other services, and how they manage to compete with other suppliers and expand their productions.

Government's monopolisation of services other than those defined in the constitution is usually the result of two different, contradictory forces. One is government's absolute advantage: there are some services which no organisation except government can afford to supply. This is a pure economic argument: there is a demand for some service, and government is the only organisation capable of meeting it at a price that consumers (or users) are willing to pay. The other is government's lack of comparative advantage: there are services for which government's production has been legalised but protection from other suppliers is required to make it profitable or affordable (i.e. a kind of infant-industry argument). This is essentially a political force because monopolisation depends on the political willingness and capacity to give such protection. Indeed, there are very few services for which governments can claim such absolute advantage, whereas they have been able to monopolise many others, or at least to limit competition significantly.

Governments' comparative advantage in the production of some goods and services can only be revealed by competition with other potential and actual suppliers. *A priori* there are few arguments to sustain that they will have such advantage in the production of particular goods and services. Since government is intrinsically a complex organisation – the specific knowledge required to perform the basic function of enforcing the law is necessarily diffused among many individuals – its expansion to perform other functions is likely to be efficient only when relevant decisions require such knowledge. But this is at best a necessary condition; there are many complex organisations other than governments, and there is a potential for creating new organisations to deal with such situations.

In comparison with other complex organisation, government has, however, a greater capacity to control the free riding that often deters collective action. This is because of its power of compulsion, another intrinsic characteristic derived from the basic function of enforcing the law, which other organisations do not have. Given the limits of other instruments to control free riding, the power of compulsion gives government an advantage at least when it is exercised within the boundaries of, and according to the processes of the constitution. General conditions under which this power is a valuable instrument for controlling free riding can hardly be defined *a priori*, however.

Government intervention in most market economies has become pervasive, but only exceptionally has it resulted in the direct production of goods and services. Actually, it appears that government's comparative advantage may be in forms of intervention other than direct production. In particular, governments have relied heavily on monetary incentives and regulation for their intervention. Both forms of intervention assume the power of compulsion. Monetary incentives, including both taxes to deter and subsidies to promote private activities, are effective when the purpose is to control the externalities associated with such activities. In turn, regulation in the form of rules and standards has complemented the legal order of the market economy either by strengthening the protection of individual rights (or entitlements), or by facilitating the exchange of property rights. Not surprisingly, direct production has been common when the power of compulsion was essential to provide merit goods (e.g. mandatory social security and elementary education).

In sum, in most market economies, competition is likely to limit the role of governments to interventions in the form of incentives and regulation, and exceptionally in the form of direct production. The political process may, however, allow for governments to monopolise the production of other goods and services, as well as for interventions in the form of incentives and regulation that are prompted by rent-seeking. In all countries with market economies, at any particular time, the scope and forms of government intervention reflect the forces of both competition and rent-seeking, especially how they have been evolving in the recent past. While competition leads to forms of government intervention that are likely to enhance allocative efficiency, rent-seeking leads to a diversion of resources to non-productive activities. The constitutional framework of the public economy should encourage competition and deter rent-seeking.

4. Accelerating the Pace of Reform

At this time we cannot assess progress in reforming government in Africa's emerging market economies. In addition to the framework outlined in previous sections, that assessment demands a substantial effort to collect appropriate information and consistent statistics.[13] Few African countries have been embarked on government reform for more than five years, and even in these few countries the process has been incoherent and the pace slow. Despite the wide circulation of progress reports, the documentation of those experiences is based more on announcements than on effective actions, and the limited analytical work has been focused on narrow issues with limited success.

Government Reform: Solvency

Since the reforms were precipitated by large fiscal and external imbalances, the initial concern was to correct them. Fiscal adjustment demanded reductions in expenditure and increases in domestic revenues but the imbalance was still large in most countries. Governments are still to achieve a sustainable level of expenditure, i.e. a level consistent with the long-term domestic revenue generated by present tax policies and asset holdings. For most countries, this conclusion is independent of how expenditure is measured; the standard measure, which underestimates the relevant level of spending, indicates that the current level is not sustainable. In other words, in the absence of a profound fiscal reform, government revenue from taxation and state-owned assets will never be enough to finance the present level of spending (alternatively, the present value of that revenue is expected to be lower than the present value of spending). Governments have then no choice but to increase revenue or reduce spending. The magnitude of these changes depends on each country's conditions, but for most countries it may be equivalent to at least 5 percentage points of GDP. Other sources of revenue, including all sources of non-budget revenue and foreign grants and concessional credits, may provide temporary relief and facilitate the achievement of a sustainable level of spending. They cannot, however, generate enough revenue for a long period of time; more importantly, since governments have been relying on these sources without making progress in achieving a sustainable level, it cannot be taken for granted that the economic cost of these sources is still affordable and/or the political costs of their conditionality acceptable to governments.

In most countries, the potential for rapidly increasing budget revenue is severely limited because of the shortcomings of their tax systems and the limited capacity of state-owned assets to generate additional revenue. Typically, a radical reform of the tax system is needed to reduce the economic cost of generating the present level of tax revenue, but such reform is likely to generate less revenue in the short-run and little more in the long-run. Rather than attempting to collect more tax revenue from today's economy, governments must ensure that the tax system is not a constraint to economic growth, and therefore they should try to shift quickly the tax burden from production to consumption. Concerning state-owned assets, governments will be able to continue to obtain significant revenue only in countries with large mineral resources and fisheries, and to generate significant additional revenue only through the privatisation of large utilities and plantations.

Governments have then no choice but to reduce their spending to achieve a sustainable level. This is not a short-term problem in which spending cuts are needed to correct a prospective financial imbalance this or next fiscal year. It is a long-run problem: to be sustainable, the new level of spending must reflect the effective demand for government services. Because the political system has not yet changed, governments have so far paid little attention to the provision of services demanded by a majority of the population, and they continue to be organised to provide only those services demanded by key but small constituencies (including foreign donors). Foreign donors and creditors have failed so far to persuade governments to take this long-term perspective of public finances.

Government Reform: Efficiency

Since governments still own many assets and control a large share of national disposable income, the efficient reallocation of these resources is a priority. On the advice of foreign donors and creditors, governments have attempted this reallocation by privatising some assets and by shifting revenue to social services and infrastructure. So far, these attempts have brought about little change.

There has been some progress in breaking government monopolies, however. In many activities, particularly agriculture and related rural activities but also services in urban centres, governments have let others enter production. Changes in the price system have encouraged individuals and small private companies to start production, even in those areas which governments had been hitherto reluctant to allow. This new production has not depended on the privatisation of state assets, but its expansion has been constrained because access to credit, which governments continue to monopolise, is still very limited. This monopoly is in turn critical for governments to raise funds at low cost and secure the financing of their unsustainable level of spending. Thus, the continued expansion of individuals and private companies to previously government monopolised production depends mainly on their own savings.

Governments continue to monopolise several manufactures, foreign trade, utilities, education, health and other areas which private companies may be interested in entering. Indeed, governments have been very reluctant to let nationals and foreigners compete in these activities. In addition, it is not obvious that private companies and non-profit organisations would be interested in entering into those activities because of the small size of internal markets, the high risk of investing in these countries, and the scarcity of managerial and technical skills. However, because of the scarcity of capital and human resources, entry of foreign companies and non-profit organisations appears to be the only way out of the current dilemma. Governments will have to choose between facilitating the inflows of capital and skilled labour, which will encourage competition with government monopolies and perhaps the takeover of these monopolies, and maintaining the monopolies regardless of the burden imposed on the incipient domestic private sector.

Foreign donors and creditors have also put emphasis on improving the technical efficiency of government monopolies. Exceptionally, governments have agreed to privatise the management of these monopolies, to allow foreigners to work as close advisers to government officials, and to reorganise state banks (including central banks). Also, governments have been more receptive to reviewing investment projects before initiating them and securing their financing, implementing new personnel policies, and improving the information systems of central and sectoral ministries. To yield significant benefit these changes will have to be properly implemented and extended to all government productions.

In a few countries foreign aid may have continued to be large enough to provide little incentive to reforms that could have enhanced efficiency. However, only exceptionally would foreign aid have been enough to offset the loss of domestic revenues, and more importantly it has been increasingly conditioned to recipient governments' commitment to reforms. Indeed, these governments have reluctantly accepted donor conditionality and often have not facilitated the effective implementation of the reforms. Notwithstanding the lack of serious analysis of its effects on government policies and economic performance, it appears that foreign aid may have alleviated the burden on low income groups – in its absence the recipient governments would have cut services to these groups rather than military spending and services to high income groups – but contributed little to encourage the reallocation of resources.

Government Reform: Institutions

The limited success in improving government solvency and efficiency can be traced back to the lack of progress in reforming government institutions. Most policy changes, including those to correct serious macroeconomic imbalances and eliminate excess demands in particular markets, have elicited limited supply responses because of the failure to implement institutional reforms. In comparison with programmes of structural adjustment in Latin America and other places, radical reform of the legal system and government has been a prerequisite for the long-term success of policy changes in Africa's quasi-socialist economies. In the absence of such reform, only extraordinary, positive changes in variables beyond government control (e.g. in the terms of trade) could have stopped and perhaps reversed the process of economic decline, but these uncontrollable changes would have hardly led to sustained economic growth.

Despite foreign donor pressure for a radical change of the political system, so far there has been little progress. Occasional, apparent exercises of democracy have not been accompanied by serious efforts to develop the institutions of constitutional government. Given the limited development of the rule of law, government involvement is a prerequisite for national and foreign companies and non-profit organisations to start business. This involvement usually centres on the creation and sharing of rents between the parties – the government side offers to impose restrictions on other potential suppliers in exchange for licensing fees – but there are few agreements because of government propensity to overestimate the rents that can be created by limiting competition. Upon the failure of government-run monopolies, Africa's governments appear to have relied on the practice of licensing government-created monopolies – the distinguishing characteristic of the mercantilist regimes that preceded constitutional democracy in Europe and Latin America – to generate revenue.

The limited development of the rule of law is also reflected in the absence of mechanisms for checking and balancing the exercise of power and for holding governments accountable. In addition to negating the idea of individual rights, the lack of such mechanisms implies that governments' decisions are not an aggregation of a majority of individual preferences but a representation of the preferences and interests of small constituencies. Except for the constraint imposed by the potential for rebellion, governments are still exercising unlimited powers. Donors have pressed governments to take account of the needs, if not the preferences, of the majority of the population, but these pressures have not encouraged the emergence of new political institutions. In the short run, donor resources may have alleviated the plight of low income people because governments have increasingly treated donors as a special constituency to be pleased to obtain their financial support,[14] but with limited prospect of a sustainable improvement in their living conditions.

Donors have also pressed for improvements in the decision-making process of government programmes and resource use. Efforts to build a capacity for planning, executing and monitoring the use of public resources have so far had little impact on economic performance. The improvements in budgetary systems have been largely in the form of better collection, processing and communication of information, which have facilitated the internal control of lower levels of the administration for the benefit of its top, political levels. In turn, line ministries and agencies have yet to develop a managerial and technical capacity commensurate with the complexity and size of the programmes they have been entrusted to execute. Finally, governments have shown little interest in improving their poorly funded and ineffective auditing systems, and no interest in setting monitoring systems based on independent reviews of their programmes and resource use.

The Pace of Reform

As shown by the experiences of other socialist economies in transition, the pace of reform is conditioned largely by political forces. This is obvious in countries where the economic transformation was preceded by radical political change. In the few countries whose political systems have changed little, the pace of reform has depended largely on their governments' willingness and ability to lead the radical transformation of their economies. It is difficult to determine *a priori* the conditions under which the governments of these countries will be willing to lead such transformation that will inevitably erode their monopoly of both political power and economic resources, but experience suggests that the increasing prospect of massive rebellion eventually forces governments to do it. This recognition often comes too late, however, and radical political changes precede economic transformation.

In Africa, despite the appearance of political reform, little has changed so far. Notwithstanding the decline in the living standards and the poor prospects of restoring sustained economic growth, other forces – including the potential for ethnic conflict and the loss of external support as a result of the end of the cold war – have driven the political process. Thus, African governments have opted for mobilising donor assistance to offset the loss of national income, with the expectation that this support will give them enough time to introduce changes needed to build new political coalitions. The changes were not intended to develop institutions, but to create and protect groups with a vested interest in the maintenance of the ruling elite. In their approach to economic reform, the strategy of African governments has closely resembled that of traditional Central American and Caribbean dictatorships, extreme examples of governments not constrained by the long-term economic performance of their countries. To conclude, in Africa's socialist economies, the pace of reform will continue to be slow as long as their governments continue to view their countries' long-term economic performance as irrelevant to the pursuit of their own interests.

Notes

1. This paper was prepared when the author was Principal Economist in AFTEF, later AFTPS. The paper does not represent the views of the World Bank. The author acknowledges the background research done by Eduardo Wallentin, Craig Mitchell, and Nigel Chalk.
2. In this paper the terms Africa and Sub-Saharan Africa are used synonymously.
3. The figures are gross estimates prepared by the author and pretend to present only an order of magnitude.
4. The Portuguese population was only 44,000 in 1940, increased to 172,000 in 1960 and doubled between 1960 and 1974. It was

5 per cent of the country's population in 1974. The per capita income of the Portuguese was well above US$4,000 in 1974 when the country's per capita GAP was around US$400. Estimates indicate that total GAP increased at the annual rate of 7 per cent between 1960 and 1974.

5.   For an analysis of Angola's post-independence economic system, see World Bank (1991), especially Chapter 2 and Annex III.

6.   It should be noted, however, that the economic value of Africa's outstanding foreign debt is substantially lower than its accounting value because of the large share of concessional foreign credits. Estimates of the grant component of new commitments indicate that even in the late 1970s and early 1980 it was well above 20 per cent for Sub-Saharan Africa, when it was negative for Latin America and slightly positive for East Asia. Later, in the second half of the 1980s, the grant component of new commitments increased to around 50 per cent for Sub-Saharan Africa. See, World Bank (1994) summary tables.

7.   In most African countries there was no monetary overhang, a typical phenomenon of socialist economies elsewhere. In Angola, however, there was such overhang and a currency reform took place in late 1990 to eliminate the excess liquidity.

8.   This means a radical break with the legal order of a socialist system. In this system, laws lay down rules of individual behaviour that are suitable to the purposes determined by a central authority. Legal rules are at best complementary to commands, but often they are subsidiary, filling the gaps left by the commands; in other words, they are part of a hierarchy's control system. Central authority's decisions are a matter of expediency, independent of their formal presentation as comments or laws. Not surprisingly, in socialist economies incentives are largely a question of motivating subordinates to pursue the goals set by superiors.

9.   This classification, used by the International Monetary Fund for its Government Finance Statistics, is based on the classification of the functions of government published by the Statistical Office of the United Nations (see IMF, 1986, p. 143).

10.   For example, Argentina's constitution has occasionally been declared null by military and even civilian governments, but

subsequent governments have restored it and have found no need to change the provisions limiting government.

11. For example, Chile's present system of presidential government differs significantly from the congressional model of the United States and other countries. In the Chilean system, the president is responsible for the initiation and execution of all government decisions and congress is responsible only for the ratification of the president's initiatives (congress has a very limited power to initiate legislation).

12. The contrasting experiences of Chile and Argentina (in Chile the phenomena have always been very limited compared with Argentina) have led to explanations based on non-institutional factors (for example, differences in forms of social interaction as a result of different ethnic backgrounds). Apparently these factors are reflected in the institutional framework of the two countries. Thus, in Chile, government officials have been accountable to a special institution (in recent years, Contraloria General de la Republica), in addition to the judiciary.

13. We lack proper measures of the seise of government in the early 1980s, i.e. just before the collapse of most African quasi-socialist economies, and their evolution in the past ten years. The all-encompassing role of government in these economies is not properly captured by the standard definition of government in the IMF's Government Finance Statistics. There are too many state enterprises and agencies not accounted for in those statistics. Furthermore, to the extent that the State's boards had monopolised the marketing of some private production, these productions may be regarded as instances of contracting out by government. Also, state banks and other state financial institutions may be responsible for financing extra-budgetary expenditures. A proper measure of the size of government must include the organisations for which the government has assumed responsibility for their financial obligations, and those for which the government exercises some real control over their decisions.

In several African countries, the significance of international donors poses a problem to define and measure properly the size of government. The accounting of all grants and concessional credits in the recipient government's budget, as demanded by international donors, makes sense only when the recipient government can at least manage the funds. If the recipient government did not control or manage the funds, then accounting for them in the budget would serve no useful purpose and would be misleading about government's command of resources. Only funds effectively allocated through the budgetary system should be accounted for in the budget; thus, when projects are managed and controlled by international donors and the 'recipient' government has been asked to finance part (usually a minor part) of the total cost of the project, the budget should account only for the funds actually committed by the government (from an economic viewpoint, the government is subsidising the donor's project and the funds should be recorded as any other subsidy).

14.   Indeed, this argument implies that donors have effectively provided additional resources to governments. Alternatively, the argument implies that donors have to pay a tax to governments to secure the execution of their preferred programmes.

References

Kornai, J. (1992) *The Socialist System: the Political Economy of Communism*, Princeton: Princeton University Press.

International Monetary Fund (1986) *A Manual on Government Finance Statistics*,Washington DC: IMF.

Rimmer, D. (1989) 'Africa's Economic Future', *African Affairs*.

World Bank (1991) *Angola: an Introductory Economic Review*, Washington DC: World Bank.

— (1994) *World Debt Tables 1993–94*, Volume 1, summary tables, Washington DC: World Bank.

3 The Macroeconomics of the Transition from African Socialism

David L. Bevan and Paul Collier

Introduction

The macroeconomic policy problem is to maintain internal and external balance by means of policy instruments which are consistent with microeconomic objectives. This is common to both socialist and market economies. However, socialist economies are distinctive in their microeconomic objectives and this in turn gives rise to distinctive choices of macroeconomic instruments. The socialist perspective implies suspicion of the market as an allocative mechanism, and suspicion of private property due both to the power and the unearned income which it confers. If the market is rejected as an allocative mechanism, the government has a choice between regulating the private agents who constitute it or replacing them with public agencies. Three microeconomic interventions have had particularly powerful macroeconomic repercussions: the allocation of credit, price controls, and the allocation of foreign exchange.

In the credit market, intervention reflected the socialist perception that the accumulation process should not be left to the market. It was believed that the market would deliver too little capital formation and that it would wrongly direct it. Intervention was intended to correct the second of these, directing loans to favoured sectors (above all manufacturing) and to favoured agents. The policy of cheap lending implied a policy of cheap borrowing which tended to reduce voluntary private savings further below what were already deemed to be inadequate levels, leading to greater recourse to forced savings. An intervention at the micro-economic level created the need for macroeconomic correction.

In the goods market, since the market was rejected as the determinant of relative prices, it had to be replaced by the administrative mechanisms of price control. With these in place the government was itself a major price setter and so was directly implicated in the inflationary process over and above its indirect

93

role in influencing aggregate monetary demand. It was therefore only a small step further for the government's administration of prices to be used for counter-inflationary purposes. Thus, an instrument which was initially designed to control relative prices easily evolved into one which attempted to control the general price level.

Markets for assets were particularly prone to intervention because they combined the suspicion of the market process with hostility towards property. Among asset markets, that for foreign exchange was the most vulnerable because it was the mechanism whereby private agents could transfer their assets outside the jurisdiction of the government. Virtually all African governments inherited currencies which were convertible, but often became wary of capital outflows. Outside the Franc Zone convertibility was usually suspended, this being the first stage in the non-market allocation of foreign exchange. Gradually, an administrative allocation process developed, combining quantitative restrictions on trade in particular goods with quantitative restrictions upon access to foreign exchange, both reflecting an increasingly complex prioritisation of activity. As with price controls, the prioritisation reflected microeconomic objectives but its aggregate implication was that trade policy (defined in this broad sense to include foreign exchange allocation) became a macroeconomic instrument.

In all these markets controls were to an extent evaded so that parallel markets co-existed with official allocation processes. Africa's socialist economies were distinguished from its market economies not just by the formal legislation of the control regime but by the severity of its enforcement. A strictly enforced regime, such as in Ethiopia, was of more consequence than a weakly enforced one, as in Ghana. However, even when illegal transactions are common, the illegality inflicts costs: firms cannot advertise their activities, cannot use the law to enforce contracts and must largely avoid formal services such as banking and insurance (Bevan, *et al.*, 1991). Because transactions are secret, parallel markets may not clear. For example, Bevan, *et al.* (1989), found that shortages were endemic on both official and parallel markets in rural Tanzania. In some circumstances the cost of illegal transactions may be so high that the market clears only at a price which excludes most of the population. Such markets are therefore far from being perfect substitutes for legal transactions. Because private activity switches from formal production at normal profits to criminal trading at high profits, the popular image of private enterprise as exploitative is reinforced.

This suspicion of the market as an allocative mechanism, of profits accruing to private agents and of the economic power arising from private ownership of assets was exacerbated in Africa by the fact that private ownership was largely in the hands of ethnic minorities. This case for public ownership reinforced that arising from allocative considerations: non-market allocations are more easily sustained when the state directly controls production decisions rather than relying exclusively upon price, trade and credit controls. As a result of the public sector acquiring this role in the productive sector, the state became the recipient of profits which became a major source of revenue mobilisation. Thus, the archetypical African socialist economy was characterised by government ownership of a wide range of productive (and residential) property, together with non-market allocations achieved either through direct public ownership of the institutions which constituted the market or through a network of controls on prices, credit and trade in those areas of the economy where private activity was still permitted. While relatively few African economies had all of these features *à l'outrance*, most of them displayed them all to some degree. In consequence, the analysis of the transition from socialism is relevant to most African economies whether or not their governments were officially committed to socialist ideology.

Except for short periods, macroeconomic policies must be compatible. By this we mean that they should jointly give rise to a sustainable balance of payments position and a sustainable budget deficit. In most African socialist economies, macroeconomic policies were not compatible by the start of the transition: budget deficits and sometimes payments deficits were at unsustainable levels. There are therefore three distinct policy problems in the macroeconomics of transition. First, the initial flow disequilibrium must be rectified. Second, the accumulated debts from past disequilibrium must be accommodated either by servicing them out of current surpluses (thereby requiring a more severe flow adjustment), or by offsetting adjustments through forgiveness, aid or default. Third, the original microeconomic interventions in the credit, goods and foreign exchange markets must be reversed. These liberalisations will have macroeconomic repercussions and to the extent that these give rise to incompatibility, other macroeconomic policies must be changed so as to offset them. The structure of the paper follows this agenda. Section 1 considers the flow disequilibrium in the budget and the experience of attempts at rectification. Section 2 considers the liberalisation of financial markets in the context of the overhang of the stock disequilibrium, namely excess government indebtedness. The argument is that rapid liberalisation of the credit market is usually not fiscally feasible because of the government's domestic indebtedness. The next two sections discuss the other microeconomic reforms, the liberalisation of the markets for goods and foreign exchange. The concluding section brings together these analyses, discussing the sequencing and co-ordination of reforms.

1. Fiscal Policy and Stabilisation

The state has two distinct roles in respect of the economy. In the first it acts as an agent in its own right, obtaining revenues – from taxation, selling goods and services, and borrowing – and using them on purchases of final goods and services, purchases of factor services, transfers and lending. It may engage in public production with outputs that are either sold or distributed without charge, and in the creation of public capital. It is always a substantial employer. In the second role, the state acts to determine the rules of the game for other economic agents and, to some extent, itself. These rules of the game are embodied partly in legislation and partly in fiat. They range from the structure of property rights such as the nature of ownership titles to land, through to the mechanics of determination of the foreign exchange rate. Together, they constitute the economic control regime. Coupled with those other features of economic interchange which are determined by practice, habit, culture and convention, this imposed control regime defines the constraints under which economic agents operate and also modifies the structure of opportunities and incentives facing them.

It is the essence of a transition from socialism that this control regime will undergo substantial modification. Some controls can simply be dismantled, allowing a less regulated, market-determined solution to evolve in replacement, but for the most part the transition requires that the act of dismantling one institutional structure be accompanied by the construction of a possibly more detailed and complex alternative. (For example, if a system in which all land is vested in the state is to be abandoned, this requires both the detailed definition of the new forms of private title, and their associated obligations and rights, and also a decision as to how and to whom beneficial ownership is to be transferred.) These changes may have profound fiscal effects, via direct or indirect impacts on revenues, expenditures and the balance between them. They may also have consequences for what is feasible or desirable in the design of fiscal structure.

A transition from socialism may also involve a substantial redefinition of the role of the state as an economic agent. It may raise questions about whether the previous scope, size and structure of the state were inappropriate, and whether the transition affords a good opportunity and possibly a requirement for change. In particular, the fiscal agenda of the transition may include the proposals that the state should exit from various production activities (privatisation); should increase the direct financing of services which it continues to provide (user charges); and should retrench various unproductive expenditures (notably on defence and on civil service employment). The transition may also need to address a number of features of the previous situation which are not specifically connected with a socialist orientation, but which are at least as prevalent in previously socialist states, and where change cannot or should not be deferred. These include an excessive degree of centralisation, with local government starved of resources (devolution); the unsatisfactory structure of revenue instruments and administration (tax reform); and, typically, the fact that the budget deficit was unsustainably large (stabilisation).

African countries exhibit a very wide range of tax-to-GDP ratios, from around 5 per cent (Sierra Leone and, previously, Ghana and Uganda) to over 30 per cent (Botswana, Lesotho). However, a number of them fall within the 15–20 per cent band and these include those with relatively reformed tax structures, such as Kenya and Malawi. There appears to be a loose consensus, which is largely innocent of any theoretical underpinning, that this is an appropriate tax target for many African countries (and, indeed, developing countries more generally). Apart from taxes, there are two sources of domestic financing for government spending. Non-tax revenue – leaving aside the special case of mineral revenues – has mainly come from parastatals and from agricultural marketing boards. For reasons both of policy (designed to extricate government from inappropriate production activities, and to face agricultural producers with world prices), and of history (mounting parastatal losses, falling world commodity prices), this component of revenue has contracted in many African countries; is unlikely to provide more than a few percentage points of GDP on average; and is in some cases negative. Similarly, domestic borrowing and seigniorage can only provide a few percentage points in the long run, though a much higher, albeit undesirable, yield is obtainable in the short run (Adam, *et al.*, 1993). In the absence of external financing, the sustainable level of public expenditure would therefore be roughly in the range 20–25 per cent of GDP.

In a number of African countries such as Ethiopia and Zambia, aid currently doubles the level of budgetary resources, from 15 per cent to 30 per cent of GDP. It is inconceivable that this level of supplementation can be maintained indefinitely so one or both of two things must eventually happen, namely domestic resource mobilisation must increase and/or government expenditure must fall. Precisely how these must be combined for long-run sustainability will obviously vary from country to country. At one extreme, expenditure could be maintained indefinitely at the 30 per cent level even if aid fell back to 5 per cent of GDP, but domestic resource mobilisation would have to be increased to 25 per cent, probably the upper limit of what is durably feasible in a representative African economy. In any event, if current mobilisation is only around 15 per cent, this type of revenue gain would take a very long time to achieve, since attempting rapid increases in effective rates may prove counterproductive for reasons both of taxpayer compliance and of political economy. (The limited exception to this general caveat is where the increase represents a recovery to previous levels following a revenue collapse; an example is Ghana in the late 1980s, when revenue was raised by nearly 8 per cent of GDP in a three year period, albeit only to around 14 per cent. Even in this type of case reversing the decline may be far from straightforward, as contemporary experience in Uganda demonstrates.) Hence the more likely scenario is one in which a substantial reduction in public spending will be required in the medium term. To the extent that aid-assisted expenditures are successfully focused into one-off categories, such as infrastructure rehabilitation or the costs of demobilisation, this may not be problematic. However, experience suggests that it is very difficult to organise public expenditure reduction in an efficient and orderly manner. In consequence, the prospect of such reductions becoming necessary in a number of African economies in the medium term must be viewed with misgivings. It is all too possible that they will be accompanied by very severe deteriorations in public service provision or by a re-appearance of virulent stabilisation problems.

In general, the problem of stabilisation overshadows all other fiscal aspects of the transition, and is considered in the next sub-section. The remainder of the section then briefly addresses the other two groups of issues which have been outlined above. It examines the issues of size, scope and structure of the state and the associated changes in these during the transition; and it looks at the extent to which fiscal outcomes are likely to be affected by the other reforms involved in dismantling the control regime.

The Deficit and Stabilisation

A major threat to many incoming governments, and to the programmes of reform to which they are committed or to which they have been induced to subscribe, is the scale and sustainability of the overall fiscal deficit. If sufficient aid inflows cannot be obtained over a sufficiently long horizon, and even then if the flows are explicitly conditional on macroeconomic performance, a stabilisation programme will have to be adopted. With the partial exception of recovery following an earlier collapse, revenues can be raised only rather slowly, and may in any case already be as high as they should be. Hence any substantial stabilisation effort is necessarily focused on the expenditure side. However desirable in the long run it is to cut the public sector wage bill, this is usually pretty incompressible in the medium run, so public expenditure cuts usually end up in savage reductions in capital expenditure or the already heavily compressed category of operations and maintenance. The short to medium run implications of stabilisation can therefore make any sort of ordered transition process difficult. It is often argued that the appropriate sequencing is stabilisation before liberalisation, primarily because attempting both together may simply abort the liberalisation programme. However, this may not hold particularly if the liberalisation programme is itself budget enhancing.

Attempting to Reduce the Fiscal Imbalance

Unsustainably large deficits had emerged by the early 1980s in African countries of all ideological persuasions (as indeed they had elsewhere in the developing world). In consequence, the typical African country was faced during the 1980s with a major challenge of fiscal correction, whether or not it was also engaged in extensive structural reforms and liberalisation. This raises a number of issues. First, and most generally, how successfully was this challenge met? Second, what were the mechanisms employed; in particular, did adjustment take place on the side of revenue, or expenditure, or both? Third, what relation did the actual adjustment bear to that which had been planned? These questions require detailed country studies to resolve them adequately, but some provisional answers are sketched here.

As to the first set of issues, the overall deficit for Sub-Saharan Africa (in per cent of GDP, unweighted) was around 9 per cent at the beginning of the decade, and was brought down only to 8 per cent in the first half of the 1980s, with little further improvement subsequently. (These figures exclude grants, which will be considered in a moment.) This minimal average adjustment was achieved by a small reduction in expenditure (from 28 per cent to 27 per cent of GDP) against a stationary level of revenue (at around 19 per cent of GDP). To all intents and purposes, no net fiscal adjustment took place in aggregate at all. The perception to the contrary reflects the fact that the flow of external grants to Africa has increased enormously over the period, and particularly since the late 1980s. In consequence the deficit requiring further external or domestic financing has fallen sharply to only a few percentage points of GDP. It is important to note that this amelioration of the financing problem does not reflect any sustained turnaround of domestic fiscal magnitudes. What has happened is a switch toward financing a relatively stationary fiscal imbalance in a way which has less immediately problematic implications, but which may not carry any promise of long-run sustainability. To the extent that reforms already in the pipeline will themselves yield a sustainable fiscal correction, this form of 'bridging finance' may be desirable and efficient. To the extent that they do not, and to the extent that donor patience in these circumstances is finite, then they simply defer and possibly exacerbate the required adjustment.

Despite what appears to be a rather stationary picture in aggregate, individual country experiences were very varied. The interesting question is whether these differences are fairly random, or whether there is anything systematic to be observed. One such 'stylised fact' is now well known; it is the relatively poor fiscal performance of the francophone relative to the anglophone countries during this decade. An obvious candidate explanation for this systematic difference is membership of the CFA Franc Zone. The members of the western and central African monetary unions have been constrained to maintain a fixed exchange rate parity with the French franc. This acted as a nominal anchor and was supposed to induce fiscal discipline and ensure low inflation. Most other African countries adopted a strategy of managing the exchange rate, which enabled them more easily to engineer the relative price shifts required to respond to terms of trade declines or to move from an inappropriate initial configuration. The costs of this strategy were commonly perceived to be the obverse of the supposed benefits of the fixed rate strategy, namely fiscal laxity and high inflation. In the event, the fiscal prediction proved very misleading, even though the associated differential inflation materialised as predicted. For example, a calculation that partitions Sub-Saharan Africa into fixed and variable exchange rate groups finds that the average deficit rose from 6 per cent to 8 per cent of GDP over the decade for the former, but fell from 11 per cent to 6 per cent for the latter (see Nashashibi, 1993). The cause of this difference was primarily that revenue contracted sharply in the latter half of the decade in the fixed rate case, while it expanded in the variable rate case. (Both groups achieved a modest contraction in expenditure). In contrast, the fixed rate countries did experience much lower (and decelerating) inflation than the variable rate group, which on average experienced high and accelerating inflation. (However, this average is misleading, since the group includes some countries with high and accelerating inflation and others with moderate and decelerating inflation.)

This evidence poses two questions. First, why should revenue performance in the fixed rate countries have been so different, particularly since expenditure outcomes have been relatively similar? Second, why should the linkage from the fiscal deficit to inflation have been so unreliable and irregular? For the first question, the most important feature is probably the combination of very heavy dependence on trade taxes with severe trade compression in the fixed rate countries. While there was a deterioration in the terms of trade in both groups of countries, this was accompanied by a substantial appreciation of the real exchange rate in the fixed rate group, in sharp contrast to the depreciation achieved in the variable rate group. The second question, concerning the nature of the link between the deficit and inflation, really involves two links: one between the overall deficit and the part that is financed from the domestic banking system; the other between the domestically financed deficit and inflation. The monetary union countries are both more restricted in their recourse to bank finance than the others, and more able to obtain external finance. In consequence, the initial inflationary impact of any increase in the budget deficit is relatively muted. In addition, inflationary expectations become embedded, with a consequent slowing down or reversal of the process of financial deepening. Once inflation becomes established, the scale of banking finance consistent with the (inflationary) fiscal equilibrium becomes smaller. Reducing an established inflation may therefore require a more or less substantial temporary overshoot. In any event, the relatively major fiscal tightening achieved in the late 1980s by many of the variable rate countries has to date yielded a rather modest disinflationary pay-off.

The second set of issues concerns the mechanisms by which fiscal correction was achieved, in those cases where some progress was indeed made. Broadly speaking, revenue gains were concentrated on domestic tax sources, both indirect and direct, with trade taxes stable or declining. This reflects the main thrust of the tax reform programmes which began to be implemented under the prompting of the donor community. However, the net revenue gains were typically small and, in many cases, were likely to remain so, since overall tax effort was as high as was consistent with the general circumstances of the economies in question. Attempts to raise tax revenue much above 20 per cent of GDP in very poor economies are likely to prove counterproductive, leading to increased smuggling, other forms of evasion, and substitution into the informal and subsistence sectors. In these circumstances, the proper role of tax reform is to reduce the deadweight losses and inequity with which a given revenue is raised, rather than to increase the total. As regards expenditure, the average patterns are clear cut. Capital expenditure is quite severely compressed (by several percentage points of GDP), with a much less marked movement in current expenditure. Within the latter category, interest costs rose (typically by a couple of per cent of GDP), and since the wage bill stayed much the same, the strain was taken up by other current goods and services, including operations and maintenance.

The third set of issues concerns the relation between the adjustment which was achieved and that which had been planned. The patterns outlined above diverged from those that had been intended, which usually included a more substantial revenue gain, some compression of the wage bill, and protection or indeed expansion of the maintenance category. The difficulty, and indeed possible inadvisability, of trying to engineer significant increases in revenue has already been alluded to as has the medium run incompressibility of the wage bill. It is not that these shifts are infeasible; several countries have demonstrated the contrary. (Indeed, in some cases, reforms yielded macro fiscal benefits as a by-product of other developments, rather than by design. For example, the tax reform in Malawi raised tax revenue by a couple of per cent of GDP, in virtue of increased elasticity to inflation, coupled with a failure to bring inflation under control.) However, these shifts are slow to achieve, and need to draw on considerable reserves of political capital to succeed.

Individual Country Experiences

Individual country experiences diverge in particular respects, but tend broadly to confirm the pattern outlined above. This is illustrated with very brief sketches of experience in Côte d'Ivoire, Madagascar, Benin, Tanzania, Uganda and Ghana. Recent developments in Zambia and Ethiopia are then considered in rather more detail.

Côte d'Ivoire devoted considerable energy during the 1980s to trying to raise its general tax revenue, which nonetheless remained stubbornly anchored in the range 20–23 per cent of GDP (excluding the important but highly volatile contribution of the price stabilisation funds). The massive fiscal correction made necessary by the excesses following the commodity boom had therefore to be focused on expenditure. Capital expenditure was slashed, from nearly a fifth of GDP to less than half that amount; however, current expenditure remained more or less stationary, with the share of the wage bill in GDP actually rising, despite a reform programme.

Madagascar also has a very low tax to GDP ratio, and has followed a flexible exchange rate policy. Given its very low initial level of tax effort, it might seem straightforward to increase tax revenue substantially. However, the tax to GDP ratio slid from around 10 per cent in the mid-1980s to around 8 per cent in 1990 and still lower thereafter, partly reflecting an unusually high dependence on trade taxes, which accounted for more than half of tax revenue. Despite this very lacklustre performance, the recorded budget deficit fell from around 3 per cent of GDP to less than 1 per cent. This was not an artefact of increased grant aid, which rose relatively little on average, nor a consequence of reduced capital spending, but resulted from a contraction in current spending. However, it has been argued persuasively (see Houerou and Sierra, 1993) that this apparent improvement is largely illusory, and that part of the true fiscal deficit has simply been transferred temporarily off budget in the form of Central Bank losses. If allowance is made for these quasi-fiscal deficits, the improvement did not in fact occur.

Benin also exhibits a very low level of resource mobilisation, running consistently below 15 per cent of GDP during the late 1980s, and falling below 10 per cent subsequently. At the same time, the overall budget deficit has been pretty stable, at around 10 per cent of GDP. As a member of the Franc Zone, it may have been more difficult to increase revenue during this period, but the apparent difficulty of even maintaining the status quo is striking.

Tanzania provides yet another example of this familiar pattern. During the 1980s, tax revenue remained stable at about 18 per cent of GDP; so did recurrent expenditure, at about 21 per cent. The substantial reduction in overall deficit (from 12–14 per cent of GDP to less than half that amount) was overwhelmingly due to a correspondingly large cut in capital expenditure. Within the recurrent budget, interest payments rose, and since the wage bill was stationary, were accommodated by a squeeze on other goods and services.

Uganda is a leading case of a country which has suffered a revenue collapse, with tax revenues falling to about 5 per cent of GDP in the mid-1980s. Given the impossibility of obtaining significant external finance at that time, and despite recourse to inflationary finance, it was inevitable that expenditure should have become severely constrained. There could be little doubt that the public sector was operating on too small a scale, and that enhanced resource mobilisation was a necessary condition for correcting this. Accordingly, the government accepted advice to undertake a thoroughgoing reform of the tax administration, as well as studying mechanisms for tax reform. Despite the inauguration of what appears to be an energetic new revenue authority, the current forecast (by the Ugandan Authorities) is for a very modest revenue gain, with total tax revenue not exceeding 7–8 per cent of GDP over the next year or two. In the meantime, any material advance in public spending has to be financed from external sources.

The picture is somewhat similar for Ghana. Having started the 1980s decade with a historically low level of revenue mobilisation of around 5 per cent of GDP, as well as many other problems, it was expected that a rapid (partial, at least) return to fiscal normality should be relatively manageable. In the event, a rapid fiscal recovery during the mid 1980s was indeed achieved, with tax revenue returning to around 14 per cent of GDP, assisted by the large scale resumption of external grants. Part of the revenue gains arose from devaluation, reflecting Ghana's then unusual position of having been constrained from acquiring much external debt. On the minus side, as in Madagascar, there were also large quasi-fiscal deficits which made the true budgetary position substantially less rosy. This is one reason why an apparently tight fiscal stance should have been associated with rapid inflation.

By way of contrast, the first sequence of attempted reforms in Zambia (1985–87) exhibits four major differences. First, the original fiscal imbalance reflected vastly over-extended spending, given reasonably adequate revenues, rather than a revenue collapse. Second, there was a huge debt overhang which made the economy extremely unstable in face of currency depreciation, and required really substantial aid inflows to make any transition – short of outright default-feasible. Third, there were widespread doubts as to how serious the commitment was to the reforms of the Zambian Government. Fourth, the required scale and reliability of external resources committed to the programme was also lacking. In effect, the fiscal and structural adjustment problems of Zambia were probably less tractable than those of many African countries, but they did not receive comparably serious attention. The consequent failure to solve the stabilisation problem in the late 1980s led to the remainder of the reform programme being aborted.

The second reform sequence began in 1989, but was temporarily de-railed by an election boom in 1991. Given Zambia's subsequent status as a pioneer of democratically legitimated transition from socialism, the fiscal evolution since then is of particular interest; it certainly provides stark evidence of both the possibilities and difficulties of rapid fiscal change. In 1991, central government revenue was 16.8 per cent of GDP, with total expenditure (excluding interest payments) at 23.5 per cent, so that the primary deficit was 6.7 per cent. In 1992 the new government succeeded in transforming these figures to 19.1 per cent, 20.4 per cent, and 1.3 per cent respectively. If the budgetary impact of the drought, and of excess copper earnings are removed, the outcome would have been still more impressive; revenue 17.3 per cent, non-interest expenditure 16.5 per cent and hence a primary surplus of 0.8 per cent. As can be seen from these figures, the overwhelming bulk of this massive fiscal adjustment came on the side of expenditure, despite a considerable programme of tax reforms. The major contributor to expenditure reduction was the virtual elimination of (non-drought related) consumer subsidies. The expected outcome for 1993 involves a further severe contraction in spending, reflecting the very tight cash budgeting procedures in place. If the budgetary aftermath of the drought is again stripped out, revenue is expected at 14.1 per cent of GDP, expenditure at 11.8 per cent, yielding a primary surplus of 2.3 per cent. The fall in revenue is largely a consequence of the severity of the fiscal squeeze. All the main economic components share in the expenditure reduction, but a near halving of the share of civil service wages in GDP is particularly noteworthy; since this has not been accompanied by a successful retrenchment programme, and the current wage is derisory, it is unlikely that this reduction can (or should) be sustained.

The scale and speed of this adjustment is remarkable; in a three year period non-interest expenditure has been halved, and the primary balance improved by ten percentage points of GDP. Since capital inflows have been more than sufficient to cover all interest payments, the central government has been able to reduce its recourse to bank financing substantially, by around 2–3 per cent of GDP in each of 1992 and 1993. Despite this tremendous reduction in domestic credit to the government, nominal reserve money continued to grow rapidly, and inflation accelerated to 200 per cent per annum.

The primary reason for this combination of very tight fiscal stance with lax monetary policy is probably mounting parastatal losses, arising in part from the reform programme itself; poor accounting makes it difficult to be certain. The scale of the resulting inflationary impact reflects the earlier loss of confidence in the currency. The Zambian transition is still under way, but remains fragile. One danger is that the fiscal squeeze is simply too tight to be sustainable; the other is that the quasi-fiscal losses will continue to prevent policy from achieving its stabilisation goal and lead to abandonment of reforms.

Finally, the newest addition to this set of fiscally adjusting and liberalising economies is Ethiopia. In this case, a very substantial temporary reduction in revenue generation (to about 15 per cent of GDP) has been made both necessary and desirable because of the unacceptable and authoritarian mechanisms of surplus extraction previously involved. Since the recovery from a state of war places a high premium on reconstruction, there is a concomitant need for high public spending. At present, the donors are prepared broadly to match domestic resource mobilisation, so that expenditure can run at around 30 per cent of GDP. However, this poses serious medium term problems of revenue enhancement or expenditure reduction when the present high degree of donor enthusiasm fades.

While domestic revenue and net capital inflow as a share of GDP may be similar to that in Zambia, the fiscal implications are very different. If rouble-denominated debt to the former Soviet Union is ignored, Ethiopia's level of indebtedness is small compared with Zambia's, and the burden of external interest due correspondingly light. Hence the rise in capital inflow has cushioned the fall in expenditure even though both domestic revenue and domestic borrowing have fallen.

The fall in domestic revenue has been sharp, from 25 per cent of GDP in 1989/90 to 20 per cent in 1990/91 and around 15 per cent thereafter. Of this, tax revenue amounts to barely 10 per cent, reflecting a somewhat primitive and as yet unreformed tax system. Non-tax revenue – mainly from state-owned enterprises – continues to provide substantial resources to central government, though not at the previous scale. Similarly, financing from the domestic banking system has fallen over the period from around 10 per cent of GDP to less than 4 per cent. Despite the high previous monetisation of the deficit, inflation has remained low and the level of seigniorage revenue high. The sharp reduction in military spending from nearly 20 per cent of GDP in 1989/90 to perhaps a fifth of that in 1992/93 also makes the redeployment of economic and social spending much easier, within a stable total of around 30 per cent of GDP. While the problems facing the Ethiopian government early in its transition are severe enough, they are at least spared the need for very sharp contraction of civil expenditures, and, as yet, the need to counter large parastatal losses.

These country examples go to demonstrate two main points. First, individual country experience is various and complex; a deeper understanding requires detailed comparative analysis. Second, and notwithstanding the previous point, there remain certain general conclusions which can be drawn even from the present overview. Several of these have already been suggested. Here, two such conclusions remain to be stressed. One is that revenue enhancement appears to be a very slow business, regardless of whether revenue is currently reasonably healthy or massively depressed. The other, and similar, conclusion is that shifts in the composition of public current expenditure are difficult to engineer and slow to execute. It follows that the short term characteristics of fiscal reform are bound to involve some combination of elevated external assistance, contraction in capital spending, and contraction in desirable as well as undesirable components of current spending. This is uncomfortable, but probably has to be faced, as does the corollary, that effective fiscal reform is likely to be an extremely protracted business.

Size, Scope and Structure of the State

The first point to establish is that there is no general presumption that the state is too large relative to the economy in socialist states in Africa, or in consequence that there is a priority to cut it back overall. It is important to distinguish between three components of the public sector, though the boundaries between them are sometimes blurred; these are the central government itself, local government and the state owned enterprises. Since the present focus is on macroeconomic aspects, the discussion is restricted mainly to central government.

Central governments in these socialist economies have often been dirigiste in nature; in some cases warfare has also induced a major extension of central government activity. However, the success with which the authorities have been able to implement the heavy associated demands for resources has varied dramatically. At one extreme, the Ethiopian government was remarkably successful at extracting surplus from the citizenry. Prior to the overthrow of the Derg in 1991, central government spending was running at around 40 per cent of GDP, even when no account is taken of Soviet supplied military hardware; and explicit revenue was running at around 27 per cent. By any conventional standard, the Ethiopian government had become too big relative to the economy; it would probably not have been feasible and certainly would not have been desirable to attempt to close the excessively large budget deficit by increasing revenue (see Bevan, 1992). At the other extreme, the catastrophic collapse of revenues in both Ghana and Uganda to a few per cent of GDP prior to reform had the effect, in the absence of any substantial external financing, of compressing central government expenditure to levels which by any conventional standard were too small relative to the economy. If 40 per cent of GDP is evidently too high, 10–12 per cent is equally evidently too low in African circumstances, unless a truly extreme view is taken of the desirability of a minimalist state.

While initial conditions vary so substantially, there can be no facile general presumption as to whether central government activities should be contracted or expanded during the transition. The specific initial conditions are likely to dominate over the orientation of the government. As regards the *scope* of central government's spending activities, broadly defined, there is little case for any large change, transition from socialism notwithstanding. The key components of central government spending have always been, in functional terms, on education, health, transport, certain welfare services, public administration and defence, and economic services. While it can certainly be argued that the balance between these components is wrong (for example, too much spent on administration and defence, too little on health) or that the total level is wrong, there can be few who would claim that the list of functions itself is wrong. The real arguments about central government spending are therefore about level and composition, not about scope.

Conclusions concerning the economic composition of spending are more robust. It is commonly argued that the wage bill is too large a proportion, and expenditure on operation and maintenance too small a proportion, of total current spending. This has been as true of over-expanded governments like the Ethiopian as of over-compressed governments like the Ugandan. The two other major components of central government spending are capital expenditure and transfers. The position on each of these is less clear cut than for wages and operation and maintenance spending. In some socialist economies, government capital formation has been excessively high, particularly in relation to the eventual output. An obvious example is the Tanzania of the late 1970s and early 1980s. On the other hand, much the same could be said of the Nigerian governments of the 1970s, though it would hardly be appropriate to classify them as socialist.

During the turmoil of the 1980s, when most African governments sooner or later ran into serious financing difficulties, capital expenditure usually became severely compressed. If earlier high rates of capital formation had left the country's capital stock in good shape, the compression need not have been disastrous though regrettable. However, the earlier capital formation, in socialist states particularly, was frequently on ill-chosen public enterprise investments in the manufacturing sector, and infrastructure was relatively neglected. The stock inherited at the start of the squeeze thus consisted of a set of unproductive manufacturing assets with no viable future, especially within a liberalised control regime, and a desperately depleted physical infrastructure. This is very much the Tanzanian story. It is also the story in Ethiopia, where the infrastructure was also hastened in its decline by the impact of war.

There have been two main categories of transfers: consumer subsidies and transfers to state owned enterprises. The losses of SOEs have been a major factor in destabilising government budgets. They have rarely been justified on allocative grounds but have usually reflected a loss of accountability and control. As regards consumer subsidies, these have often been excessively large. However, in countries where the redistributive capacity of the direct tax/transfer system is very weak, and where distributional issues are important, the government may need to rely on indirect taxes (and subsidies) and on public expenditures to achieve its distributional goals. Indeed, the transition from socialism may have

the apparently paradoxical effect of increasing the transfer component in the explicit budget. In many socialist regimes, very substantial
transfers are made off budget by the manipulation of prices. Thus,
the Ethiopian government of the 1980s heavily taxed peasant producers by making forced purchases of grains at artificially low prices,
and subsidised the population of Addis Ababa by selling them, also
at low prices. This substantial rural-urban transfer did not pass
through the budget. It may well be an implication of the transition
that total transfers should be reduced, but it is also an implication
that what transfers are retained should be routed through the tax/
expenditure system.

Associated with the retreat in Africa from highly controlled
socialist systems to more market-based forms has been a growing
disillusionment with the institutions of the state. This has partly
taken the form of rejection of one-party systems in favour of
pluralistic, more fully democratic ones: it has also taken the form of
rejection of a system of government seen as distant, over centralised
and often predatory. The central government is often quite reasonably perceived as having been captured by particular interest
groups or ethnic minorities and being insensitive to the wishes or
interests of the majority. This has been true of African governments
of all types of ideological persuasion – or presentation – but it has
been especially true of governments flying a socialist flag. Ethiopia
and Tanzania provided particularly powerful instances of the sub-
ordination of rural interests to urban interests, and of the wholesale
autocratic interference in individual lives associated with villagisation and resettlement programmes. The transfer of various expenditure responsibilities to lower tiers of government has become a
major policy commitment in a number of countries (including
Uganda, Ethiopia, and Nigeria). It will probably have powerful
consequences for the delivery of public services and possibly for
macroeconomic policy. However, in none of these countries has the
process gone far enough, for long enough, to permit an assessment
of the outcome to be made.

African governments in general, and socialistically orientated
ones in particular, have poured substantial resources into the
enterprise sector, sometimes on a wholly owned basis, sometimes
in partnership, usually with foreign capital. This has often been
accompanied by wholesale distortion of the fiscal structure and of
the trade regime to ensure profitability or – all too frequently – to

reduce losses of enterprises which were ill-conceived, poorly executed, badly managed and overstaffed. A virtually universal response has been to look to privatisation as a way of extricating the government from what is seen as a costly and inappropriate involvement. This whole question has been extensively studied both within the African context and more generally (see, for example, Adam, *et al.,* 1992). Privatisation occupies a central position in the agreed policy agenda, there are now privatisation agencies in place in many countries, and much preparatory documentation has been prepared. However, to date the scale of privatisation accomplished in Africa is trivial. Whether it proves to be a policy which fails to fly at all, one which has a limited but useful pay-off, or one which transforms the productive sector while yielding substantial fiscal benefits remains to be discovered. In the short run, at least from the fiscal perspective, there can be little doubt that tighter accounting procedures for parastatals (the so-called hard budget constraint) will prove of much greater significance. The desirability of wholesale privatisation as a solution to the fiscal problem has been overstated, and its feasibility exaggerated. In many cases the government will have no option but to choose between continued state operation and closure. In consequence, it is important that attention be less heavily weighted on privatisation and more heavily weighted on problems associated with improved commercialisation: better accounting; more sales orientation; labour shedding; redefinition of markets and products and so on. To a large extent, the liberalisation programme itself will have the consequence of enforcing this type of change, but careful attention to it during the transition will ensure that a larger proportion of the truly viable concerns survive the process.

Fiscal Effects of Liberalisation

So far the discussion has turned on changes which arise directly from the changed perception of the role appropriate to the state as economic agent, or from the view that the previous performance of the state was unsatisfactory, given this role. However, a major component – very likely the major component – of the transition from socialism is the partial dismantling of the control regime itself. This involves a package of liberalisation policies which are not themselves explicitly fiscal, though they may have fiscal consequences as a by-product, and it is important that the management of fiscal policy during the transition takes these into account and takes steps if necessary to accommodate them.

The three main groups of liberalising reforms analysed in the later sections of this paper are financial, price and trade reforms. The fiscal implications of financial reform are discussed in Section 2. One of the several reasons given there for being extremely cautious about financial reform, particularly in terms of liberalising the interest rate, is that it is likely to have a substantial adverse fiscal effect for rather limited gains. In practice, the seigniorage that the government obtains from financial repression may be several times as large as that obtained from the inflation tax. If it is felt nonetheless that full financial liberalisation is desirable, it is important that the scale of the associated fiscal loss is computed, and an alternative instrument capable of generating equivalent revenue is installed. If these budgeting implications are neglected, financial liberalisation may destabilise the economy.

The fiscal implications of price de-control are discussed in Section 3. One effect, via the demand for money, is not to alter the deficit directly, but to reduce the amount of it that can be monetised for a given rate of inflation. To the extent that price controls were accompanied by subsidised supplies, the joint abolition of controls and subsidies will obviously be deficit reducing. However, these types of arrangement may take place largely off budget, as in the Ethiopian example given previously.

Finally, consider the fiscal implications of trade liberalisation. These arise through three distinct channels. Most directly, there are the revenue effects of trade taxes themselves, and the impact on the foreign exchange budget of the currency depreciation which accompanies liberalisation. Somewhat less directly, there are the induced revenue and expenditure consequences that follow from the wholesale shift in relative prices (of importables, exportables, non-tradeables, wages) and associated volumes that are the whole purpose and intention of liberalisation. Most indirectly, there are the changes to profitability of the public sector manufacturing enterprise which may be off budget initially, but are likely to come on budget sooner or later.

All of these effects can go either way, so that trade liberalisation can improve or worsen the fiscal situation. As this discussion implies, this theoretical ambiguity means that the likely budgetary consequences of liberalisation must be estimated as an empirical matter in a country-specific way. Since what are involved are wholesale general equilibrium effects, this may be a fairly difficult exercise. Furthermore, the transitional impact on the deficit during adjustment may differ from the fully adjusted equilibrium impact.

This means that the structure and sequencing of trade liberalisation measures (the relationship between quota and tariff changes, for example) are likely to prove difficult to evaluate, and to differ depending on the economic and fiscal structure of the country concerned and on the initial trade regime. However, it should be stressed that there is no general presumption that trade liberalisation need threaten the budget; indeed it can be conservatively designed to improve it. While it would be far more secure and comfortable to undertake a liberalisation from a stable platform, there need be no presumption that the two processes cannot be undertaken simultaneously.

2. Asset Market Liberalisation and Financial Policy

Recall that there are three distinct sets of macroeconomic policy problem in the transition from socialism: rectification of disequilibrium flows; accommodation of debt overhangs; and the repercussions of liberalising markets. Financial policy during the transition bears on all three of these objectives. The nominal anchor inefficiently provided by price controls under socialism is commonly replaced by monetary targeting which has its own problems. The accommodation of the domestic debt overhang has implications for the liberalisation of the credit market. Finally, the liberalisation of the credit market risks financial shocks while not offering a short-run efficiency gain.

Monetary Targeting and its Variants

In socialist Africa the short term macroeconomic policy target was the level of foreign exchange reserves and the policy instrument used to achieve it was the rationing of imports. The post-transition objective is for the short term target to be the growth of the money supply and the instrument to be the alteration of bank lending through open market operations. However, during the transition phase the two conditions necessary for this strategy to provide a nominal anchor are not met.

First, because of the lack of markets in government financial instruments and the low level of discretionary foreign exchange reserves, the money supply is in effect directly determined by the budget deficit. The logic of monetary targeting applied in this context is therefore to target the fiscal deficit directly. This is currently being followed in some transitions. For example, in Uganda since 1992 expenditure has been tied to revenue in the preceding month. This has successfully reduced inflation from 230 per cent to zero in twelve months, without significant lost output, GDP growing by 7 per cent over the same period. This remarkable disinflation was feasible because, as a result of the past history of instability, there were few long term contracts or loans. Hence, despite the disinflation being unexpected it did not cause large transfers or changes in relative prices due to nominal rigidities. In such economies, targeting can thus have a high pay-off.

However, such fiscal targeting runs foul of a second necessary condition, namely that the demand for money should be stable. During the transition from socialism there are likely to be large changes in the demand for money, especially if financial markets are also liberalised.[1] Hence, the mapping from the money supply to the price level is unreliable. In the early stages of the transition the provision of a nominal anchor should not be an objective. As discussed in Section 3, if price controls have produced a monetary overhang, the price level should be allowed to rise. However, once this has happened, the demand for money may be abnormally low because of fears of inflation. At this stage a nominal anchor is needed. While the fiscal deficit may be the appropriate instrument, the correct target is not the deficit itself but the CPI, as long as it is reliably measured.

Ethiopia and Uganda provide examples as to why such targeting might be more appropriate than fiscal or monetary targeting. In Ethiopia the private sector has accumulated enormous domestic currency savings during the period of socialism. A successful transition would involve a switch in private portfolios from these liquid assets into fixed investment. Thus, recovery can be expected to lead to a fall in the demand for money. When this occurs, the maintenance of price stability requires a corresponding fall in the money supply. Monetary and fiscal targets might be comfortably met and yet the economy experience a serious bout of inflation.

The obverse case occurred in Uganda during 1993. The recovery in confidence in the currency consequent upon the attainment of price stability induced a rise in the demand for money, which could be accommodated by increased supply with causing inflation. Should the nominal money supply fail to increase (by means of a fiscal deficit), private agents achieve their desired increase in real money balances through a decline in the price level. This would be a highly inefficient means of increasing the money supply, raising the real wages of those whose nominal wages are not flexible downwards (such as public sector employees) and increasing the real liabilities of the government.

Having argued that it is more appropriate to target the price level directly during the transition than some fiscal or monetary aggregate, we now consider whether there is any alternative to using fiscal policy for its attainment. All alternatives involve the government varying its net liabilities and at best this can only be a short-run policy. However, because fine-tuning government expenditure on a monthly basis can reduce its efficiency, a short-run substitute is desirable. Domestic markets for financial assets are likely to take many years to develop because, during the transition, the government lacks reputation. An alternative is to vary the sale of government-owned assets. However, the markets for real assets such as commercial and residential property are not well suited to fine-tuning. The only asset market which is sufficiently well developed to withstand fine-tuning of government sales is that for foreign exchange. When prices are rising too rapidly, sales of foreign exchange should be progressively increased and correspondingly slowed if prices are falling. This is a viable policy only if it is confined to fine-tuning and if the government has adequate reserves. Otherwise, the best that can be done is to target the CPI, fine-tuning the fiscal deficit to achieve the target.

Financial Liberalisation and the Budget

We now argue that increasing nominal interest rates is inappropriate in a socialist banking system. The argument is that because virtually all the borrowing is by the public sector, the attainment of positive real interest rates is essentially a fiscal problem. A big-bang move to positive real interest rates is therefore dependent upon a drastic improvement in the fiscal position, whereas an increase in nominal interest rates will actually worsen the budget. If drastic fiscal improvement is not feasible, then the attainment of positive real interest rates can only be gradual. We illustrate this with the example of financial liberalisation in Tanzania.

An Example: Tanzania

Consider the role of the Central and commercial banks in Tanzania during the socialist phase. The commercial banks were publicly owned and their lending was directed as part of the planning process. Over 80 per cent of bank lending was to the public sector, narrowly defined. Most of this lending was to meet the recurrent deficits of the marketing boards, that is, it had no counterpart in asset accumulation. The commercial banks funded this lending from two sources: deposits and borrowing from the Central Bank. The Central Bank in turn financed its lending by printing money. The upshot of this structure was that the conventional distinction between outside and inside money was made inapplicable (see Collier and Gunning, 1991). The liabilities of the government (that is, outside money) were the deposits of the commercial banking system plus private holdings of currency (commercial bank holdings of currency had not meaningfully left the government and so were not liabilities). There was virtually no inside money. The banking system was thus marketing government liabilities and distributing the proceeds to various public spending agencies. This both closed down the more usual functions of financial intermediation and constituted a parallel budgetary process. The latter was particularly important during the liberalisations of the mid-1980s, for an apparently modest fiscal deficit was much larger when proper account was taken of commercial bank lending. Collier and Gunning estimate that correctly defined, the increase in outside money was four times larger than implied by the conventional definition of currency outside the Central Bank. Further, in the Tanzanian context, an increase in the nominal interest rate had a direct and substantial consequence for government expenditure without achieving any improvement in the allocation of loanable funds. Interest rates on bank time deposits were raised from 4 per cent to 29 per cent. Since these were liabilities of the government, at the margin it had to increase outside money in order to cover the higher cost of servicing its domestic debt. Yet the demand for money was insensitive to the interest rate (there was not even substitution out of call deposits) and so the increased supply of money was inflationary. The extra expenditure on debt service was therefore ultimately financed by an inflation tax on holders of non-interest-bearing money. Since around three quarters of money holdings were in this latter category, and given the absence of rural banks, virtually all peasant money holdings were of this form; the result was a reduction in the real interest rate for most savers, which financed an increase in the real interest rate for a minority. This financial liberalisation thus produced inflation and regressive transfers without any offsetting benefits.

The error in the design of the Tanzanian financial liberalisation was to miss the centrality of fiscal policy. In the Tanzanian context the move to non-negative real interest rates for savers could only be achieved by fiscal action: less spending or more revenue. Financing positive real interest rates for a minority of savers by transfers from a majority was pointless. Even with such a fiscal correction (which would have worked by lowering the rate of inflation, thereby raising the real interest rate on all money holdings) the only aspect of financial liberalisation which would have been achieved would have been to raise returns for savers. While we will argue that this may generate real benefits, despite the evidence on very low interest elasticities of savings, there would need to be a further step before the gains arising from financial intermediation could be realised. This would require (and as argued below, this is only a necessary but not a sufficient condition for financial intermediation) an additional fiscal correction, since the government would need to reduce its dependence upon borrowing in order to leave the banking system with some funds to allocate to private enterprises. In a slowly growing economy this implies that the government must actually pay back some of its debts to the banks, not merely refrain from further borrowing, that is, it must run a budget surplus. Since at the start of the 1980s the Tanzanian budget deficit was around 10 per cent of GDP, the fiscal correction needed for financial liberalisation was enormous. Realistically, it could only be achieved gradually, and so domestic financial liberalisation could only be achieved gradually. Given the arguments for delaying an opening of the capital account until after domestic financial reform (essentially, that if the capital account is opened first savers will transfer deposits out of the country), this implies that financial reform in its entirety must, in such circumstances, be a slow process.

Creditworthiness and Financial Intermediation

It is now generally accepted that financial liberalisation will not make a major short term difference to savings rates (see Fry, 1988 for a survey of evidence) and so gains depend upon an improvement in the allocation of capital arising from financial intermediation. Here we argue that Africa's socialist economies lack the intangible capital of reputation and cheap information channels which are required for a well-functioning credit market and that these can only be acquired gradually. In the African socialist economies the commercial banking system has usually been publicly owned (Zambia being the exception). As discussed in the Tanzanian example above, these institutions are not really banks but rather extensions of the government budget process. Attempts to recapitalise them while leaving them in public ownership are unlikely to turn them into banks: the problem is not that they have become undercapitalised, but that they do not confine lending to those loans which satisfy commercial criteria. Thus, the *sine qua non* of a functioning credit market is the entry of private banks. However, this is not sufficient: properly run banks would be unlikely to lend significant amounts to profitable investment. In the final part of this section we discuss the dangers that banks will not, in fact, be properly run.

Even in developed economies with highly advanced financial markets it is now established that a large majority of investment is financed by retained earnings, and that of the other forms of financing, by far the most important is bank lending (Mayer, 1991). Equity markets tend to provide negligible or even negative flows of new money into investment. Further, theories of financial control emphasise that there are sound reasons for most financing being in the form of short term bank loans. Until firms acquire reputations which can function as collateral substitutes, creditors must keep managements on a short leash or else the latter will have an incentive to embezzle or waste external funds. Hence, attempts to develop longer-term funding instruments, whether through development banks or corporate bond markets, are likely to fail. A final corollary is that the borrowing units which need to emerge in the process of development are firms, not projects. That is, reputations (which are the capacity to borrow in excess of tangible collateral) are vested in management teams and corporate structures rather than in projects. If the country is very short of good management teams it will not meet the conditions needed for any financing other than short-leash lending.

Socialist Africa faces insuperable short- and medium-term problems which preclude significant financial intermediation by soundly run private banks even where they are present. For example, in Zambia for long periods the private banking system has been running very high levels of liquidity by world standards and above those required by regulations. Evidently, it is short of credit-worthy loan proposals. This need not indicate that there is a shortage of high-return opportunities for investment in the economy, but rather that there is a failure in the mapping from high-return projects to creditworthy loans.

Why Private Banks would be Reluctant Lenders

In assessing creditworthiness, private banks take three values into account. The first is the value of intangibles, essentially the reputation of the firm ('goodwill'), which is an indicator of how much owners would lose by default, and so a measure of their incentive not to do so. The second is the value of the firm as owned by the bank, that is, its value in the event of default. The bank can either sell the firm as a going concern or realise its break-up value. The third is the bail-out value offered by the government to avert political costs. One problem of creditworthiness in post-socialist Africa is that the pertinent value is liable to be the bail-out value since the government may be assumed to be unable to stand aside. If private banks lend on this collateral then the allocation of credit is no more efficient than under socialism: since the collateral is the prioritisation of the government, private credit allocation simply mimics government wishes. Until the government can convince private banks that the bail-out value is negligible, financial liberalisation cannot begin to be efficient. However, even once this problem is overcome, the pertinent value for collateral is then likely to be the break-up value, at a heavy discount upon the purchase price of the assets.

The reputation of the firm is likely to be of limited value so that it only provides an incentive for managers to avoid default on small loans. This is the case generally in Africa because many firms have short lives, partly due to high macroeconomic volatility. However, it is particularly so in socialist Africa because private firms have been discouraged and public firms have had neither the need nor the opportunity to demonstrate managerial skills in the context of a market economy. For example, in Ethiopia, industrial decisions were taken in the ministries and enterprise-level officials were more akin to administrators in a bureaucracy than managers in a firm. In Zambia, though less extreme, the structure of authority through the boards of publicly owned holding companies up to the central committee of the then ruling political party, gave plant-level managements little discretion. The lack of an existing structure of firms also limits the value of the post-default firm as a restructured enterprise, since those in a position to do the restructuring (that is, able entrepreneurs) lack the reputations with which to secure finance, and those with the finance, that is the banks, lack the expertise to restructure the firm. This drives the value of the firm for the purpose of assessing creditworthiness down to the break-up value of its tangible assets.

In turn, this break-up value is unusually low in Africa and especially in socialist economies because the specific investments have an unusually low degree of marketability. In Africa, markets in capital goods are liable to be thin due to the low level of investment, the low level of wealth, and the small size of the economy.

The Consequential Pattern of Lending during Transition

An implication is that in the early post-socialist period, African economies have neither the enterprises nor the asset markets which are needed to convert profitable opportunities for projects into creditworthy propositions for banks. The failing lies not with the banks but with the economy. A further implication is that the financial intermediation which can take place beyond this narrow base in the post-transition period is likely to be socially inefficient.

The normal allocative efficiency properties of financial intermediation are features of long term equilibrium. In such an equilibrium the flow of new lending to a firm will broadly reflect

David L. Bevan and Paul Collier

and be determined by the incremental net value of the firm. This increment might arise both because the firm is generating higher-than-expected profits on its existing projects and because the borrowing permits a profitable project to be undertaken. In either case there is some link between the flow of finance and the likely capacity of the firm to use that finance. In Africa's socialist economies the initial allocation of credit across enterprises is likely to be far removed from the essential characteristic of such an equilibrium, namely that the firm's liabilities reflect its gross worth. Hence, when private banks are introduced and normal commercial considerations of creditworthiness apply, the flow of new lending becomes determined not by the expected value of the new projects which the lending will finance but by the opening pattern of disequilibrium between outstanding loans and asset valuations. At one extreme the entire corporate sector may have negative net worth: for example, it might have been subject to price controls and so never have accumulated profits, while carrying heavy liabilities with respect to its workforce. At the other extreme, if there is an explosion in the price level, the net worth of all firms may become substantially positive as their liabilities are eroded. More generally, if private banks look to bail-out values and break-up values, the firms which are best placed to borrow in a liberalised financial system are those which are well connected to the government or capital intensive. This is likely to be diametrically opposed to the socially appropriate allocation of the capital stock.

A Policy Implication

The conclusion from this is that in the short to medium run following a transition from socialism there is very little scope for socially useful financial intermediation. Not even in highly developed financial markets are significant amounts of funds provided to enterprises purely on project prospects detached from reputation and default valuation. Reputation largely means the track record of the management team in generating profits in a market environment, so that in socialist Africa management teams cannot possess reputation. Since out of equilibrium default valuation has no relationship to the profitability of prospective projects, credit allocation based on creditworthiness considerations will not improve the social efficiency of investment allocation. Indeed, on the contrary, it is likely to worsen it. The alternative to financing investment from credit is to finance it from the retained earnings of the firm. The flow of retained earnings in the post-reform economy is by far the best indicator of the competence of the management team and of the net advantage which the sector in which the firm is located has received from the reform. Recall that even in developed economies a very high proportion of investment (typically around 80 per cent) is financed through retained earnings. Adding financial intermediation onto this environment simply enables those firms with high bail-out and break-up values to borrow the profit streams of other firms. Some of the firms which wish to do this will be borrowing because they are making losses: motivated by hopes of improvement; by a strategy of gradual depletion of the firm; or of managerial embezzlement; wishing to realise and distribute the net worth of the firm while it is still positive. Hence, the expectation should be that financial intermediation would transfer funds from socially profitable to socially less profitable uses. Three preconditions are necessary before financial intermediation can improve the allocation of capital. The government must have convinced banks that bail-out values are very low; firms must have acquired reputations so that creditworthiness can be assessed upon prospective returns rather than just on break-up valuations; and the break-up valuations themselves must have adjusted broadly so as to be correlated with prospective returns. These requirements gradually come to be met over time as long as firms live or die out of retained earnings. Financial intermediation should only be a longer-term objective in the transition. While the lack of scope for financial intermediation might seem a serious constraint upon investment, the considerable opportunities for the repatriation of previous capital flight means that, unusually, new firms (established by business families with access to such funds) may have a ready supply of financing.

The Scope for Financial Shocks

While the gains from financial liberalisation are at best modest and long term, policy makers need to pay attention to short run dangers of financially generated shocks. The composition of the banks in a newly liberalised financial market is likely to be highly unusual. If the government is reluctant to permit the entry of the large foreign banks, then the private banks will all be newly established. Unregulated banks without large previous investments in reputation have an incentive to embezzle depositors' funds. The implication of government deposit guarantees (which the government cannot avoid being present in an implicit fashion) is that cautious banks will get driven out by high-risk banks. Yet the central bank is as unskilled in the task of supervising the financial prudence of the banking sector as it is in the completely distinct function of restraining the government. Stiglitz (1989) argues that to some extent it might be possible to overcome these problems of the lack of reputation of banks by relying upon foreign banks. However, if foreign banks simply do not find creditworthy opportunities, then either they will be the only banks and remain highly liquid, or banks without reputations will rely upon implicit or explicit government guarantees to bid deposits away from them. The very high level of non-performing loans in Africa's banking system, often related to embezzlement by directors rather than by government-directed lending, does not augur well for the avoidance of financial crashes arising from bad loans in liberalised and *de facto* unregulated banking systems.

3. Price Decontrol

The price level is closely monitored by African governments because of its political sensitivity. For example, the decisive intervention which undermined the Zambian liberalisation (the instruction by President Kaunda to appreciate the exchange rate) was apparently motivated in part by the rise in the consumer price index. Socialist governments have usually attempted to restrain inflation by means of price controls. Apart from the consequences of this policy for the real economy, it biases the index. As a result, the behaviour of the index during liberalisation is an unreliable guide to the price level and hence to policy. The inflation which provoked the intervention of President Kaunda was in part spurious. The effects of price control on the index are discussed in the first part of this section. In the second part we turn from issues of measurement to the determination of the price level. We consider how the transition from socialism alters the demand for money. Finally, we set out the implications of this change for the real economy, and in particular, for agricultural supply response.

Price Controls and the Consumer Price Index

The Consumer Price Index (CPI) is an attempt to proxy changes in the cost of living. We consider two causes of bias in the CPI during the transition: failure to capture changes in the range of choice, and misweighting of goods.

Changes in the Range of Choice

In the transition from socialism there is a dramatic change in the range of consumer choice for two distinct reasons. First, trade liberalisation – and in particular the move from quotas to tariffs, and from positive to negative lists – permits a wider range of consumer goods to enter the country. Second, and probably much more important, price decontrol at the consumer level converts markets from the seller's market of excess demand to the buyers' markets prevalent in market economies. Shops, instead of selling out as soon as goods arrive, or holding stocks beneath the counter for privileged customers, keep goods on display. In a shortage economy, within reason, consumers buy what they can get, making compromises with what they would prefer, whereas in a market economy they can approximate much more closely to what they really want. Economics has two ways of depicting this: consumers might have a 'taste for variety', wanting to buy several different types of a product (such as not always eating the same meal); or their tastes (or needs) might differ one from another (people need differing sizes of clothes), so that providing only a narrow range of choice condemns most people to buying goods with characteristics substantially different from those which they would prefer. These are not alternatives, rather they reinforce each other since both are manifestly reasonable descriptions of choice. The onset of shortages thus causes technical regress in the capacity of the consumer to transform expenditure into utility.

Equivalently stated, the price of achieving a given level of utility has increased. This rise in the price of achieving a given level of satisfaction should be reflected in the CPI, but current compilation procedures fail to do so. Thus, during the widening of choice consequent upon price decontrol, the CPI will exaggerate the true rise in the cost of living. The magnitude of the effect depends upon the scope for substitution between products which remain available and those which become unavailable, but illustrative calculations for Tanzania (Collier and Gunning, 1990) suggest that it may be very large. They show that the availability of eight products in the typical shop improved so much during the period 1983–88 that the range of choice (i.e. how many products could be found) more than doubled.

By the same argument, during the intensification of price controls and shortages, the failure to capture the welfare-reducing effects of a narrowing range of choice implies that the CPI understates the rise in the cost of living. This is compounded by the procedures used in statistics bureaux when a good previously included in the CPI ceases to be available. Typically one of three choices are made. The least damaging is to calculate the price series for that group of commodities omitting the product which has disappeared. For example, if a particular brand of imported shirt disappears, the increase in the price of clothing will be calculated on the basis of the rise in the price of all observed clothing items, while clothing will retain its old weight in the overall CPI. This gives rise to a downwards bias because the shadow price (and indeed in all probability the actual parallel market price) of this brand will have risen more than other items which are still in plentiful supply. A more biased correction, chosen in Nigeria and Tanzania, was to replace the imported shirt with a domestically produced shirt with no allowance made for quality differences. Thus, if previously the imported shirt sold at a premium over the domestically produced shirt, the substitution would show up as a fall in the CPI. The third, and most biased correction, is to retain the missing product in the CPI but to use the last observed price as the notional current price. This was the strategy adopted in Ethiopia with eleven imported products which had disappeared by the early 1980s but which continued to be given their notional constant price. By 1992, Ethiopia was undoubtedly the cheapest place in the world to buy these eleven products except that they were not available. In this case, the move to market-clearing and the reappearance of the eleven products at current prices would clearly give rise to a spurious increase in the index.

Changes in Weights

Price controls change the true weights on goods in the CPI basket, but the actual weights used are maintained unaltered. This produces a major bias. The weights are generally taken from some pre-shortage consumer expenditure survey. The actual weight on controlled items will fall since less is spent on controlled goods both because lower quantities are supplied and because the relative price is lower. By keeping the unchanged weight, the CPI exaggerates the contribution of price control to moderating the rise in prices and conversely exaggerates the increase in prices brought about by decontrol. The counterpart to the over-weighting of price controlled items is the under-weighting of goods purchased on the parallel market. For example, in Zambia during the period of price controls in the late 1980s, the official price of a box of matches was 40 per cent of the parallel market price. The CPI had only one weight for matches, and only one price, namely the official price. Yet both because matches on the official market were scarce and because they were cheap, the bulk of the expenditure on matches was probably at parallel prices. As controlled prices are increased, more expenditure takes place at official prices and less at parallel prices. In calculating the true overall effect of this on the price level a useful benchmark is to imagine what would happen were the velocity of circulation of money unaffected (an assumption relaxed in the next sub-section). The increase in expenditure on officially priced goods would be offset by reduced expenditure on other goods. Since prices on parallel markets are highly flexible they would in consequence fall. The rise in official prices would be precisely offset by the fall in parallel prices so that the true price level would be unaltered. However, since the CPI over-weights those goods which rise in price (official goods) and under-weights those which fall (parallel goods), the measured CPI will rise. Bates and Collier (1992) estimate that during the Zambian price decontrol of 1984–86, while the CPI rose between 1984 and 1986 by 108 per cent, the price level rose by 76 per cent (correcting for the bias in weights).

The Demand for Money during the Transition from Socialism

So far we have suggested that were the velocity of circulation of money unaffected, price decontrol would not alter the average price of goods: rises for official goods being offset by falls for parallel ones. On top of this, the widening of choice lowers the cost of living for given prices of goods. We now relax the assumption that the velocity of circulation is unaffected.

Money Demand during Stochastic Shortages

Price controls cause shortages and these in turn can alter the demand for money. A central distinction is between deterministic and stochastic rationing, both of which can be found in socialist regimes. Deterministic rationing means the controlled allocation of scarcity at the household level, such as can be achieved by formal rationing systems with coupons or some other precise indicator of entitlements. Households know how much they will be able to purchase at controlled prices, namely the amount specified on their coupons, and so money holdings over-and-above this can only be used for non-controlled expenditures. By contrast, under stochastic rationing the household is not certain of how much it will be able to purchase at controlled prices because it depends upon how much the household can find available. Under such a system the household has an incentive to devote resources to search. Since the search does not augment the total stock of available resources, this is a form of rent-seeking. If the household engages in search it does so in the hope that it will find. Should it find, it must then purchase. In order to purchase, the household must proffer money. Thus, the household must hold money balances for transactions purposes not just sufficient for its expected expenditures but for its hoped-for expenditures should its search activities turn out to be unusually successful. Thus, under stochastic rationing the transactions demand for money rises relative to actual expenditure. Equivalently, the velocity of circulation declines.

The Asset Demand for Money

A second reason for the tendency of velocity of circulation to fall during rationing (which applies regardless of the form which the rationing takes) relates to money's role as an asset. As discussed above, the restriction of choice over substantial areas of consumption during rationing regimes implies that the unit cost of consumer satisfaction is high. If agents anticipate that the rationing regime is temporary, then they will accumulate assets rather than simply switching their expenditure into whatever goods and services (including leisure) remain unrationed. Since the purpose of this asset acquisition is to switch back into consumption once goods become available, the assets must be liquid. The range of liquid assets in socialist economies is extremely narrow. Most financial asset markets such as those for equities and private bonds are suppressed, as are those for many real assets such as housing. Thus a desire to save in the form of liquid assets is likely to spill over into a demand for money.

This deferral of consumption by the acquisition of liquid assets is likely to be matched by a deferral of investment. The socialisation of the economy enormously reduces the scope for profitable private investment. However, it quite probably does not reduce the scope for large profits. As the conventional opportunities for profit in the productive economy are reduced, the scope for profits through trading are probably substantially increased as markets are disrupted and competition reduced, giving rise to much wider marketing margins. Private entrepreneurs thus continue to make profits, but lack the opportunity to use them for investment. To the extent that they still desire to save (and consumption opportunities are very limited) they will therefore hoard liquid assets. Whether this translates into a demand for domestic currency depends upon its reputation. In Ethiopia, during the period of socialism, there was a continuous and substantial build-up of real money balances relative to GDP. The most likely interpretation of this seems to be that trading profits were accumulated in currency. By contrast, similar circumstances of market disruption in Uganda coincided with a collapse in the demand for domestic currency. There was probably an equivalent build-up in liquidity, but because of a lack of confidence in the Uganda shilling, this took the form of dollar holdings.

Liberalisation and the Price Level

Hence, both the transactions and the asset demand for money can rise in response to price controls. The consequence for the government is that it is able to acquire resources as a counterpart to the extra money which it supplies. Thus, the rent-seeking monetary accumulation at the level of the household has, paradoxically, a socially useful function for the government. Further, the less credibility the price control policy has (that is the more it is seen as about to end) the greater is the incentive for monetary accumulation rather than leisure or expenditures upon other goods.

The converse of this is that when prices are decontrolled the demand for money falls back to its normal level in relation to expenditure. It is this change in the transactions demand which pushes up the price level. Because this is a counter-intuitive way of viewing why price decontrol is inflationary, it is worth seeing why it would be possible to have price decontrol without inflation. Suppose that during the price controls, there are intense shortages and these all take the form of deterministic rationing. Further, because the controls are seen as permanent, there is no incentive to acquire assets. In this case there is no monetary build-up. The frustrated demand for controlled goods has a precise counterpart in second-best purchases of other goods and perhaps additionally in leisure. If there is no monetary build up then price decontrol cannot raise the price level, only change the price structure, lowering the price of non-controlled flexibly priced goods and services to offset the increase in the price of controlled items.

Just as the transactions demand for money falls once the stochastic rationing of consumption is ended, so the asset demand for money falls once investment recovers. For example, in Ethiopia, once deregulation creates profitable opportunities for investment and confidence returns sufficiently for private agents to switch their portfolios into them, there will be a concomitant switch out of domestic money. Hence, precisely the private behaviour which marks a successful transition, namely a recovery of investment, has inflationary consequences.

We consider three African examples of changes in the demand for money caused by shortages: Zambia, Tanzania and Angola.

Example 1: Zambia

In Zambia, shortages set in at the start of the 1980s and intensified until the reform of late 1985. The rationing was stochastic: that is, there was little attempt to secure predictable access to goods at the level of each individual household. Prior to the onset of shortages the velocity of circulation of cash to private consumption had gradually being rising. However, with the onset of shortages in the early 1980s the velocity of circulation started falling and by 1984, the last full year of shortages, was 21 per cent below trend. Had the liberalisation of prices in late 1985 simply returned the velocity of circulation to its previous trend, velocity would have risen by 34 per cent over its 1984 level. By 1986 this adjustment had happened, the velocity rising by 37 per cent. If the rise in velocity was indeed due to decontrol then we may conclude that decontrol caused a once-and-for-all increase in the price level of around 34 per cent.

Example 2: Tanzania

In Tanzania there is quite good evidence that rationing was stochastic, especially in rural areas. Further, we have time series data on the severity of shortages. In twenty towns around the country, regional statistical officers and their staff gathered price data for a wide range of consumer goods. As shortages emerged, some prices could not be observed and the bureau staff recorded these failed attempts at finding a price on their primary data sheets. Collier and Gunning (1990) computed the ratio of these failed attempts to the total attempts to record a price. The change in the index is a guide to the time path of shortages in the economy, revealing a continuous and substantial deterioration in availability from 1978 until 1982 and a small further deterioration until 1984. In 1985, the year after price decontrol, there was a dramatic improvement in availability approximately back to the 1978 level, and thereafter less dramatic further improvements. The velocity of circulation followed a similar pattern. It fell continuously from 8.0 in 1978 to a low of 5.3 in 1982. From this level it recovered slowly but fairly continuously, rising to 7.4 in 1985 and reaching 9.2 by 1988. Again, if the rise in the velocity from its trough is attributable to decontrol, then the decontrol raised the price level by 74 per cent.

Example 3: Angola

In Angola, by contrast to Zambia and Tanzania, the rationing system was deterministic – at least in urban areas where most of the consumer goods were sold. Households were given specific entitlements to spend small parts of their wages at government shops, purchasing at very low official prices. The remainder of salary could only be spent on the parallel market where hyper-inflation set in. In rural areas where very few consumer goods were dispatched, rationing was more stochastic, but as a result of a change in government policy, transactions largely reverted to barter. In the early 1980s the government became worried by the implications of the monetary overhang in rural areas. Because of reduced deliveries of consumer goods to rural areas, peasant holdings of money became inefficiently large and peasants started to reduce them. Thus, in 1984, the value of crop purchases by the government was only 30 per cent of the value of government dispatches of consumer goods to rural areas: peasants were selling money back to the government (Azam, *et al.*, 1994). As a device for defaulting on this rural monetary overhang, the government changed its policy so as to require peasants to sell crops in order to purchase consumer goods, refusing to sell goods only in exchange for money. Hence, neither for urban nor rural households was there an incentive to accumulate money balances relative to expenditure. To the extent that there remained a rationale for peasants to hold savings for when official goods supplies were unpredictably large, the appropriate asset switched from money to crops: by the late 1980s, peasants were reportedly holding very large stockpiles of unsold coffee. Thus, the tendency to barter in rural areas and to hyperinflation in urban areas both produced a decline in real money holdings by contrast to the build-up in Tanzania and Zambia. Paradoxically, this makes decontrol much less inflationary in Angola. Indeed, since the velocity of circulation should fall, any increase in the CPI would be because of the mismeasurements discussed in the previous sub-section.

4. Trade Policy Reform in the Transition from Socialism

If the essential feature of socialism is the non-market allocation of resources, most African governments have pursued socialist trade policies. Even governments ostensibly highly hostile to socialism, such as that of Kenya, have allocated foreign exchange through bureaucratic rather than market processes. Indeed, the focus upon state ownership of foreign exchange rather than state ownership of enterprises might almost be the defining feature of African as opposed to East European socialism.[2]

Since socialist trade policies are found across Africa in otherwise non-socialist economies, to an extent the problems of liberalising socialist trade policies are general African problems of trade liberalisation. This is how they are analysed in sub-section 2, which focuses upon the macroeconomic problems of policy co-ordination. This sub-section sets out the basic framework, drawing upon the monetary approach to the balance of payments, which is used in much of the subsequent analysis. The transition from socialist trade policies may, however, be more difficult if other areas of economic activity have also been socialised. This is taken up in sub-section 3, which turns to the concept of incredibility. All governments face potential problems of credibility in trade liberalisation but Africa's socialist governments face particularly severe difficulties: that is, the general difficulties of reforming an initially socialist trade policy are amplified if the government is more broadly socialist.

The potential gains from trade in the small and specialised economies of socialist Africa are considerable. We focus upon the policy transition needed to bring them about. First, we identify two conditions which must be met: compatibility and time consistency. A breach of either of these makes the attempt incredible, inducing dysfunctional private responses. In maintaining compatibility the government has a wide array of macroeconomic choices. While not all of these are equally efficient, choice among them is a second order problem in macroeconomic policy when compared with compatibility itself. Fully socialist economies have an additional problem in that often they do not start from monetary equilibrium. Any excess supply of money must be removed by price decontrol prior to or synchronised with the trade liberalisation to avoid chronic payments deterioration. This section therefore pre-supposes that the liberalisation of the goods market discussed in Section 3 has already been achieved. Time consistency, by contrast, may require wide ranging changes in the political order, because it is not a matter of government sincerity but of the forces which bring pressure to bear on policy choice. In socialist economies, in which the social groups which would normally support liberal trade have been marginalised and in which the intellectual atmosphere has been hostile to market-based resource allocation, the government evidently faces acute difficulties. We contrast Eastern Europe, where revolution and decolonisation have provided a context in which radical policy changes are credible, with the aid-induced reformism of socialist Africa.

Compatible and Incompatible Trade Liberalisations

If trade policy is altered, it will generally have macroeconomic repercussions so that other policies need to be altered in order to maintain equilibrium. This section sets out a taxonomy of the various policies which can be adopted in order to maintain external balance during a trade liberalisation and gives African examples of particular options.

The Conditions which a Socialist Trade Policy Violates

The core of a socialist trade policy is not simply the restriction of trade but the form which restrictions take. Although trade is directly taxed (tariffs and export taxes) consistent with a general distrust of market mechanisms, it is also restricted by import quotas, import bans and foreign exchange rationing. A double hurdle system is common in which the importer first has to satisfy commodity-specific trade restrictions (usually a positive list in which only certain goods are permitted) and then has to gain explicit authorisation for foreign exchange from the Central Bank, a stage which can be fine-tuned according to the availability of foreign exchange. Such a trade policy violates four equalities each of which is needed for efficient resource allocation and which are jointly the objective of liberalisation. First, the value of a dollar of imports at the margin should be equated across all uses. This is violated because the explicit tariffs, and more importantly the price effects of quotas and foreign exchange rationing, give rise to very different rates of implicit nominal tariffs. Second, the cost of generating a dollar of exports should be equated across all export activities. This is violated because the prices set by marketing boards and the differential scope for smuggling jointly imply a wide range of rates of implicit export taxation. Third, the cost of economising on a dollar of imports by domestic production of substitutes should be equated across all import-competing activities. This is violated because the combination price controls, soft budgets of some parastatals, and the implicit nominal tariffs on competing goods and inputs give rise to a wide dispersion of rates of effective protection. Fourth, the marginal value of using a dollar of imports should be equated to the marginal cost of earning a dollar, which in turn should be equated to the marginal cost of economising on a dollar. This is violated because, on average, imports and import-substitute production are subsidised (at different rates), whereas exports are taxed.

It is worth stressing that the objective of trade liberalisation is the attainment of these four aspects of allocative efficiency because the very concept of trade liberalisation has often been misunderstood in African applications. Following the import compressions of the early 1980s, the trade liberalisations of the late 1980s have often been interpreted as import expansions. This is a natural interpretation of an aided liberalisation, for the aid secures a temporary expansion of imports. Temporary (unsustainable) aid can at the most achieve the first of these sets of equalities (although it usually fails to do so), but risks fundamentally violating the fourth.

Such a system violates the first, third and fourth of the equalities required for allocative efficiency through trade. Because agents cannot express the intensity of their excess demands for foreign exchange, the allocation system is intrinsically denied the information needed for efficient allocation.

Why an Uncoordinated Trade Liberalisation Worsens the Balance of Payments

A trade liberalisation tends to worsen the balance of payments unless other measures are taken. To see why this is so, it is useful to describe this system through the monetary approach to the balance of payments. Normally, a balance of payments deficit is the automatic counterpart of an excess supply of money. However, in those African economies in which socialist trade policies have been combined with widespread price controls, this is not the case. As discussed in more detail in Section 2, the counterpart of price controls and shortages of goods is that there are excess holdings of money. These excess holdings are not equilibrated by inflation because of price controls, and do not cause a balance of payments deficit because of import controls. In such an economy, an import liberalisation, combined with the maintenance of quantitative restrictions on other goods, will cause a switch from excess money holdings into imports and so worsen the balance of payments. This tells us that, in socialist economies, trade liberalisation must be preceded by, or synchronised with, price decontrol. Although there is no analytic case against synchronisation, it is easier to see the liberalisation problem by decomposing it analytically into two stages, first price decontrol, and then trade liberalisation. Price decontrol is discussed in Section 2. Here we consider an economy which has already made the transition to market-clearing prices in domestic goods markets. That is, the fully socialist economy has made the transition as far as, say, Kenya in which a socialist trade policy co-exists with overall market-clearing.

With money now only held willingly, the link between an excess supply of money and a balance of payments deficit is re-established. The impact effect of a trade liberalisation will be on the demand for money. The monetary approach is particularly suitable for African economies like Kenya. Because the range of alternative financial assets is unusually limited, while inflation is well below hyperinflation rates, the demand for money can usually be regarded as well behaved and transactions-driven (the first application of modern econometric techniques to African demand for money functions (Adam, 1992) establishes just such a function for Kenya.) Further, because policy interventions in the goods markets are so complex, specific and rapidly changing, it is far easier to grasp the implications of policy for the demand for money than for the aggregate demand for goods which is its counterpart.

For monetary and hence payments equilibrium, the demand for money must equal its supply. If the demand for money (Md) is driven by transactions needs, as it largely is in such economies, then it can be represented as a function of the price level (P) and aggregate real expenditure (E):

(1) $$Md = Md(P,E) = Ms$$

In turn, the price level is composed partly of non-tradeables and partly of tradeables. Usually, exportable goods do not form a large share in African consumption and so the dominant component of tradeables as far as the price level is concerned is importables. The domestic price of importables is related to the world price by the exchange rate and the totality of import restrictions as set out in equation (2):

(2) $$Pm = Pm^* . e . (1 + t)$$

where Pm = the domestic price of importables; Pm^* = the world (dollar) price; e = the nominal exchange rate in units of domestic currency per dollar; and t = the implicit tariff equivalent of the import restrictions.

A trade liberalisation does not directly impact upon the prices of non-tradeable goods, and so its immediate effect upon the price level is via its effect upon the price of imports. The relaxation of import restrictions can be represented as a reduction in the implicit tariff rate, t. If no other policies are changed, this directly lowers the price of imports, Pm. In turn, this lowers the price level, and this lowers the demand for money. For a given money supply there is then an excess supply of money, and so a payments deficit.

The fundamental policy problem is how to preserve payments balance that is, how to maintain macroeconomic policy compatibility by changing other policies. The menu of alternatives divides into those policies designed to raise the demand for money back up again, and those which are designed to lower the supply of money, and is set out in Figure 1. The rest of this section discusses these possibilities.

Figure 1:
Policy Options for Making a Trade Liberalisation Compatible

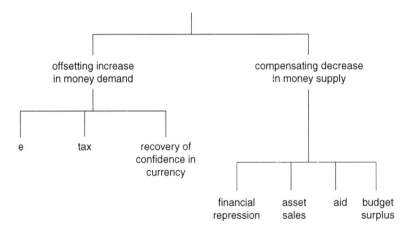

An Offsetting Increase in the Demand for Money 1: Devaluation

The demand for money can be prevented from falling if the price level is prevented from falling. One means of achieving this is by a depreciation of the nominal exchange rate. The price level is then preserved if the depreciation of e precisely offsets the reduction in *t* brought about by the trade liberalisation. Indeed, the way to think of this is that the depreciation of *e* permits a lower *t* consistent with payments balance. Note that in such a devaluation the price level does not rise and so the balance of payments does not improve. This is the fundamental difference between a trade liberalising devaluation and a payments improving devaluation. In the latter, which is the conventional analysis of the effects of a devaluation, trade policy is held constant so that the devaluation raises the price of importables, thereby raising the price level. This in turn increases the demand for money, causing an excess demand for money and so a payments surplus. Sometimes policy makers wish both to liberalise trade and to improve the balance of payments. In this case the devaluation must be shared between a price-increasing effect and a tariff-reducing effect. More commonly in Africa, as discussed further below, a trade liberalisation is synchronised with a deliberate worsening of the balance of payments due to an increase in programme aid. Such a package is price-reducing: the tariff-reducing effect is less than fully offset by devaluation.

Now, return to the case in which the trade liberalisation is precisely offset by devaluation. If the implicit tariff rate, *t*, were common across all imports, then the key relative price change in the economy would be a rise in the domestic price of exportables both absolutely and relative to both importables and non-tradeables. If exportables are not consumed domestically (e.g. copper in Zambia) the gains from liberalisation would then depend entirely upon the scope for shifting resources out of the two latter sectors into exports. Typically, African policy makers regard enhanced production by the export sector as the major, or even the only reason for trade-liberalising devaluation. However, this is to take an excessively restricted view of the sources of gains. We will take two African examples in which there are gains even if export production is unalterable.

Nigeria: Gaining from Trade Liberalisation without Increasing Exports

In the first case, the only gains arise because the structure of implicit tariffs pre-liberalisation will usually be highly variable, and liberalisation will alter the structure of relative prices among importables and enhance resource allocation as a result. A classic example of trade liberalising devaluation in which the gains could only be of this latter type was the Nigerian devaluation of 1986. The Nigerian experience is important in three respects. First, consider its impact upon the price level. Prior to the policy change, policy makers had believed that a large devaluation would be highly inflationary. Possibly this was due to thinking through the wrong analytic framework: as discussed above, a payments-improving devaluation as opposed to a trade liberalising devaluation must indeed be inflationary. However, in Nigeria, despite a huge change in the exchange rate there was no discernable impact upon the consumer price level. Second, there was no increase in imports either in the short run or over a longer horizon. In the short run this was because the liberalisation was unaided, the Nigerian government declining a proffered IMF facility. This is particularly important because unaided trade liberalisations have been rare in Africa, although common elsewhere. Even in the medium run there was no significant impact upon the total value of imports because exports were virtually exogenous since they were so dominated by oil, a situation which will take many years to alter. The medium-run exogeneity of exports is particularly interesting because it removes two sources of gain from liberalisation: intra-export allocation and export versus other sector allocation do not significantly improve. In Nigeria, the gains from liberalisation therefore accrued from better allocation of imports; better allocation within import-substitute production; and a better balance between imports as an aggregate and import substitution as an aggregate. Judging by the change in Nigerian growth performance post-devaluation, these gains were enormous. GDP has been rising at around 8 per cent p.a. since 1987, a faster rate than at any time during the previous two decades, including the period of the oil boom. There are two limitations to using the Nigerian growth performance as an example of the benefits of trade-liberalising devaluation. First, the National Accounts data are weak so that the growth rate is disputable. Second, there is a problem of attribution: the growth may have been generated by other factors. However, although other policies were also changed, the exchange rate trade reform was manifestly the centrepiece of policy reform and so, to the extent that the improved performance is policy-dependent, it is reasonable to attribute much of the growth to this cause.

Ethiopia and Kenya: Increasing Exports without Changing Production

In the second example the gains arise because not all exportable production is actually exported. Hence, as a result of the liberalising devaluation there is scope for substitution out of the consumption of exportables, permitting higher exports with unchanged production. The example of where such a gain is likely to be important is the Ethiopian devaluation of October 1992. Ethiopia's main export is coffee but it is estimated that around 45 per cent of production is consumed domestically. The devaluation raises the domestic price of coffee to consumers (since producers will only sell locally for around the price they can get for exports) and so induces a reduction in consumption as consumers substitute into other drinks or simply drink their coffee weaker. To take it to the extreme, it would be possible almost to double Ethiopian coffee exports without any change in production. Further, consumption substitution is something which can occur much more easily and speedily than reallocations in production. While Ethiopia is unusual in having such a high domestic consumption of a primary commodity, there are many examples of where exports could be increased by substitutions in consumption, most notably in textiles. Here, the Kenyan experience is illuminating. Offshore, in Mauritius, the textiles sector has become a highly successful export product. In Kenya, where the incentive structure is much less favourable for exports, the textiles sector spans firms which depend upon inefficient import substitution and firms which are so highly efficient that they are able to export profitably even under the present incentive structure. Thus, the equipment and the labour force is in place for a rapid switch to a larger share of exports in total textile production should the incentive structure change.

The above examples illustrate that the benefits of trade liberalisation are not confined to enhanced export production. However, in the longer term there are opportunities for export growth even in economies such as Nigeria in which currently virtually all exports are oil-related. A useful contrast is with Indonesia, where different incentive structures and public investments have cumulatively enabled the economy to reduce oil dependence to around 60 per cent of total exports. Some of this has been in labour intensive manufactures and processed agricultural exports such as plywood, but even in primary commodities Indonesia has been remarkably successful. Indonesian exports of cocoa now exceed those of Nigeria, whereas 25 years ago cocoa production was negligible in Indonesia while it was Nigeria's dominant export.

An Offsetting Increase in the Demand for Money
2: Indirect Taxation

We now return to the menu of policy alternatives for the achievement of a compatible trade liberalisation. Recall that our basic problem was that a trade liberalisation reduces the demand for money by lowering the price level. An alternative means of preventing the price level from falling other than by depreciating the exchange rate is the imposition of 'consumer taxes such as the value-added tax. This has direct revenue implications but it also gives rise to a different set of relative price changes. The key difference between a devaluation and a value-added tax is that the import-substitute sector gets hit much harder with a value-added tax. To see this return to equation (2). In the simplest case in which all the implicit tariffs are uniform, the exchange rate change will precisely offset the implicit tariff reduction, leaving the domestic price unaltered. The import-substitute sector still gets squeezed in this case but not, at least, as a result of a fall in the price of its output. The squeeze occurs because, to the extent that it was able to import capital goods and intermediate imports duty-free at the old exchange rate, it now has a cost increase on these items. Further, since the export sector is more profitable it will bid away resources, including labour.

There is thus a striking contrast between compatibility achieved by devaluation and compatibility achieved through a value-added tax. The point of a value-added tax is that it raises prices to consumers without raising them to producers. Hence, even if the value-added tax is confined to import-substitutes (so that consumers do not notice the difference between it and a devaluation) it confers no benefits on producers. Hence, producers face a squeeze due to a fall in the price of their output equal to the reduction in implicit tariffs. Offsetting this, they do not get squeezed through higher prices of imported inputs since the exchange rate is now not depreciated.

In the more general case in which implicit tariffs differ, this result is somewhat weakened. Because production will be highest and consumption lowest on those items which bear the highest implicit tariff rates, the average implicit tariff will be higher when weighted by production than when weighted by consumption. Since the objective of a compatible devaluation is to maintain a constant the demand for money, and the latter is much more sensitive to consumption than to production, the devaluation need only offset the fall in the average price of importables weighted by consumption. This implies that the compatible devaluation involves some fall in the production-weighted implicit tariff, so that import-substitute firms get squeezed somewhat by falling prices of output as well as by rising costs of inputs.

To summarise the contrast between the two policies, compatibility achieved by devaluation will raise the nominal price of exportables by the extent of the devaluation and slightly lower the nominal price of importables (weighted by production), leaving the nominal price of non-tradeables unaffected upon impact. Compatibility achieved by value-added tax will leave the nominal price of exports unaffected, and will lower the producer-price of importables and/or that of non-tradeables, depending upon where the tax is levied. Both, by design have the same impact upon the consumer price index and hence upon the demand for money. To the extent that there are nominal rigidities in the labour market, the value-added tax strategy shifts resources into the export sector by creating unemployment in the other sectors, whereas the devaluation strategy shifts resources primarily by firms in the export sector being able to bid workers away from their employments in the other sectors.

An example of an attempt to achieve a compatible trade liberalisation through the use of a value-added tax was the Kenyan liberalisation which began in 1989. That this liberalisation attempt was subsequently reversed does not necessarily indicate that the use of a value-added tax was misconceived. The nature of the potential problem is as follows. Often tariffs, implicit plus explicit, are initially very high: in Kenya they averaged around 110 per cent. Lowering them to the modest levels at which they will not involve high inefficiency costs therefore implies a large fall in that part of the price level made up of protected goods. Since value-added taxes are generally levied in the range of 10–20 per cent, they must be much more broadly based than the implicit tariff to leave the average price level unaffected. But a broadly based value-added tax is going to imply a quantum increase in government revenue unless it is offset by reductions in other taxes which do not lower the price level, i.e. income tax and corporate taxes. Income taxes generate so little revenue in Africa that in practice the offsetting change would be a reduction in corporate taxes. The resulting package of trade liberalisation, cuts in corporate taxes and the imposition of a broad-based value-added tax might be quite a desirable fiscal alteration. In francophone Africa, where exchange rate policy is ruled out, it is certainly worth promoting. However, the difficulty is that there is no fiscal equivalent to an auction. That is, if a quantum trade liberalisation is desired, an auction or similar floating rate is a device in which the magnitude of the devaluation required to maintain compatibility is found by the market rather than needing to be estimated by the government. By contrast, there is a danger that the government (or its advisers) will miscalculate the fiscal change needed for a given trade liberalisation. One way around this, since fiscal changes cannot be fine-tuned week-by-week, is to raise taxes year-by-year until the point at which quotas cease to be binding. That this requires a sustained commitment to trade liberalisation makes the policy more demanding of the government but, as we will see, thereby precludes those liberalisation attempts most likely to end in costly reversal.

An Offsetting Increase in the Demand for Money 3: Confidence

Socialist economies in transition have a potential advantage in achieving compatibility because they may experience a persistent increase in the demand for money as confidence in the currency is gradually restored. A current example of this process is Uganda. During the years in which money was a poor store of value and subject to periodic confiscation through currency reconstructions, households learned to economise on holdings of real money balances. Since the attainment of price stability, confidence in the currency has increased (albeit from a low base) and the real value of money holdings has risen substantially relative to expenditure (i.e. the velocity of circulation has decreased). There is a similar opportunity in Angola where real money balances fell to extremely low levels as the economy retreated into barter and dollarisation. In these economies the transition from other socialist economic policies can therefore contribute to the macroeconomic accommodation of trade liberalisation, although the affect is intrinsically gradual and so not suited to big-bang trade liberalisation. Further, it is not a universal feature of socialist African economies. In Ethiopia, which was unusual in combining socialism with fiscal conservatism, the long term price stability thereby achieved induced a large accumulation of real money balances and so there is no further scope for raising the demand for money by means of restoring confidence. There is a similar lack of opportunity in francophone Africa.

An Accommodating Increase in the Money Supply

Devaluation and value-added taxation both achieve compatibility by offsetting the fall in the price level brought about by liberalisation. The broad alternative strategy is to allow the price level to fall, and with it the demand for money, and to achieve compatibility by reducing the money supply. There are four strategies for reducing the money supply but all of them have the disadvantage that the impact effect of the trade liberalisation now falls only on prices in the importables sector. Instead of raising the price of exportables relative to the producer prices of both importables and non-tradeables, which is achieved by a devaluation and can be achieved by a broad-based value-added tax, the price of both exportables and non-tradeables initially rises equally relative to importables. This generates excess supply in the non-tradeable sector the elimination of which requires a fall in the nominal price of non-tradeables. However, this price fall in turn reduces the demand for money and so in addition to the reduction in the money supply needed on the impact of the liberalisation in order to avoid a payments deficit, there is a further gradual reduction needed as the price of non-tradeables falls to the new market-clearing level. Since the fall in non-tradeables prices can only be induced by excess supply, this method of achieving compatibility involves unemployment in the non-tradeable sector.

If the liberalisation is done in the context of significant inflation actual downward movements in nominal prices may not be needed on a substantial scale, merely a departure from a counterfactual price increase. However, if the trade liberalisation is large and the initial inflation rate is modest, then substantial nominal price falls are required. The Franc Zone is the best example of this type of adjustment through money supply reduction inducing a falling price level. Because in Africa there is an unusually large small enterprise sector and generally rather weak labour unions, this strategy is much more feasible than in other parts of the world. The most acute downward nominal rigidities are probably in the public sector itself. Nevertheless, these might be sufficiently severe to make adjustment a long-drawn out and costly process. A final disadvantage with such falling-price strategies is that they confer a windfall upon those who hold government nominal liabilities. Some of the Franc Zone governments have large liabilities to their citizens in the form of payments arrears. Since the capacity of the government to service its liabilities is not increased, any increase in the real value of those liabilities merely increases the extent to which the claims must be discounted against their face value. The increase in the real face value of liabilities, precisely offset by a devalued prospect of repayment is entirely counter to appropriate management of excessive liabilities.

The above problems are common to all mechanisms of compatibility achieved through money supply reduction. Now consider in turn the four mechanisms by which such a reduction can be achieved.

Money Supply Reduction 1: Financial Repression

The first is to reduce the money supply through changing the rules governing bank lending. An increase in the minimum cash-to-deposits ratio of the banks can force them to reduce lending and hence inside money (claims of one private agent on another private agent), for a given level of outside money (claims by private agents on the Central Bank, most notably cash). However, raising the cash to deposits ratio is like a tax on the banking system: the banks are required to hold non-interest-bearing government liabilities against part of their loan portfolio and so must charge borrowers more and pay depositors less. In the limiting case in which the cash to deposits ratio is raised to unity, the banking system has been closed down as an institution of financial intermediation and is essentially a retail outlet for government liabilities. Thus, compatibility achieved by raising the cash-to-deposits ratio secures trade liberalisation at the price of financial repression. In most of socialist

Africa (Zambia being an exception), the banking system is already subject to such a high degree of financial repression that there is little or no further scope for increasing its severity. Nor is it sound policy to achieve liberalisation in one market by increasing restrictions in another one.

Money Supply Reduction 2: Asset Sales

The second strategy is to reduce the money supply through the sale of government-owned assets. In developed economies the principal assets used are financial typically bonds. However, such markets are largely absent in Africa (or else the only holders are public agencies essentially part of the government). However, in some African countries, especially those which have been most socialist, there is scope for selling real assets. Striking examples are Ethiopia and Angola, where in addition to productive assets (ownership of firms) the government owns the entire stock of residential and commercial buildings. While it may be impossible to create a bond market in these economies except in the longer term, there is considerable scope for selling public assets. The sale of productive public assets should primarily be determined by issues of management of the enterprises rather than by macroeconomic considerations of financing. However, the sale of property as opposed to enterprises is particularly well suited to macroeconomic requirements. The uncertainty about future inflation, which is essentially the factor which precludes the rapid emergence of bond markets in formerly socialist economies, actually makes property more saleable: the more that agents fear a burst of inflation, the higher the prices they will be prepared to pay for real assets. Further, in all the socialist economies of Africa there has recently been a housing market so, at the most, the issue is one of revival. Indeed, generally the housing market has not been fully suppressed. In Ethiopia, for example, the rent-controlled publicly owned housing stock gave rise to the practice of key money paid by new tenants to previous tenants.

Money Supply Reduction 3:
Programme Aid and the Franc Zone Mechanism

Whereas the first two strategies for money supply reduction have been stock-adjustment effects, which can be executed quickly, the remaining strategies work through flows. The change in the flow supply of money depends upon the current account of the balance of payments: a deficit giving rise to a reduction as government liabilities are purchased by the government for foreign exchange, and the fiscal position; a budget surplus directly reducing the government's liabilities. Consider reduction in the money supply achieved through a balance of payments deficit. This is broadly what is happening in the Franc Zone, the payments deficit being financed by France. Residents of francophone Africa sell surplus CFA francs to the two regional central banks in exchange for French francs, which the regional central banks have been lent by the French Treasury. In anglophone Africa the capacity to do this is normally extremely limited.

Aided trade liberalisations have an economic rationale primarily through providing a means of achieving a reduction in the money supply. In effect, the aid is used by the government to sell foreign exchange to private agents, buying back domestic currency liabilities. Temporary aid can thus achieve a sustained trade liberalisation. However, this mechanism is open to all the criticisms which apply more generally to money-supply reduction strategies. In addition, the notion that aid reduces the 'costs of adjustment' seems to be seriously misplaced. Because aid substitutes for exchange rate depreciation, the import substitute sector is hit harder by aided trade liberalisation than by a trade liberalising devaluation. The temporary expenditure gain for private agents, which is the counterpart of the aid inflow, accrues not to the import-substitute sector (the sector whose interests are damaged by trade liberalisation) but to agents who hold money, since the aid permits a lower price level. Since the private sector is a net holder of money, on average, private agents gain. However, the fall in the price level involves a transfer from private debtors to private creditors, which approximately corresponds with a transfer from the formal corporate sector to households. Since the import substitute sector is usually dominated by corporate rather than household producers (who predominate in the non-tradeable and export sectors) the enhancement of the real value of money balances may actually worsen the position of the sector over and above the direct effect on the price of its output.

Money Supply Reduction 4: Budget Surplus

The final strategy for money supply reduction is to reduce the budget deficit relative to its counterfactual. The problem with this strategy, over and above the obvious difficulty of implementing it, is that it produces only a gradual reduction in the money supply whereas a quantum trade liberalisation gives rise to an immediate quantum reduction in the price level and hence in money demand. Thus, this strategy cannot avoid a temporary period during which the balance of payments deteriorates except by making the trade liberalisation itself gradual. But a gradual trade liberalisation driven only by a fiscal improvement is probably extremely vulnerable to arrest and even reversal. It is probably the least likely strategy to be seen as durable since there are so many pressures on expenditure which inhibit a sustained fiscal improvement. A general criticism of money supply reduction through fiscal policy as a means of making a trade liberalisation compatible is that policy makers should be judging the appropriate fiscal deficit by other criteria. A sound macroeconomic policy would involve some explicit or implicit rules of deficit financing which would gradually become credible by adherence. The establishment of a reputation for consistent fiscal policy is an enormous asset for a government and is difficult to acquire. Temporary suspensions of this rule for other objectives, even temporary fiscal improvements, weaken the perceived adherence to the rule.

Co-ordination of Policies

The above discussion has considered seven strategies for maintaining macroeconomic compatibility during a trade liberalisation. These options are not exclusive: a government could, for example, combine consumer taxes with exchange rate devaluation to partially offset the fall in the price level, while using some programme aid to reduce the money supply. A major problem, however, is that it is not feasible to provide accurate measures of the extent to which different policies need to be changed in order to offset a trade liberalisation of a given magnitude. This is an advantage of switching to a floating exchange rate (combined with whatever other policies the government might choose to retain compatibility). In effect, the government then leaves one policy instrument to be set by the market in such a way as to be compatible with whatever trade policy it chooses. Other than by this means, quantum trade liberalisations are prone either to incompatibility or to speculative fears of incompatibility, because the government lacks other policies which can be fine tuned to rectify incipient depletion of foreign exchange. This is indeed why quantitative import restrictions have been so common under fixed exchange rates in Africa, since they offer the opportunity for fine tuning which, in economies with better developed financial markets, is provided by interest rate policy. The conclusion is, that if a government is not prepared to float the exchange rate, it should not lead with specific large trade liberalisation measures, but let trade liberalisation occur piecemeal in the wake of accommodating changes which improve the balance of payments. However, as will be seen in the next section, a government which embarks upon a quantum liberalisation combined with floating still has the opportunity for fatal policy errors.

Credibility in Trade Liberalisation

Macroeconomic policy choices are constrained by the need to maintain credibility. Incredible policies induce private agents to make intertemporal choices which can be socially highly costly, as will be discussed in this and the next section. Here we discuss two reasons why a trade liberalisation might be incredible and show that they lead to different private responses which are, in each case, damaging. The analysis makes extensive use of the example of the Zambian liberalisation of 1985–87.

We begin with the causes of incredibility in trade liberalisations. Sufficient conditions for a trade liberalisation to be perceived as credible are unknown and unknowable. However, both experience and theory give us important insights into the necessary conditions. There are two such conditions: compatibility and time consistency. Compatibility has already been discussed above. If a liberalisation is incompatible, i.e. involves unfunded payments disequilibrium, it is liable to be unsustainable.[3] The consequences of incredibility generated by time inconsistency and by incompatibility are somewhat different. However, they have in common a disincentive to incur fixed investment in the export sector, which destroys the longer-term growth prospects which are central to the rationale for trade liberalisation. First, consider incredibility due to incompatibility.

Incredibility due to Incompatibility

If private agents recognise that the reform is incompatible, then they can anticipate that some policy must be changed. One possibility is that the liberalisation will be reversed; another is that the exchange rate will be depreciated. In either of these events, imports will become dearer to private agents in domestic currency. However, which choice of achieving compatibility the government takes will determine how relative prices alter: devaluation raises the price of all tradeables; protection benefits only importables. A belief that the package is incompatible therefore gives rise to a belief (held with the same degree of certainty as that of the incompatibility) that imports are temporarily cheap; but to uncertainty as to the future sectoral structure of incentives. This is a disastrous combination of expectations. The expectation that imports are temporarily cheap encourages a rational response of hoarding imports of durable goods, whether these be consumer goods or intermediate imports. The uncertainty concerning the future structure of incentives discourages fixed and sectorally irreversible investment in preference for liquidity. The two expectations work in conjunction: the reduction in fixed investment helps to finance the hoarding of imports.

While all African economies attempting trade liberalisations are liable to encounter doubts concerning whether reforms are compatible, the socialist economies are probably particularly vulnerable. There are far less pertinent data with which to make informed guesses about how much other policies need to be altered; and the government is likely to include supporters of socialist policies, encouraging 'compromises' in which concessions are made which are in aggregate incompatible. This is, indeed, the problem in our first example.

Example 1: Zambia, April–September 1986

An alarming example of this effect was the attempted liberalisation of the Zambian trade regime 1985–87. The Zambian trade liberalisation was initially achieved by the move to auction in September 1985. If import quotas are removed as they were in

Zambia, an auction automatically allows the exchange rate to make a compatible adjustment (as it did in Nigeria a year later), hence, superficially, it seems unlikely that the Zambian experience can furnish an example of an expectation of incompatibility. Unfortunately, however, the government surreptitiously moved away from the auction system in April 1986. The President wished to have an appreciated exchange rate (from 7 kwacha per dollar to 5), and ordered the Governor of the Central Bank to deliver this result. The Governor refused to manipulate the auction system and so resigned along with the Minister of Finance and the President's economic adviser. The new Governor initially achieved an appreciation to 5 kwacha by the device of disallowing bids on technicalities. This was followed by a strategy of running down the reserves. However, since the reserves were soon exhausted, he began to sell foreign exchange which the Central Bank did not yet possess. As a result, a 'pipeline' built up, that is a queue of those who had purchased foreign exchange at an agreed 'auction' price but who could only take delivery of the dollars some weeks subsequently once the Central Bank had purchased them. This strategy was blatantly incompatible: the government was selling more dollars than it was buying and accumulating dollar liabilities. As such it was evident that dollars were temporarily cheap: the government could not maintain the policy for long. Further, it was an open question whether compatibility would be restored by a depreciation of the kwacha or by a reversal of the trade liberalisation. Thus, both the ingredients were in place for the socially costly asset behaviour which we predicted above. It indeed appears that there was a shift from fixed investment and into import hoarding. During 1986 there was an unprecedented accumulation of inventories (almost all of which would be imported intermediate inputs) which, remarkably, were three times the value of gross fixed capital formation (normally, inventory accumulation is very small relative to gross fixed capital formation).

Example 2: Kenya, 1980

A further African example is the Kenyan trade liberalisation of 1980. This was incompatible in that quotas were relaxed without exchange rate adjustment. During the liberalisation the level of reserves fell rapidly, so that the unsustainability of the policy was manifest to well-informed private agents. Data on imports of consumer goods reveal a substantial alteration in their composition. Total private consumer imports increased by only around a quarter in 1980 compared with the previous year. However, imports of consumer durables doubled.[4] This is consistent with stockpiling behaviour by private agents in anticipation of a subsequent rise in their domestic price brought about by a collapse of the policy. Those who held the belief were proved right. By 1981, imports of consumer durables had fallen to only a third of their 1980 level, so that market-clearing prices must have risen considerably. Whereas the policy error in Zambia could reasonably be blamed on the President (who was presumably trying to make a small concession to the opponents of the liberalisation while preserving the policy), the Kenyan liberalisation seems to have been a technical error by the World Bank (which at the time was wary of discussing exchange rate policy, seen as the preserve of the Fund).

Incredibility Due to Time Inconsistency

Having seen that incompatibility is an important source of incredibility, we now turn to time inconsistency. This is an acute problem, possibly the most fundamental one, in the transition from African socialism. A policy change is time inconsistent if the government has a clear incentive to reverse it once private agents have acted on the expectation that it will be maintained. Suppose that the balance, of political power in society is such that the export sector is not strongly represented and so is heavily taxed. Suppose further that, for whatever reasons, the government has over-exploited this tax base so that it has gradually diminished: as the capital invested in the export sector has depreciated it has not been replaced so that production has declined. At some point the revenue will have diminished to such an extent that the government forgoes little current revenue loss by reducing taxes on the sector. Further, if only private agents will believe that the change in incentives is permanent, they will invest in the now profitable export sector again. The government therefore has an incentive to promise that the change in incentives is permanent. However, should the investment take place, the government again has an incentive to impose taxes on the export sector. Because all agents can see that the government would have such an incentive, the promise of sustained liberalisation is time inconsistent. As a consequence, even if the government embarks upon the liberalisation, private agents will not be 'fooled' into making irreversible investments in the export sector. This applies even if the government has genuinely changed its mind on the long term desirability of export taxation. The government's policy is incredible not because ministers might be lying, but because future ministers, if rational, will reverse the policy.

The reason that time inconsistency is likely to be a far more acute problem in the transition from African socialism than in the transition from East European socialism, is because in Africa, governments have not been toppled by anti-socialist popular revolutions. Sometimes governments have indeed been toppled, as in Ethiopia, but the issue which precipitated government defeat was not primarily socialism. The nearest Africa comes to an anti-socialist revolution is probably Zambia: here the new government has a much easier task of establishing its credentials for fundamentally different long term economic policies from those of its predecessor. At the other extreme, the Angolan government has a long record of explicit and strong commitment to socialist trade policy and has been re-elected. For its policy changes to be credible, it must persuade private agents that either its long term interests have fundamentally changed, or that its past policies were not furthering its long term interests.

A time inconsistent but compatible liberalisation will not generate speculative accumulation of imports. To see this, return to equation (2). If the liberalisation is compatible, the exchange rate has been depreciated so as to offset the reduction in the implicit tariff. Time inconsistency implies that there is a rational belief on the part of private agents that this policy switch, e up and t down, will be reversed: the exchange rate will be appreciated and implicit tariffs will be increased. However, just as compatible trade liberalisation does not give rise to a generalised cheapening of imports, so its reversal does not give rise to a generalised increase in their domestic price. There is no incentive for hoarding.

Example: Zambia, September 1985–April 1986

Zambia during the period September 1985 – April 1986 is probably an example of this unlikely-sounding conjunction of time-inconsistency and compatibility. Because during this period the auction was not manipulated, macroeconomic policy was compatible. However, there were very good grounds for being sceptical that the liberalisation was time-consistent. The overwhelming majority of the cabinet had opposed the liberalisation attempt and this reflected the balance of interests within the ruling political party. Indeed, the most puzzling feature of the liberalisation attempt is why, politically, it happened at all. Apparently, the President was persuaded that it would reduce corruption (a not unreasonable belief); there was the attraction of receiving extra aid (which in the event appears to have been used for debt repayment and so did not significantly alter the capacity to import); and there was the need to be seen to take some initiative to improve the economy. However, the spectacle of UNIP implementing a massive trade liberalisation under the auspices of the IMF was so intrinsically unlikely that it could hardly be regarded as durable.

An indication that the huge speculative accumulation of inventories was the result of the incompatibility of macroeconomic policy – which started in April 1986 and became increasingly acute until the policy reversal of May 1987 – rather than the time inconsistency which was present from the inception of the policy in September 1985, is that the speculation appears not to have set in until July 1986. The evidence for this comes from borrowing by manufacturing firms (the ones best in a position to accumulate speculative inventories of imported inputs) from the commercial banks. Between September 1985 and June 1986 their level of additional borrowing was entirely in line with their past behaviour. Suddenly, in mid-1986 their borrowing exploded to around ten times its normal rate,[5] suggesting that this was the period from which speculative accumulation commenced.

Consequences of Speculation

Speculation is thus not an inevitable consequence of incredibility, but rather is generated when incredibility is caused by incompatibility. Speculation is fatal to trade liberalisation because it is usually self-fulfilling. The speculative purchase of imports depletes the reserves and so advances the date at which policy must be changed to one which is compatible. Indeed, as the date is advanced, so the rate of return on speculation rises, since the imports need not be hoarded for such a long period before getting the windfall arising from their increased value. Suppose that there is no consensus among private agents as to the likely duration of the liberalisation. Those who regard it as long lasting will, as a result, see the expected rate of return from speculative hoarding as lower than those who expect a swift policy reversal. Even if initially only a few agents regard the return as higher than the opportunity cost of the funds which will be tied up by the imports hoard, their speculation can rapidly induce a crisis. The speculation by these agents reduces the reserves. This in turn brings forward the dates at which all the other agents anticipate policy reversal and so raises their expected return from hoarding. For some agents this increase pushes them over the threshold at which hoarding is more profitable than alternative uses of funds and the behaviour of these agents further depletes the reserves. This sequence does not inevitably unravel the liberalisation: it depends upon the distribution of expectations of policy reversal and upon the sensitivity of the rate of return upon hoarding to the date of policy reversal. However, it creates the potential for an accelerated descent into macroeconomic crisis due to speculative asset movements, which radically changes the timing of collapse of incompatible regimes.

Example: Zambia, July 1986–May 1987

The Zambian experience provides a salutary lesson in how a policy mistake can interact with speculation. This completes the story of the collapse of the Zambian attempt at trade liberalisation. The speculative demand for imports induced the Central Bank to sell dollars yet further into the future, so that the 'pipeline' extended to ten weeks. In effect, by creating the pipeline the Central Bank was setting up a forward market in foreign exchange and taking a position in it, namely, a set of commitments to supply dollars at a previously agreed price. As the time came for these commitments to be honoured, they pre-empted sales by the Central Bank on the spot market, so that forward sales rapidly crowded out spot sales. For example, if a central bank sells 20 per cent more dollars than it has, in its first auction it will sell $20 forward for every $100 it sells on the spot market. In its second auction these forward sales will be the first claim and so only $80 can be sold on the spot market, leaving $40 of forward sales unless the bank abandons its attempt to sell 20 per cent more dollars than it is purchasing. By the third auction spot sales have shrunk to $60 and forward sales have grown to $60. By the sixth auction all sales are on the forward market. Further, not all these sales can be honoured at the next auction and so the forward market is extended from just being the interval between adjacent auctions: the bank now has liabilities further into the future. Because speculative demand for dollars was so large in Zambia, despite these extra sales of dollars on the forward market, the Central Bank had to depreciate the exchange rate quite rapidly. Had there been no pipeline, this exchange rate depreciation would have restored compatibility: after all, the incompatibility had arisen from a relatively modest appreciation of the exchange rate from a market equilibrium rate of seven kwacha per dollar, to a government determined rate of five. Under speculative pressure the rate soon reverted to seven and continued to depreciate further. The reason that depreciation back to the previous equilibrium failed to restore compatibility was because the forward commitments created large central bank losses, which depreciated the equilibrium rate. On average, over the period May 1986 to May 1987, the period of speculative pressure, the exchange rate depreciated by 25 per cent every ten weeks. Hence, the pipeline on average implied that the Central Bank was buying dollars for 25 per cent more kwacha than the price at which it was selling them. This produced a massive Central Bank loss on its foreign exchange transactions. In the period May to December 1986 the bank lost around one billion kwacha. At the start of 1986 the entire stock of 'outside money' in the economy (i.e. monetary liabilities of the Central Bank) was only two billion kwacha. Hence, the inadvertent creation of a position in the forward market caused a 50 per cent increase in the base of the money supply. This naturally caused inflation. The inflation in turn worsened the fiscal position. The government had a commitment to a fixed nominal price of mealie-meal maintained by subsidy. The inflation sharply reduced the real price of mealie-meal, thereby making this commitment much more expensive. This additional claim upon the budget worsened the fiscal deficit and so further fuelled inflation.

By late 1986, the Zambian authorities were thus faced with a nightmare situation in which inflation was accelerating due to monetary expansion caused partly by Central Bank losses and partly by the deteriorating budget. The inflation was in turn depreciating the exchange rate needed for compatibility. Had the government not intervened in the foreign exchange market in April 1986, the auction rate might gradually have depreciated in line with a small underlying fiscal deficit to around eight kwacha per dollar by the end of 1986. The 50 per cent increase in the money supply caused by Central Bank losses implied that the equilibrium rate would instead have been around 12 kwacha. The additional deterioration caused by the budget implied that it would be even lower than this, perhaps around 14 kwacha per dollar. However, the fundamental dilemma of the Central Bank was that even by reverting the exchange rate to a compatible level it would not arrest the inflation. Suppose, taking further the above numerical example, that the central bank abandons its attempt to sell 20 per cent more dollars than it receives and now sells only the dollars it receives at a market-clearing price. It cannot, however, deliver these sales on the spot market, because of its backlog of liabilities. All that happens is that the change of policy prevents the pipeline from lengthening further. All the Bank's trading remains in the forward market. Since it is buying dollars at a higher price than the price it has previously agreed for the dollars which it is currently delivering (i.e. the forward sales which have now come due), it continues to make losses. These continue to fuel inflation and so the exchange rate needed for compatibility continues to depreciate. Forward sales in a depreciating market imply continued losses. Hence, reverting to a compatible exchange rate (which the Zambian Central Bank did during late 1986) is insufficient of itself to arrest the process of collapse initiated by a relatively brief and modest departure from compatibility. To arrest the decline, the Central Bank must clear its commitments in the forward exchange market. To achieve this, it must temporarily sell fewer dollars than it buys.

There are two ways for the Central Bank to achieve this. The most desirable solution is for the private agents who accumulated speculative hoards of imports to be induced to run them down again. The reversion of the exchange rate to its compatible level indeed removes the original incentive for these hoards: the decline in the exchange rate, and the concomitant increase in the domestic market-clearing price of importable goods, means that the expected windfall gain which was the rationale for the speculation has now occurred. Hoards are now excessive to normal requirements and so there is a rationale for decumulating them. However, the original speculative incentive for hoarding imports has now been replaced by a different incentive for retaining them. The increase in the rate of inflation implies that unless nominal interest rates on bank loans are correspondingly increased, real interest rates have turned heavily negative. It is thus profitable to be a debtor: holding real assets such as durable imports which maintain their real value, while monetary liabilities lose their real value. To induce agents to dishoard, the government must therefore raise nominal interest rates sufficiently high to keep real interest rates significantly positive. However, if the government is a substantial borrower from the banking system, this increase in nominal interest rates might itself deteriorate the fiscal balance, a subject which we discuss in a later section. If the government is able to induce agents to dishoard then the demand for dollars temporarily falls. Thus, at the compatible exchange rate the central bank is temporarily indeed able to buy more dollars than it sells and so pay off the backlog of its liabilities. If the government is not able to induce dishoarding, then the only other way open to it to pay off the backlog is temporarily to depreciate the exchange rate even below the level needed for compatibility. That is, the previous disequilibrium of over-valuation has to be offset by a corresponding period of under-valuation.

If the Central Bank implements neither of these strategies then it will continue to make trading losses which increase the money supply. The only remedy then for the government would be to offset these losses either by running a fiscal surplus or by selling assets. In Zambia, there was an attempt at least to reduce the fiscal deficit by raising the mealie-meal price during December 1986. This led to riots which caused the government to reverse the attempt. The actual policy reversal, the following May, occurred because the government could no longer tolerate the rapid depreciation of the exchange rate and accelerating inflation. The riots are commonly identified as the key point from which the liberalisation attempt failed. However, on our analysis, by this stage the government had virtually no hope of salvaging the reform.

The key lesson from the Zambian experience is of the damage done by the inadvertent taking of a position by the Central Bank in the forward exchange market. Had the government merely adopted a temporarily incompatible exchange rate by running down its reserves, confining all its transactions to the spot market, it would still have provoked the wave of speculative import purchases but it would have been able to end this simply by reverting to the equilibrium rate and it would not have incurred trading losses. The speculation might even have reversed itself once the compatible exchange rate had been re-established. The attempt to deal with speculation by forward trading created running losses such that even when the exchange rate was depreciated to a rate which would otherwise have been compatible, the very act of depreciation so inflated the money supply as to make the depreciation insufficient.

Credibility as a Constraint

We have seen that a trade liberalisation needs to be credible. Even aside from the acute problem of speculation, if private agents suspect that the policy is likely to be reversed, they will not invest in the export sector, defeating one of the allocative objectives of the reform. Of the two conditions we have identified as necessary for credibility, one is far more difficult to achieve than the other. Compatibility, while not always easy, is nevertheless a fairly precise and technical condition. It was evident at the time that the Zambian government was breaching compatibility by building up a pipeline of foreign exchange sales. By contrast, time consistency is deeply problematic. Arguably, it is only met if the political and social forces which made trade restrictions a favoured policy in socialist Africa are themselves changed. It is not enough for the government to be sincere about reform; the government has to create a political environment in which the dominant pressures are for policy maintenance.

5. Conclusion: Interactions and Sequencing

In the previous sections the interactions between, and sequencing of, reforms have been discussed piecemeal. Here, we draw together these discussions. First, we summarise the interactions. With four policy areas – trade and financial liberalisations, price decontrol and fiscal reform – there are twelve possible interactions, and we consider each of them. We then consider the sequencing of reforms.

Interactions

Fiscal/Trade Interactions

Because quantitative restrictions have been the dominant instrument of trade policy in socialist Africa, trade liberalisation can be budget-improving. This can happen in three ways. First, the overall volume of imports normally increases as a result of trade liberalisation. Second, relaxation of quotas usually changes the composition of imports towards higher tariff items. Both of these effects increase tariff revenue for a given tariff structure. Third, some of the rents from quotas can accrue to the government if tariffs are increased to replace them. Offsetting these positive effects, tariff reform may involve a reduction in the average level of tariffs. Hence the fiscal consequences of trade reform are *a priori* ambiguous, and quantitative forecasts are likely to be inaccurate.

The consequences of fiscal reform for trade policy are likely to be benign because the general direction of fiscal reform is to switch from trade taxes to domestic consumption taxes. This is because a common underlying objective of both sets of reforms is to improve allocative efficiency.

Fiscal/Financial Interactions

The fiscal consequences of financial reform are likely to be adverse, at least in the short term. Socialist governments have typically used the banking system as an extension of the budget, making heavy use of artificially cheap credit to finance their own deficits. The increase in domestic interest costs may destabilise the budget, requiring a larger swing in the primary budget balance than would otherwise have been necessary. By the same argument, successful fiscal reform generates the surplus which makes financial reform affordable.

Fiscal/Price Decontrol Interactions

The consequences of price decontrol for fiscal policy depend on whether the social groups which lose are compensated. First, consider the case where no compensation is made. The fiscal impact then depends upon the relative importance of consumer and producer price interventions and the way in which they were combined. Consumer price controls may be equivalent to either on or off-budget expenditures. Producer price controls are equivalent to off-budget revenues when the government is the purchaser. When the public sector is the producer (so that the government is indirectly the seller), price controls may be equivalent to either on- or off-budget expenditures. If the government holds consumer prices down without equivalently depressing producer prices for its own purchases, as it did in Zambia, the subsidy becomes a budget expenditure. If it finances the subsidy by purchases from producers at low prices, as was done in Ethiopia, off-budget revenues are financing off-budget expenditures. Simple abolition of controls may therefore be budget neutral or even budget damaging, but in the more usual configuration (such as the Zambian one) are likely to be budget enhancing.

Now consider the case in which compensation is paid. Since the compensation is now on budget, the fiscal impact depends upon whether it was previously off budget. There are two reasons why the government may make distributional expenditures. It may be politically necessary to compensate the social groups which lose from decontrol. Additionally, however, the government may have distributional objectives, in particular the alleviation of poverty. The achievement of distributional and allocative objectives through public expenditure rather than direct price interventions is an instance of the same government objective being achieved more efficiently and transparently by switching to more conventional instruments. When compensating expenditures must be made, price decontrol may be feasible only through fiscal reform.

Trade Liberalisation/Price Decontrol Interactions

Trade liberalisation and price decontrol work together. An essential part of the mechanism whereby trade liberalisation improves resource allocation is that domestic prices of tradeables should approach world prices. Alterations in the exchange rate and tariffs will therefore be frustrated unless domestic prices are able to reflect them. Indeed, they may be counterproductive, giving rise to large trading profits and losses which do not reflect social returns. For example, devaluations combined with price maintenance on the part of export marketing boards simply produce a transfer to the marketing boards, rather than increasing the incentive to exporters, a phenomenon experienced in Tanzania during the 1980s. Conversely, if the import-substitute sector is prevented from raising prices in response to higher input costs, needless bankruptcies will ensue. In addition to these microeconomic arguments, a trade liberalisation without price decontrol would produce a severe temporary payments deficit as all the excess supply of money was removed through extra imports rather than through inflation. However, price decontrol without trade reform may remove the one check on monopoly pricing. In the face of import bans, the market-clearing domestic price may be very high. Price decontrol without trade liberalisation would therefore induce resources to move into the activity, when quite possibly (without excessive protection) resources would be shed by it. Finally, we noted that trade liberalisation helped to reduce the true cost of living by widening the range of choice, a complement to the effect of price decontrol.

Trade/Financial Liberalisation Interactions

Trade liberalisation may be a source of financial shocks. The change in the exchange rate will raise the domestic currency valuation of foreign currency debts and to an extent raise the need for working capital. The latter effect is most problematic if the reform is done against the background of financial targeting, so that the banks cannot extend credit. Such a contractionary effect would, however, be avoided if instead of targeting the money supply, the government targets the price level directly as we have suggested.

Where the government has substantial domestic financial liabilities and cannot afford to liberalise the domestic financial market, neither can it afford to liberalise the capital account. Capital account liberalisation would produce a portfolio switch into higher-yielding foreign assets. Even when domestic financial liberalisation has been achieved, an opening of the capital account might produce an outflow if foreign assets are perceived as safer; however, the act of opening the capital account might itself increase confidence in domestic assets. The balance of advantage depends upon the relative size of non-government domestic and foreign financial assets. Because the opportunities for over-invoicing and smuggling were well developed during the previous policy regime, there have already been large capital outflows. Uganda and Angola probably represent extreme cases in which there are substantial assets held abroad and very few non-government holdings of domestic financial assets. The policy problem is then to induce repatriation and so there is little to lose and much to be gained from opening the capital account. An opposing example is Zambia, where although there have been capital outflows, there are also large domestic holdings of financial assets.

Financial Reform/Price Decontrol Interactions

Often the starting position of parastatal enterprises in socialist economies is, that due to price controls, they make losses which are then compensated by directed lending (which cannot be repaid and so is in reality a transfer) from the banking system. The two policies are in this respect complements. Financial reform without price decontrol will therefore convert book losses into needless bankruptcy. Conversely, in the absence of any financial reform, price decontrol in conjunction with trade liberalisation will lose much of its potential impact upon resource allocation. Post-reform, some firms will find themselves making large losses. It is important that such firms should contract rather than continue to face a soft budget constraint, otherwise resources will not be released from activities in which they should not be deployed. Hence, the urgent financial reform is to limit the capacity of the publicly owned banking system to lend. By contrast, as discussed in Section 2, the expansion of the system of private credit is not urgent since it can only be a long term goal. A phase in which existing enterprises are short of credit is probably necessary. Liquidity held abroad may provide the means for private entrepreneurs to finance new activities, which are in any case bound to be on a modest scale in the early years of transition. The phase of contraction of socially costly activities will probably precede the phase of expansion of socially profitable activities by several years.

Sequencing

The preceding analysis has suggested some policies which should be synchronised and others which must be sequenced. We now bring these together to indicate a critical path of reform.

The first question is whether the economy is in a condition from which it can embark upon liberalisation or whether prior steps must be taken to stabilise it. Were there a large underlying fiscal deficit which was being restrained by the control regime from destabilising the economy, then there would be a strong argument for achieving some degree of fiscal rectification prior to liberalisation. However, there is no general presumption that socialist control regimes work in this way. Where they do not, since the changes in the control regime will have large and uncertain impacts upon the fiscal balance, it is more appropriate to embark upon liberalisation while fiscal reforms are underway.

We first set out the opening phase of the transition. We have argued that price decontrol should be synchronised with trade liberalisation and that both should be synchronised with tightened control upon the lending practices of public banks. This means abandoning the nominal anchors used during the socialist phase, namely the price level and the exchange rate. Hence, the first phase of transition is characterised by a removal of nominal targets on the price level and the exchange rate. The price level will usually rise by an uncertain amount to market-clearing levels, and the exchange rate will depreciate by an uncertain amount in response to the removal of quantitative restrictions. Both the foreign exchange market and the goods market will reach market-clearing levels swiftly once controls are removed, so that the phase without any nominal anchor need not last for longer than a few months. For example, in rural Tanzania, goods markets were already clearing a few months after price decontrol. The first phase need only be longer than this if the decontrol is gradual.

In the second phase a nominal anchor is re-established. We have suggested that the most appropriate nominal target at this stage is the price level, since the money demand function is likely to alter in an unpredictable way. The policy instrument we have proposed for this phase is government expenditure adjusted on a high frequency basis (for example, monthly as in Uganda).

In the third phase, the nominal anchor is unchanged but reserves are added as a second policy instrument, enabling the frequency with which government expenditure is adjusted to be reduced. If at the end of the first phase reserves are sufficient for this role, then the second phase can be skipped. Otherwise, the accumulation of reserves must be achieved during the second phase.

In the fourth phase, the demand for money function stabilises. The fiscal position improves sufficiently for domestic financial reform to be feasible. Domestic confidence is sufficiently restored for the government to be able to establish a substantial domestic debt market on which open market operations are possible. As a result the nominal anchor can be switched from the price level to monetary targeting, and the use of foreign exchange reserves can be supplemented by open market operations, enabling the time path of government spending to be determined by allocative considerations.

In the final phase, domestic firms are building sufficient reputations for a substantial private credit market to be viable so that competitive private banking can be introduced, and confidence in the government permits an open capital account. (Recall that we have argued above that when the government has little to lose the capital account may be opened earlier than this.)

The implication of the above sequence is that neither the nominal target nor the instrument for its attainment is constant during the transition. Those which are eventually appropriate cannot be used in the early phases. The nominal anchor must first be suspended before being reintroduced, and even then it should take different forms in different phases. The array of instruments used for its attainment gradually expands, permitting the rather costly strategy of high-frequency changes in public expenditure to be abandoned. In this sequence the macroeconomic role of aid is partly to augment the reserves enabling the economy to go straight from the first phase to the third.

Notes

1. Elsewhere in Africa the demand for money has been shown to be stable; see Adam (1992) for an analysis of Kenya.
2. Since the value of foreign exchange relative to GDP was far higher in Africa than in Eastern Europe, whereas the value of enterprises relative to GDP was far lower, this different focus of policy may have reflected not so much the different ideological views of the world taken by African and East European governments, as appropriately altered strategies for a reasonably common objective of control over the 'commanding heights' of the economy.
3. Strictly, a liberalisation could be incompatible but sustainable if offsetting policies gave rise to a payments improvement leading to sustained reserve accumulation, but policy makers can readily live with this sort of problem.

4. Imports of consumer durables are proxied by cars and televisions; see Bevan, *et al.* (1990), Figure 5.9.
5. Inflation in mid-1986 was modest and so virtually all of this was an increase in real terms.

References

Adam, C. (1992) 'Specification of a Demand for Money Function for Kenya', *Journal of African Economies*, 1 (2).

Adam, C., W. Cavendish and P.S. Mistry (1992) *Adjusting Privatisation: Case Studies from Developing Countries*, London: James Currey.

Adam, C., B. Ndulu and N. Sowa (1993) 'Efficiency Gains versus Revenue Losses: Liberalisation and Seigniorage Revenue in Kenya, Ghana and Tanzania', CSAE, mimeo.

Azam J.-P., P. Collier and A. Cravinho (1994) 'Crop Sales, Shortages and Peasant Portfolio Behaviour', *Journal of Development Studies* 30 (2).

Bates, R.H. and P. Collier (1993) 'The Politics and Economics of Policy Reform in Zambia', in R.H. Bates and A.O. Krueger (eds) *The Political Economy of Reform.*

Bevan, D.L. (1992) 'Fiscal Aspects of the Ethiopian Transition', CSAE, mimeo.

Bevan, D.L., P. Collier and J.W. Gunning (1993) *Agriculture and the Policy Environment: Kenya and Tanzania*, Paris: OECD.

— (1993) 'Economic Policy Towards External Shocks in Developing Countries', *European Economic Review.*

— (1991) 'Parallel Markets: Illegality, Information and Rents',*World Development.*

— (1990) *Controlled Open Economies*, Oxford: Clarendon Press.

— (1989) *Peasants and Governments*, Oxford: Clarendon Press.

Bevan D.L., P. Collier and T. Mengistae (1992) 'The Ethiopian Transition', mimeo CSAE, Oxford.

Burgess, R., and N. Stern (1993) 'Taxation and Development', *Journal of Economic Literature'*, XXXI (2).

Colletta, N.J. and N. Ball (1993) 'War to Peace Transition in Uganda', *Finance and Development.*

Collier, P. and J.W. Gunning (1992) 'Aid and Exchange Rate Adjustment in African Trade Liberalisation', *Economic Journal*, 102.

— (1992) 'The Liberalisation of Price Controls: Theory and an Application to Tanzania', in S. Fischer and A. Chhibber (eds) *Economic Reform in Sub-Saharan Africa*, World Bank.

— (1991) 'Financial Liberalisation in a Socialist Banking System', *World Development*, 19 (5).

Collier, P., S. Radwan and S. Wangwe (1986) *Labour and Poverty in Rural Tanzania*, Oxford: Clarendon Press.

Dercon, S. (1992) 'Household Strategies to Cope with Income Fluctuations: an Analysis of the Effects of Producer Price and Asset Market Intervention on Cotton Producers in Tanzania', D.Phil. thesis, University of Oxford.

Eshetu, C. (1992) 'Ethiopia at the Crossroads: Reflections on the Economics of the Transition Period', mimeo.

Eshetu, C. and M. Manyazewal (1991) 'The Macroeconomic Performance of the Ethiopian Economy, 1974–90', mimeo.

Faini, R. and J. de Melo (1990) 'LDC Adjustment Packages', *Economic Policy*, October.

Fry, M.J. (1988) *Money, Interest and Banking in Economic Development*, Baltimore: Johns Hopkins.

Getachew, G. (1991) 'Fiscal Policy in Ethiopia', mimeo.

Gillis, M. (ed) (1989) *Tax Reform in Developing Countries*, Durham: Duke University Press.

Harrigan, J. and P. Mosley (1990) 'Evaluating the Impact of World Bank Structural Adjustment Lending', *Journal of Development Studies*, 27 (3).

Le Houerou, P. and H. Sierra (1993) *Estimating Quasi-Fiscal Deficits in a Consistent Framework: the Case of Madagascar*, World Bank, WPS 1105.

Mayer, C. (1990) 'Myths of the West', in Hubbard (ed.) *Information, Investment and Capital Markets*, National Bureau for Economic Research.

Nashashibi, K. (1993) *Fiscal Performance in Sub-Saharan Africa in the 1980s under Alternative Strategies: Fixed and Variable Exchange Rates*, Washington DC: IMF (FAD).

O'Connell, S. (1992) 'Effects of an Own Funds Imports Scheme', *Journal of African Economies*, 1 (1).

Roemer, M. and S.C. Radelet (1991) 'Macroeconomic Reform in Developing Countries', in D.H. Perkins and M. Roemer (eds) *Reforming Economic Systems in Developing Countries*, Cambridge MA: Harvard University Press.

Shiferaw, J. (1992) 'An Overview of Macroeconomic Development in Ethiopia', mimeo.

Stiglitz, J.E. (1989) 'Financial Markets and Development', *Oxford Review of Economic Policy*, 5 (4).

Tesfaye, A. (1992) 'Reforming the Ethiopian Tax System', mimeo.

Teshome, M. (1991) 'Financing of Government Agricultural Expenditure in Ethiopia' mimeo.

Udry, C. (1992) 'Risk and Insurance in a Rural Credit Market: an Empirical Investigation in Northern Nigeria', mimeo, Northwestern University.

Wallich, C. (1993) 'Fiscal Decentralisation; Intergovernmental Relations in Russia', *Studies in Economies in Transition*, No. 6, World Bank.

World Bank (1990) *Ethiopia's Economy in the 1980s and the Framework for Accelerated Growth*, Washington DC: World Bank.

— (1991) 'Tanzania Economic Report: Towards Sustainable Development in the 1990s'.

— (1987) *Ethiopia: Export Action Program*.

4 Exchange Rate Management in Liberalising African Economies

Paul Collier and Jan Willem Gunning

1. Introduction

Until quite recently almost all African countries operated fixed exchange rate regimes, either unilaterally or as members of the Franc Zone. Economic reform, particularly in formerly socialist countries such as Ethiopia, has usually led to abandonment of fixed exchange rate systems, often under pressure from donors. It is, obviously, not inevitable that liberalisation should involve the giving up of the fixed exchange rate policy, but there are several reasons for focusing on this case. First, in most African countries the fixed exchange rate regime was in many ways the centrepiece of the control regime: it was the decision to maintain an overvalued exchange rate that made the adoption of other controls (foreign exchange rationing, import licensing and, in many countries, price controls) almost inevitable. In view of the prominent position of the exchange rate regime, it would be extraordinarily difficult for a government to achieve credibility for its liberalisation programme if it were to maintain a fixed exchange rate. For example, at present the Zimbabwean liberalisation programme is not fully credible precisely because the Central Bank has recently (February 7) made it clear that it intends to maintain something like a fixed exchange rate regime. Secondly, African economies are very vulnerable to external shocks, such as changes in commodity prices. When a fixed exchange rate regime is maintained in the process of liberalisation, then adjustment to such shocks will typically either involve endogenous changes in trade policy (so that trade policy is tightened in response to an adverse shock) or it may destabilise the budget (either because the shock accrues directly to the government or, indirectly, through changes in government revenue). In either case the liberalisation may fail. Finally, it is extremely difficult to determine the appropriate exchange rate during a process of transition: informational requirements alone would reduce the policy's credibility. We therefore restrict ourselves to the case where liberalisation involves a move towards a market-determined exchange rate. In this paper we discuss how foreign exchange markets have been organised, for example, how a foreign exchange market can be made competitive when there are few domestic banks and when the government controls a large part of the supply of foreign exchange. This is the topic of the next section. We argue that the conjunction of *bureaux de change* with an inter-bank market is probably superior to an auction. In Section 3 we discuss the nominal anchor role sometimes provided by fixing the exchange rate. Section 4 discusses the role of a flexible exchange rate policy in transferring external shocks from the government to the private sector. Section 5 concludes by illustrating the trade-off between the nominal anchor and transfer effects of different exchange rate policies.

2. Organising a Foreign Exchange Market

There are several design problems in creating a market in foreign exchange. First, the agents which make the market in developed countries, namely private banks, are largely or entirely absent. The government should naturally be wary of creating a market in which there are only a very few private players because of the scope for collusion, and so a desirable design feature is that the market should be competitive. Second, the government is itself the major agent in the market. Indeed, in many cases of transition it is virtually the only recipient of foreign exchange in the economy and so virtually the only primary source in the market. This gives the government enormous potential power to influence the market should it wish to do so. Paradoxically, this can be a serious problem for the government. Because it has so much power, private agents cannot trust the government not to use it, and this lack of trust constrains the government more than if it did not have the influence over the market in the first place. That is, the government may well be in a position in which its apparent strength is in fact a weakness. Hence, a desirable design feature is likely to be one in which the government visibly forsakes some of its potential scope for market intervention. Third, different systems of foreign exchange marketing generate very different degrees of documentation. The 'paper trail' created by foreign exchange sales matters for two reasons. Doc-umentation constitutes a basis by which the government can increase the degree of enforcement of its trade taxes. Indeed, in some African transition circumstances they have proved to be the only mechanism for enforcement of border controls. Further, import documentation is demanded by donors for the release of programme aid. Different foreign exchange marketing arrangements therefore make it easier or harder to meet donor requirements. Fourth, different foreign exchange marketing arrangements imply differing degrees of openness of the capital account, *de jure* or *de facto*. An opening of the capital account will generally change the demand for domestic money. As we discuss, in some African transitions it will reduce money demand, and therefore be inflationary, whereas in others it will increase it and so be deflationary.

We begin by considering examples of the transition to a foreign exchange market in Nigeria, Uganda, Zambia and Ethiopia. To date, in each case, the preferred institutional arrangement has been a government-run foreign exchange auction, although the detailed design has differed between them.

In the Nigerian auction only banks could participate, but along side the auction was a legalised *bureau de change* market. Unlike the African socialist transitions, there were a very large number of banks involved. Nevertheless, the auction was far from competitive. Banks agreed beforehand on bids and were encouraged by the government to keep the auction price of dollars low. The banks were not entitled to on-sell this foreign exchange at the higher market clearing rate. Had the banks adhered to this rule, the rationing which had previously been done within the Central Bank would now have been done by the commercial banks: rationing would have been privatised but not eliminated. The agents who purchased foreign exchange from the banks would then have received the rents on the subsidised foreign exchange either by importing goods and selling them, as under the pre-auction system, or by on-selling the foreign exchange to the bureaux at the market-clearing rate. In fact the banks were able to evade the rule and sell to customers at approximately the bureau rate. This was achieved by a variety of devices. For example, the foreign exchange would be on-sold by the bank at the auction rate, but only to those customers who had previously deposited large balances with the bank in an account which offered an interest rate well below the market rate. The effective price of the foreign exchange was thereby increased by the forgone interest. Effectively, by conniving in this cartel, the government handed over a substantial part of its oil revenue as rents to the banks. The spread between the auction and the bureau rate varied over time from close to zero to a maximum at which around 40 per cent of the potential revenue from government sales of foreign exchange was accruing to the banks. The rapid growth of the banking system in Nigeria was largely due to the immense profitability of access to the foreign exchange auction. The banking cartel which kept bids low in the auction was enforced by the Central Bank. Were a commercial bank to exceed the guide price which the Central Bank informally indicated would be acceptable, it received no allocation of foreign exchange. Thus, although the procedure was termed an 'auction', during such periods it had few of the features which define an auction. The Central Bank chose this policy for a variety of reasons. Partly, there was a desire to keep the official exchange rate as appreciated as possible. Mainly, however, the government wanted to transfer rents to the commercial banks. In turn this was partly because the balance sheets of the public banks had been badly eroded by poor lending and this was a means of improving them, and partly, it was a mechanism for corruption: one reason why bank lending was 'poor' was that the repayment of loans was sometimes not intended, even by the bank.

The Ugandan auction was inaugurated early in 1992. As in Nigeria, only banks could bid but instead of there being around 120 banks there were only five. However, since the banks bid on behalf of clients, the underlying market is more competitive than implied by the limited number of primary purchases. There is no rationing of clients and only very narrow spreads between the bank buy and sell rates. Hence, the Ugandan auction is competitive despite there being only five primary purchasers whereas the Nigerian is non-competitive despite there being more than a hundred. There is, however, as in Nigeria, a spread between the auction rate and the bureau rate, although it is narrower at around 12 per cent. The common phenomenon, the spread, is due to quite different causes: rent allocation in Nigeria, and the tax consequences of documentation in Uganda. If an importer purchases dollars through the auction (via a bank) then the bank issues a letter of credit to the importer, sending a copy to the Central Bank. The Central Bank therefore has evidence that a particular importer will be importing goods from a particular exporter. In due course, this evidence can be reconciled with customs documentation to check that the goods have entered the country through official channels and so paid import duty. Acquisition of dollars through the auction thus generates a paper trail which increases the danger of detection should the import be smuggled. This can be contrasted with dollars purchased from a *bureau de change*. Until August 1993 the bureaux could sell foreign exchange up to $4,000 at a time with no significant documentation. By purchasing at several bureaux it was therefore possible to amass very large amounts of dollars for imports which could then be smuggled, so avoiding duty. The Ugandan border is extremely porous since customs officials have for many years accepted bribes rather than enforce duty and, as part of the civil service, are paid wages which are so low as to give them little alternative. Hence, dollars purchased on the *bureau de change* market were qualitatively different from those purchased in the auction. Importers would only purchase on the auction market at a discount because of the greater likelihood of payments of duty. The remarkable implication of this is that the government was in effect paying its own import duty. The apparent subsidy on dollars bought in the auction was a government pre-payment of the tariff revenue which it subsequently collected back once the good was imported. A corollary was that the spread between the auction and bureau rates was not itself a distortion, but was rather a symptom of the failure to enforce the collection of duty other than through foreign exchange documentation.

In mid-1993 the government came under pressure from the IMF to unify the two rates through the creation of an inter-bank market. The Central Bank would sell to the banks not as agents for the bids of importers, but as purchasers in their own right. The banks would therefore be free to sell to the *bureaux de change*. With no other change, the implication of such a move would have been that the rate would have been unified at the bureau rate. The Central Bank would have sold its dollars to the commercial banks. The commercial banks would have sold their dollars to the bureaux. The importers would have purchased from the bureaux and then smuggled their goods through the border. At the extreme, the customs service would collect no revenue, but this would be recouped by the government since its dollars were selling for a higher price. Of course, in practice, the customs service would not be able to get away with collecting no revenue for the government, and so revenue would not have fallen so drastically. In fact, the government implemented additional changes designed to get the bureaux to generate a paper trail which would approach the effectiveness of the auction. At the time of writing it remains unclear whether this will be effective. A disadvantage of this approach is that it is in a sense a resurrection of the apparatus of foreign exchange control: those purchasing from bureaux must now complete Central Bank documentation as in the former period, when they applied to the Central Bank for permission to acquire foreign exchange. While the new procedure is not planned to be used for the limitation of access to foreign exchange, the private sector may well sense that it has that potential. Indeed, this is implied by the reaction of the private sector when it first discovered that the auction was to be abolished and replaced by an inter-bank market. Far from being reassured that this was the final step on the road to complete foreign exchange liberalisation, which was the IMF rationale, the private sector substantially increased its bids for dollars in the auction. According to the commercial banks, this reaction was due to a sense in the private sector that once the auction was removed it would be easy for foreign exchange rationing to be re-introduced.

We have implied that the removal of the spread between the auction and bureau rates by the simple move to an inter-bank market is immaterial: the government gains revenue from its sale of dollars and loses it from customs. If, instead, convergence is achieved by the extension of documentation on foreign exchange sales to the bureau, as is currently being attempted in Uganda, the policy should enhance revenue but at the cost of increasing doubts about the persistence of unrestricted access to foreign exchange. However, the ideal way to achieve convergence is to switch the import duty enforcement mechanism from sales of foreign exchange to imports of goods. In this way the apparatus of foreign exchange control does not need to be used, yet revenue is enhanced. This requires the reform of the customs service, which in turn requires more generalised civil service reform. Hence the objective of exchange rate unification, which superficially appears to be achievable simply by swift alterations in the official market for foreign exchange, turns out to need reform in an area of the real economy which is highly politicised and can only be achieved gradually.

So far it seems that there is nothing to be lost by unification: in the worst case, the government loses customs revenue but regains it through higher receipts on its sales of dollars, and in the other cases total revenue is increased. However, this is before we allow for a quite distinct use of import documentation, namely the verification by donors that programme aid has been spent on legitimate purposes. The present donor practice, in Uganda as elsewhere, is to verify eligible imports by means of proof of payment and border control documentation. In Uganda, this has the bizarre consequence of making imports financed by dollars purchased from the bureau eligible for counting as evidence that programme aid has been legitimately spent. Even if all the aid were to be embezzled into Swiss bank accounts, and if the government were able to enforce border controls, the imports financed through the bureau would 'verify' that aid had been well spent. This alone is sufficient to demonstrate that the present donor verification procedures are inappropriate. Unfortunately, since the Ugandan government cannot enforce border controls, its only means of generating import documentation to satisfy the donors is by means of the auction. The auction generates the paper trail which provides some evidence at the border that goods are entering the country. Even with the auction the volume of documentary evidence is extremely limited, so that the renewal of tranches of programme aid is quite precarious. The abolition of the auction therefore generates the severe risk that the post-auction paper trail generated by the bureaux will be inadequate to maintain the flow of programme aid. Indeed, by mid-1993 the government was in a difficult position with the IMF threatening that failure to abolish the auction would be punished by its refusal to certify the economic reform programme as eligible for further donor lending, thereby triggering a cessation of aid, whilst compliance with the IMF risked breaching the documentation requirements of the other donors funding import support, with the same consequence. This problem would be entirely avoidable were the donors to move to a more appropriate and more accurate system of import verification. While the present attempt to generate a paper trail within Uganda is not only extremely difficult, and, as shown above, quite spurious even if achieved, the appropriate method is already used by the Ugandan bureau of statistics. After careful investigation it determined that the monitoring of imports from data gathered at the Ugandan border was infeasible, and so it uses Direction of Trade data on exports to Uganda. This information is available swiftly and is far more reliable. Since it is largely generated by the statistical services of the donor countries it is curious as well as dysfunctional that the donors do not choose to use it for verification purposes. Were they to do so, the only substantial obstacle to the move to an inter-bank market in Uganda would be removed.

We now turn to an early failed African foreign exchange auction, that of Zambia, which started in 1985. In Zambia, unlike in Nigeria and Uganda, both banks and firms could bid. The auction was initially quite successful, until April 1986 when President Kaunda decided that the exchange rate ought to be 5 kwacha per dollar (compared with the auction rate at the time of 7). This led to the resignations of the Minister of Finance and the Governor of the Central Bank. In an attempt at moral suasion, bids were published in the newspapers: the government hoped to shame firms into submitting lower bids for foreign exchange. The new Governor tried to achieve the desired appreciation of the kwacha by selling more dollars than he had. As a result, there was a growing delay between the date of sale of dollars in the auction and the date of delivery. In effect the Bank of Zambia was selling dollars forward and was making increasingly large losses as the auction price of dollars continued to rise. One of the rationing devices involved changes in the documentation required. The requirements were changed continually and firms would suddenly find themselves disqualified from bidding on the grounds of having failed to satisfy some new criterion. (This method could be used in Zambia since the number of potential bidders was large. In most African auctions the maximum number of bidders was already quite small at the outset, e.g. only a few banks qualifying, so that changes in qualification requirements offered little scope for government intervention.) As a pipeline built up the system lost credibility[1] and over a period of a year the kwacha depreciated from 7 to 21K/$. The Central Bank made a loss of about K1 billion, equivalent to about half of the monetary base. The auction was not terminated until May 1987[2] but its credibility was already forfeited in mid-1986. By May 1987 Zambia had returned to foreign exchange rationing and import quotas.

Ethiopia inaugurated a foreign exchange auction only in August 1993. The auction is held once every two weeks. Participation is not limited to banks. A firm wishing to import can put in a bid which must be accompanied by full documentation on the intended use of the foreign exchange and a 100% deposit in local currency. The Central Bank checks whether the proposed imports are allowed. If the bid is successful the foreign exchange is disbursed against an invoice for the imports so that the dollars acquired cannot be diverted to other uses.

We now consider further the properties of foreign exchange auctions. First, there are many variants on the auction model. One, which was briefly employed in Zambia, is the Dutch auction. In a Dutch auction the seller practises price discrimination: bidders are served in the order of their bid prices, starting with the highest bidder. Each bidder acquires the quantity he requested at the price he offered, rather than at a cut-off (or marginal) price and successively lower bids are honoured until the supply of foreign exchange is exhausted. Some governments prefer this system, believing that it will generate more revenue. However, the system introduces two types of inefficiency. First, imports and exports are treated differently. While exporters typically get a fixed price for the foreign exchange they surrender, importers on average pay a (higher) auction price. Hence the Dutch auction introduces a wedge equivalent to a trade tax. Secondly, different importers obviously pay different prices and this in itself is a source of inefficiency.

Second, we return to the problem of competitiveness. If only banks are allowed to bid it is inevitable that during the transition from socialism there will be few primary private purchasers, as in Uganda. One policy option is to encourage the emergence of new banks, as in Nigeria. However, since there is little experience with the supervision of banks this is dangerous. Ponzi-like schemes (based on the chain letter principle) have recently sprung up in Romania and in Serbia. This could easily happen in socialist Africa since capacity for and experience with bank regulation is lacking. Another possibility is to allow non-bank agents to participate in the auction. For example, in Ethiopia any firm wishing to import can participate (banks acting only as agents of firms). The experience of Uganda suggests that even if there is only a limited number of primary purchasers this is not likely to generate collusion, since there are many underlying purchasers from the banks.

Third, we return to the problem of government interference. In many cases, as in our Zambian example, government intervention, leads to uncertainty. As Roberts (1989, p. 128) stresses,

Frequent rule changes on access, eligibility, auction type and, above all, amount sold have caused uncertainty among bidders and, where they have occurred, a tendency to hoard imports. The authorities have countered this by insisting on seeing evidence of eligible transactions or outstanding payments obligations – as happened in Zambia, Guinea and Nigeria.

A government-run auction is likely to suffer from credibility problems in any case and this will be reinforced if the rules are changed. Private agents will see the current arrangements as temporary and respond by hoarding imports, just as when trade liberalisation is seen as temporary (Calvo, 1987). Such speculative imports may then trigger a balance of payments crisis.

The challenge therefore is for the government to devise a foreign exchange market which is more difficult to manipulate than an auction. The government has an interest in binding itself in this way because only by forgoing the power of intervention can it reassure private agents of the continuity of market-clearing. Zimbabwe provides a recent example of a failure to reassure private agents. Effective January 1, the government established what was described as an inter-bank market, as a step towards a market-determined exchange rate. While initially this was interpreted as the government passively accepting the rate which would be determined in competition between the banks, after a month it became clear that the Central Bank had chosen a central rate, had set a five per cent spread either way and was not willing to allow banks to transact outside this range. Hence, effectively, the inter-bank market is a continuation of the fixed exchange rate regime under another name, with the role of the banks reduced to that of retailers. As yet the system is not tested so that it is not known whether the Central Bank will adjust the rate in case of excess demand for foreign exchange or, alternatively, will try to defend the chosen rate, e.g. by bringing back some form of foreign exchange rationing. At the moment the government's credibility is reduced as private agents assign some positive probability to this latter case. The government can legalise the parallel market by permitting *bureaux de change*. Bureaux can deal only in cash and this sets limits to the extent of arbitrage between bureaux: indeed considerable price dispersion is observed, even with a very large number of bureaux.[3] However, as the Nigerian experience shows, the existence of bureaux is insufficient to prevent very large distortions in the official market. It is intrinsically difficult for the government to curb its own power in a market in which it is itself the dominant seller. However, one important distinction is between markets in which it is merely the dominant seller, and those in which it is the only seller. Auctions have the latter characteristic, whereas an interbank market has the former. Hence a feasible check on the capacity of the government to manipulate the exchange rate is to allow some transactions in the same market as that in which the government participates, but in which the government does not take part. Auctions fail on this criterion since the government is the sole seller. *Bureaux de change* also fail because the government does not participate in the market. Further, in the bureau market arbitrage is necessarily limited so that there is no single price which can be published. However, an inter-bank foreign exchange market[4] meets the criterion. At any one time there will be a single inter-bank exchange rate, and banks will buy from each other only at the same price which they are willing to pay to the Central Bank. This does not completely prevent the Central Bank from selling to the commercial banks at a price below the inter-bank rate, but it makes it more evidently a misapprop-riation of funds if it does so. The declared policy of the Central Bank should be to sell at the inter-bank rate, and this rate should be published daily. A breach of the policy then either involves suppressing the inter-bank market (so that there are no transactions at a price different from the official price), or publishing an inter-bank rate which differs from the stated policy. In other words, there is an element of self-discipline because the government cannot intervene inconspicuously as it can in an auction. The Zimbabwe example illustrates that an inter-bank market is no guarantee for the absence of government intervention. But it does reduce the scope for manipulation. If the government had publicly declared it would accept the rate determined in the inter-bank market, then the policy of the Reserve Bank of Zimbabwe of not allowing a rate outside the range determined by itself would clearly be a violation of the declared policy. An inter-bank market differs from a bureau market not only because the government participates in it, but because banks are not limited to cash transactions and so will hold foreign exchange as an asset to a much larger extent than bureaux.[5] Inter-bank transactions can be done by telephone so that arbitrage is easier than between bureaux. If, in addition, banks are allowed to buy and sell directly from bureaux then the two markets will become integrated with the price effectively set in the inter-bank market and the bureaux rate adjusting. Since the number of bureaux is typically very large relative to the number of banks, allowing the banks to deal with the bureaux also makes the market more competitive.

The asset-holding role of banks has important consequences should the Central Bank attempt to have an over-valued exchange rate. Suppose the Central Bank tries to appreciate the rate by temporarily offering more foreign exchange to the banks than is sustainable. It does this by depleting the reserves. As we have seen, when this is done in the context of an auction, as in Zambia, private importers recognising that the policy is unsustainable, accumulate speculative hoards of imports. With an inter-bank market, this speculative role is transferred from importers to the commercial banks. This has three advantages. First, the banks are much better informed than importers as to the sustainability of a strategy. Second, they are able to speculate on a larger scale and more quickly, since they do not need to speculate through transactions in goods but can simply buy foreign exchange. This means that an unsustainable Central Bank strategy will unravel much more quickly. Third, whereas speculation by importers leads to socially costly hoarding of goods, speculation by banks simply privatises the foreign exchange reserves: dollars are transferred from the Central Bank to the commercial banks. Hoarding of imports is socially costly because they depreciate, they have an opportunity cost in interest forgone on foreign assets, and goods are selected for importation on the basis of their durability rather than on their underlying priority for the economy. The transfer of reserves is not costless, since it amounts to a transfer to private agents from the Central Bank, but the foreign exchange remains available to be used appropriately rather than on hoarding. The inter-bank market thus adds a further discipline on the Central Bank since if it wishes to prevent the reserves being privatised, it must avoid unsustainable policies.

If the Central Bank is constrained by the presence of an inter-bank market and still wishes to appreciate the exchange rate without depleting its reserves, it has one potential mode of intervention which can be highly dangerous, namely the creation of a forward market. It is probably unwise for a government in the early phases of a transition from socialism to set up a forward market, since it creates the scope for the Central Bank to achieve an appreciation of the currency in the spot market by selling foreign exchange in the forward market. While the Central Bank is constrained in the spot market since it cannot sell more dollars than it possesses, there is no such constraint in the forward market: the Central Bank can enter into contracts to deliver any amount of dollars at some future date even if it currently has no reserves. When that future date arrives, however, the bank must either purchase the dollars on the spot market or default. If it purchases them on the spot market having previously sold them too cheaply on the forward market, it will incur a loss. There is no limit to the losses which an unwise Central Bank can incur once it has a forward market in which to operate. The only fully credible position for the Central Bank is therefore not to permit a forward market, or failing this, to ban itself from transacting in the market by declaring that no forward transactions entered into by the Central Bank are legally enforceable.

The final design issue we consider is the implication of *de facto* opening of the capital account for the demand for money. It is evident that with an open capital account the government loses a degree of freedom in that interest rates cannot be held below world levels without inducing a capital outflow. Where the government has significant volumes of domestic debt at variable interest rates, such as through the Treasury Bill market or through directed lending to public entities on the part of the commercial banking sector (Collier and Gunning, 1991), then raising domestic interest rates is fiscally costly and so must be co-ordinated with changes in fiscal policy. Hence, just as convergence between the auction and bureau exchange rates might depend upon civil service reform, so the opening of the capital account might require reductions in public expenditure. However, the more important point is that even with domestic interest rate adjustment, opening the capital account will still change the demand for money. We take two extreme cases of transition to illustrate the different possibilities.

The first is where opening the capital account *de jure* does not lead to a capital outflow because throughout the period of the control regime there has already been *de facto* convertibility. This would apply in Uganda and Angola. Domestic inflation was so high and the controls sufficiently lax, that the transition started from a position in which private agents had most of their financial assets in foreign exchange. In this case the legalisation of convertibility can hardly reduce the demand for domestic currency and is more likely to increase it. Since most assets are already out of the country, by removing penalties for taking them out, there is increased inducement to repatriate some of the assets. By contrast, in other African control regimes enforcement was more effective, and there were large public corporations which had no option but to abide by the legal requirement to hold assets in domestic currency. This would apply in Zambia and Ethiopia. In both cases there was a very large parastatal sector under the close supervision of the government and so there were large domestic currency holdings. The introduction of convertibility into this environment produces a stock-adjustment out of domestic currency as agents adjust their portfolios to the pattern which they have previously desired but not been able to achieve. This produces a once-and-for-all reduction in the demand for money. As Adam *et al.* (1993) show, this shifts the Laffer curve, which describes the yield from the inflation tax, to the left (see Figure 1).

Figure 1:

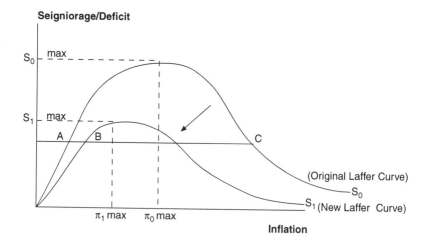

If the government was previously operating below the revenue-maximising rate of inflation, as seems probable in Ethiopia, then this is inflationary but not unstable: the government simply needs to accept a higher inflation rate in order to generate the same amount of resources (the economy moves from A to B). However, suppose that the government has been over-using the inflation tax, as in Zambia (point C), in the sense that the inflation rate is higher than the revenue-maximising rate. Now the introduction of convertibility will push the economy into accelerating inflation, since there is no higher rate of inflation at which the same amount of resources can be generated. To escape from the problem, the government must achieve a quantum leap to a much lower inflation rate (at which it may be feasible to generate the same level of resources as during the control regime). Such a quantum leap would require some spectacular and draconian behaviour on the part of the government to signal that future inflation would be much lower than in the past, despite the current tendency for inflation to accelerate. This has been precisely the problem faced by the Zambian government during 1992/93. The Ethiopian government has not yet introduced full convertibility and it may be unwise to do so given the very large holdings of domestic currency.

3. Transitional Floating and Nominal Anchors

In the longer term, all governments need some nominal anchor, although the choice of anchor varies enormously. The most sustained and widespread nominal anchor was the gold standard, but that has now been universally abandoned. Several countries have evolved a wage standard in which the government, in negotiation with unions, fixes the rate of nominal increase in wages and other variables are left free to adjust to it.[6] Some countries operate a money supply standard, in which an independent central bank is charged with the task of setting the money supply in such a way as to achieve an inflation target, the highest profile example being Germany. Some countries operate a fiscal standard in which there is a constitutional requirement to balance the budget, an example being Indonesia. A variant on these, currently common in Africa, is donor conditionality, in which the role of an independent central bank or a constitution as an agency of restraint on the government is replaced by threats from donors (Collier, 1991). Other countries operate a foreign exchange standard, in which the government commits itself to supply foreign exchange at a fixed price in domestic currency, a recent example being the European Monetary System. In Africa there is an interesting and important hybrid of the last four standards through the Franc Zone. The exchange rate has been fixed, there is an independent, supranational central bank, and membership includes rules of fiscal discipline. African socialist governments attempted to operate on a foreign exchange standard but found that they could adhere to it only by increasing trade restrictions. This has created a need for a transitional phase, in which the nominal anchor of the exchange rate is abandoned so as to permit the liberalisation of trade restrictions and it is this transitional phase of floating by various mechanisms which we have discussed above. However, in addition to the transition from trade restrictions, there must also be a transition to a more viable nominal anchor and this has implications for exchange rate policy. If, for example, the government chooses a wage standard, then the transitional exchange rate policy can be left in place permanently. If, however, the government chooses a foreign exchange standard, or some hybrid involving the exchange rate, such as the Franc Zone, then the floating phase is only transitional.

If the new anchor is a pure foreign exchange standard, then there is likely to be a reversion to the pre-reform problem of a drift into trade restrictions, the anchor being validated by an endogenous trade policy. If a fixed rate is adopted unilaterally there exist no strong incentives for a government to make policies compatible, other than by varying trade policy and rationing access to foreign exchange (Collier and Gunning, 1993). However, a variant on the hybrid anchor constituted by the Franc Zone may avoid these problems. The fixed exchange rate is combined with automatic financing of deficits (thereby avoiding the temptation to use trade policy) and fiscal discipline. In some African transitions from socialism, membership of the Franc Zone is a policy option, either because the country is a member already, or because it has some prospect of being permitted to join. For example, Equatorial Guinea (not a former French colony) was accepted as a member, while Madagascar, having formerly been a member, might be able to rejoin. In other African transitions it may be possible to construct an entity similar to the Franc Zone. For example, Angola and Mozambique were previously members of the Escudo Zone, while the countries of anglophone Africa were usually members of regional currency boards equivalent to the two regional Central Banks of the Franc Zone. It may therefore be possible to reconstruct these institutions in modified forms with donor participation (Collier, 1992).

The main advantage of a hybrid along the lines of the Franc Zone is macroeconomic stability. Inflation has been much lower (and less variable) in the Franc Zone than in the rest of Africa. This consideration is important for some (but not all) of the countries now involved in the transition from socialism. Some do not have a recent record of high inflation rates, and in those cases there may be less need for elaborate institutional anchors. In the next section we suggest that an important reason for preserving exchange rate flexibility where the cost in terms of loss of anchor is not high, is that a floating rate provides an excellent mechanism for transferring trade shocks from the public to the private sector.

4. Foreign Exchange Markets and Adjustment to External Shocks

External shocks present a serious policy problem to many of the African governments in transition. Many of them receive a large part of their revenue from undiversified primary exports and are therefore vulnerable to volatility in commodity prices. An extreme case would be the dependence of the government of Angola on oil revenue.

During the socialist phase the exchange rate is fixed and the common way of dealing with external shocks is to vary trade policy: trade restrictions are liberalised during a boom, tightened during a slump. Shocks are thereby passed on to the private sector, but in a damaging form. The relative price of exportables in terms of importables is affected, not just because of the change in the world relative price but also because of the change in trade policy. Hence this form of transfer creates a distortion. Also, by lowering the domestic price of importables, Dutch Disease is reinforced: profitability of the imports substitute sector is reduced unnecessarily.[7]

The move from a fixed exchange rate with an endogenous trade policy to a floating rate preserves the effect that shocks which directly hit the public sector, such as a fall in the oil receipts of the Angolan government, are transferred to the private sector. By contrast, the use of the exchange rate as an anchor coupled with the abandonment of an endogenous trade policy implies that the revenue shocks stay in the public sector.

African governments are not well suited to bear large revenue shocks. The policy consensus of the 1970s and early 1980s, which held that shocks are best handled by governments, is now eroded. The underlying assumption that private agents would not respond appropriately to temporary positive shocks has been refuted by empirical evidence (Bevan *et al.*, 1987, 1989, 1990, 1993). Private agents do seem to recognise temporary positive shocks (and hence to save) so that there is no case for a custodial government role. Hence, when shocks accrue in the first instance to private agents (e.g. in the case of agricultural commodities when producer prices follow world prices) there is no case for transferring the boom to the public sector through stabilising taxation. Conversely, it is desirable that a boom which accrues to the government (e.g. an oil boom) is transferred to the private sector. When a positive shock reaches the private sector indirectly, as a transfer from the public sector, the temporary nature may be less clear. Indeed, where there is evidence of low private sector savings rates in response to positive shocks (e.g. in Cameroon and in Ghana; Bevan *et al.*, 1993b), the shock reached the private sector in a form in which information on its temporariness was lost. For example, in Cameroon during the oil boom the extent of the rise in government revenue was deliberately shrouded in secrecy. The boom was transferred to the private sector, but this was largely done through increases in public expenditure so that it was difficult for private agents to judge whether the transfer was permanent. This was even more difficult in Ghana where a boom was transferred in the form of higher public sector wages; obviously public sector employees might well consider their wage increases as permanent. Hence the purpose of a transfer from the public to the private sector can be served only if the form of the transfer preserves this information.

Not only do private agents save windfalls, but when the public sector invests a windfall it appears to get rather a low return on the investment. This is partly because government implementation capacity is limited and so, when it attempts to do too much, many projects deteriorate.[8] Hence transferring a boom to the private sector is likely to lead to higher returns on windfall investment. Additionally, government spending is slow to decline post-windfall and so is peculiarly ill-suited to be responsive to external shocks. There is, therefore, a reasonable case for the government to adopt a policy rule which has the effect of transferring as much of an external shock as possible to the private sector. Private agents are both more likely to make appropriate savings responses and more likely to get a satisfactory return upon investment.

A floating exchange rate has just this effect of transferring public shocks onto the private sector (Collier, 1993). Consider an economy such as Nigeria, where virtually all foreign exchange revenue accrues to the government. Under a floating exchange rate system, if the government sells its oil dollars, then shocks due to changes in the oil price reach the private sector as changes in the exchange rate. The government does not attempt to build up foreign exchange reserves but sells all windfall foreign exchange (a 'sell-as-you-go' policy). When foreign exchange earnings are high, the domestic currency price of a dollar is low, and so government revenue tends to be stabilised. Since private agents can observe changes in world oil prices and will know the policy rule, they will correctly interpret the shock. The exchange rate can change for reasons unrelated to the oil price. But when private agents observe a cheaper dollar in conjunction with an oil price boom, they are justified (given the policy rule) in seeing one as cause of the other.

Negative shocks will also be passed on to the private sector: when government foreign exchange receipts are low, the domestic currency price of foreign exchange will rise, again stabilising public revenue. For example, during the oil price fall of 1986 the entire loss in real income accruing to the Nigerian government was passed on to the private sector by the large depreciation of the currency (Bevan *et al.*, 1993). The private sector is better able to reduce its expenditure rapidly than the government, but probably less well able to borrow. Hence the argument for transferring negative shocks to the private sector may be weaker than that for transferring positive shocks. However, even if a government correctly perceives a negative shock as temporary and wishes to respond to it by dissaving on behalf of private agents, the attempt may simply be interpreted as either a failure to adjust to a slump or as a loss of fiscal control. Only governments which had previously built up a reputation of fiscal prudence seem to have succeeded in this role.

Botswana being an example (Hill, 1991; Bevan *et al.*, 1993b). However, the African economies in transition either never had such a reputation or, as in the case of Ethiopia, a change in the regime has made the reputation acquired in the past irrelevant.

As with Dutch Disease, the transfer of a shock to the private sector will affect some groups positively (e.g. producers of non-tradeables in case of a windfall) and others negatively (e.g. producers of non-booming tradeables). In that sense, overall volatility (reflecting the effect of the shock on aggregate income plus changes in individual incomes resulting from transfers between agents) is increased by transferring the windfall as opposed to saving it. This is not to argue that shocks must be transferred to the private sector through the exchange rate, only that this is one of the options which satisfies the condition of transparency. It is obviously possible, in principle, for a government to adopt another transfer mechanism and to signal the policy rule clearly to private agents. However, in practice, governments have usually been unsuccessful in doing so.

5. Conclusion

To summarise, starting from a fixed exchange rate sustained by severe trade restrictions, there must be a transitional phase in which the exchange rate is floated. The government has a history of inter-vention in the foreign exchange market and the design of a market mechanism suitable for this transition phase must take into account both the temptation of the government to continue intervention in some form or other, and the perception of the private sector that this is likely to happen. We have suggested that the creation of an inter-bank market combined with *bureaux de change* offers some check on the government, but that ultimately, if the government wishes to undermine a market system, it always has the power to do so.

During this transition, the government abandons its nominal anchor and needs to devise a replacement. The creation of a nominal anchor is far from easy for a sovereign government, but one advantage of including the exchange rate as part of a nominal anchor package is that it is a highly public number which the government wishes, politically, to keep constant (unlike, say, the money supply which is an unpublicised number, about which only technocrats care). The government therefore faces a choice as to whether the exchange rate is again fixed as part of the re-creation of a nominal anchor, or the float continued.

The choice of strategy depends in part upon the balance between the gain from the establishment of a credible anchor and the gain from retaining a device for the transference of shocks to the private sector. At one extreme are countries such as Ethiopia without an inflationary reputation. In this case, a Franc Zone type of arrangement is a low priority, while the floating rate offers the advantage of passing on shocks.[9] At the other extreme is Uganda. Here, virtually all export revenue (coffee) directly accrues to the private sector so that there is no need for a floating rate on grounds of shock management, while price stability has been achieved only very recently after a period of hyperinflation. Hence, in this case, an institutional arrangement which helped to lock the economy in to low inflation might be very useful. The same is true for Guinea Bissau. However, there are intermediate cases where the two considerations conflict. In Angola there is a case for floating, since oil accrues to the public sector, but there is also a history of inflation and hence a case for an institution such as the Franc Zone. Whether or not the maintenance of a floating rate system is appropriate must therefore be judged on a case-by-case basis.

Notes

1. There can be no doubt that the loss of credibility was due to government intervention in the auction. However, some commentators disagree. For example, Wulf (1989), in a lengthy account of the history of the auction, never mentions the government's intervention and writes

   the continuous attacks on the authorities during the whole auction period gave rise to doubts about whether the system was sustainable. (p. 514)

2. The rate was then fixed at 8 kwacha per dollar, a higher price for dollars than that to which President Kaunda had objected.
3. Osei (1993) shows that quotes between bureaux vary sufficiently for profitable opportunities for arbitrage to exist. This is

presumably because arbitrage is itself costly when cash has to be moved between locations.

4. Inter-bank markets have been established in several African countries, including Guinea and Zaire. Roberts (1989, p. 125) states that in Guinea,

> there [is] an inter-bank wholesale market and a free retail market so that auction rates reflect market fundamentals.

This picture is too rosy. In the Guinea 'auction' buyers of foreign exchange specified the quantity they wanted, but not the price. The Central Bank set a fixed exchange rate (not necessarily a market clearing one) and the World Bank (1990) correctly describes the system as an auction only in name. In Zaire, as Roberts stresses, the inter-bank market was manipulated.

5. Since the bureaux are restricted to cash, holding foreign exchange is more costly than for banks: the bureaux forgo interest.

6. This is the strategy advocated by Dornbusch for disinflation during Latin American transitions.

7. Indeed, some countries have chosen to adopt a countercyclical trade policy during shocks for this reason. For example, Senegal tightened trade policy during a positive shock in the 1970s (Azam, 1990; Bevan *et al.*, 1993b).

8. This is also true for non-African countries. For evidence on investment in oil producing countries see Gelb (1988).

9. In Ethiopia, a large part of foreign exchange earnings – namely coffee export revenue – already accrues to the private sector directly. However, a considerable part – mainly aid flows – does not. Since aid is subject to shocks, the argument for using a floating rate to deal with shocks continues to apply.

References

Adam C.S., B. Ndulu and N.K. Sowa (1996) 'Liberalization and Seigniorage Revenue in Kenya, Ghana and Tanzania', *Journal of Development Studies*, 32 (4): 531–553.

Azam, J.-P. (1990), 'The Groundnuts and Phosphates Boom in Senegal (1974–1977)', mimeo, CERDI, Université d'Auvergne.

Bevan, D.L., P. Collier and J.W. Gunning (1987) 'Consequences of a Commodity Boom in a Controlled Economy: Accumulation and Redistribution in Kenya, 1975–1983', *World Bank Economic Review*, 1: 489–513.

— (1989) 'Fiscal Response to a Temporary Trade Shock: the Aftermath of the Kenyan Coffee Boom', *World Bank Economic Review*, 3: 359–78.

— (1989a) *Peasants and Governments: an Economic Analysis*, Oxford: Oxford University Press (Clarendon Press).

— (1990) *Controlled Open Economies: a Neoclassical Approach to Structuralism*, Oxford: Oxford University Press (Clarendon Press).

— (1993) *Nigeria: Policy Responses to Shocks, 1970–1990*, San Francisco: ICS Press, for the International Center for Economic Growth.

— (1993a) 'La politique économique face aux chocs externes dans les pays en développement', *Revue d'économie du développement*, 1: 5–22.

— (1993b) 'Trade Shocks in Developing Countries: Consequences and Policy Responses', *European Economic Review*, 37: 557–65.

Calvo, G.A. (1987) 'On the Costs of Temporary Policy', *Journal of Development Economics*, 27: 245–61.

Collier, P. and J.W. Gunning (1992) 'Aid and Exchange Rate Adjustment in African Trade Liberalisations', *Economic Journal*, 102: 925–39.

— (1991) 'Financial Liberalisation in a Socialist Banking System', *World Development*.

— (1993) 'Trade and Development: Protection, Shocks and Liberalisation', in D. Greenaway and L.A. Winters (eds) *Surveys in International Trade*, London: Macmillan.

Collier P. (1991) 'Africa's External Economic Relations, 1960–90', *African Affairs*.

— (1992) 'EMU and 1992: Opportunities for Africa', *The World Economy*.

— (1993) 'The Simple Analytics of an Oil Fund', mimeo, Oxford: CSAE.

Gelb, A. and associates (1988), *Oil Windfalls: Blessing or Curse?*, New York: Oxford University Press.

Hill, C.B. (1991) 'Managing Commodity Booms in Botswana', mimeo, Williams College.

Osei K.A. (1993) 'Foreign Exchange Bureaux in the Economy of Ghana', Nairobi: AERC.

Roberts, J. (1989) 'Liberalising Foreign-Exchange Rates in Sub-Saharan Africa', *Development Policy Review*, 7: 115–42.

World Bank (1990) 'Republic of Guinea Country Economic Memorandum', Report No. 877–GUI, 2 vols.

Wulf, J. (1989) 'Floating Exchange Rates in Developing Countries: the Case of Zambia', *Journal of Modern African Studies*, 27: 503–19.

5 The Impact of Liberalisation on Private Investment

Paul Collier and Jan Willem Gunning

1. Introduction (Africa)

In many contexts extra investment is seen as socially more desirable than extra consumption, while private investment is seen as more productive than public investment. Since private investment has invariably been very scarce in socialist Africa, it is therefore increasingly becoming a natural objective of government policy. This paper argues that the private investment response is likely to be highly policy-dependent, and that in many circumstances it will be socially sub-optimal.

We set out first the inheritance from the socialist period, since the private response to transition partly reflects the consequences of previous choices. Socialist economic policies affect the stock of assets which the productive part of the economy acquires. Once the economy is liberalised, the privately optimal portfolio changes. We distinguish between four routes by which socialist policies alter the asset portfolio. These four effects cumulatively give rise to an altered pattern of long-run equilibrium behaviour. Our eventual focus is on post-socialist private investment behaviour. Since, in the socialist economy, private agents are excluded from large parts of the productive economy, private agents do not initially control much of the asset stock. However, during the transition there is a shift of the socialised part of the productive economy back under private or quasi-private control. Public assets may be sold off, or public enterprises subjected to an approximation of the discipline of the market. Thus, by one or other of these routes, the existing stock of assets in the productive economy is shifted, if not into private ownership, at least into a decision framework which simulates private optimising behaviour. Hence private decisions are influenced not only by the new structure of incentives but by the inherited capital stock in the productive sector which, *de facto*, they now control. Therefore, in addition to a change in the long-run equilibrium behaviour of investment in the productive economy, there

193

is a stock-adjustment effect as the inappropriate inherited capital stock is added to and subtracted from until the new desired capital stock is reached. In the transition phase, it is this stock-adjustment effect which will be dominant and hence it is the primary focus of the paper. We begin in Section 2 by identifying how the capital stock of the productive sector is altered by socialist policies. Section 3 then considers private behaviour during the transition phase as the capital stock is gradually adjusted. The crux of the argument in this section is that private investment is likely to be low for a long period. Section 4 draws out the implications of this analysis for the measurement of the response of the economy during the transition, which indicators can (and cannot) be trusted by policy makers. In Section 5 we discuss those public policies which might be appropriate during the transition and, in particular, whether private investment might be encouraged, and how. Section 6 concludes.

2. The Inherited Stock of Assets

We now distinguish four routes by which the socialist policy regime alters the privately optimal composition of the asset portfolio. We consider a sequence of choices, beginning with that of financial assets versus investment; then investment in inventories versus that in fixed capital; and finally, various choices in the composition of fixed capital.

Financial Assets Versus Investment

The socialist policy environment drastically reduces the incentive for private agents to invest, but may actually increase private savings, the corollary being that the private portfolio switches from fixed to financial assets. There are obvious reasons why there is a decline in private investment during socialism. Large sectors of the socialist economy are designated as the exclusive preserve of public activity, and so private investment opportunities in them are precluded. In those sectors in which private activity is permitted, profits are liable to be heavily taxed, and there is the danger that assets will be confiscated. The effect on savings is, however, ambiguous. Although private activity is restricted, and changes character, that which remains may well be highly profitable. The regulation of markets creates wide margins and so makes illegal trading highly profitable.

Hence, while profits from formal productive activity are likely to be severely reduced, profits from trading are likely to increase substantially. Since these private profits are largely uninvested, there are three possible uses for them: consumption, leisure or savings. Socialist economies are not conducive to high levels of luxury consumption on the part of private traders. Such goods are scarce, and even if acquired, conspicuous consumption risks investigation by the government, and theft. For example, a recent anthropological study of Asian traders in rural Tanzania found that they deliberately gave an appearance of poverty in order to reduce these risks (Wilson, 1993). If traders can neither invest nor consume, then they may choose simply to earn lower incomes and take extra leisure. However, they have some incentive to save. Trading activity might itself require a high degree of liquidity, and the entrepreneur might anticipate that the system will at some stage be reformed or that he will emigrate, in either eventuality savings thereby becoming spendable. Hence, in socialist economies there might be a sizeable private demand for financial assets.

The choice facing the agent is between the legal acquisition of domestic financial assets, cash or bank deposits, or the illegal acquisition of foreign assets. Since domestic nominal interest rates are invariably fixed at very low levels during the socialist phase, the degree to which domestic assets are less attractive than foreign assets will largely be determined by the domestic inflation rate. In Ethiopia, where the government maintained low inflation so that there was only a slow rate of depreciation of the birr on the parallel market, domestic financial assets were not substantially less attractive than foreign assets. Through the socialist period there was a large and sustained accumulation of domestic currency and bank deposits relative to GDP. In Angola, where the inflation rate was high and variable, the implicit tax on domestic financial assets was penal. Real balances declined. In Tanzania, where the inflation rate was fairly high but not penal as in Ethiopia, there was a substantial accumulation of domestic currency relative to GDP.[1] In each of these economies there was presumably also substantial acquisition of foreign assets, although this is much less observable. This partly took the form of foreign currency being held in the economy, and partly of foreign bank accounts and other assets. The evidence that such illegal holdings of foreign assets are substantial is inevitably sketchy. In Ghana and Uganda, where dollar deposits are now allowed in domestic banks, quite sizeable amounts of money have already been repatriated into these deposits in Uganda $50m. Additionally, in 1992 there were private inflows of remittances into Uganda of around $200m. While some of this repatriation would have been of earnings from employment abroad or illegal exports, much of it is likely to reflect the repatriation of previous capital outflows.[2] Similarly, in Tanzania during the coffee boom of the late 1970s, Bevan *et al.* (1990) estimate that around half of the windfall (the largest that the economy has ever experienced) was shifted out of the country through over-invoicing. Currently, in Angola the unofficial export of diamonds is also likely to imply a build-up of assets held abroad. The general point is that there should be a presumption that in socialist economies private agents are highly liquid, possibly in domestic currency but also in foreign assets. The low level of private investment is, at least in part, a portfolio switch into liquid assets.

Inventories Versus Fixed Investment

The socialist economy changes the composition of investment from fixed investment to inventories. This is because the return on inventories rises as a result of the shortages endemic to non-market allocation of imported inputs. During intense foreign exchange rationing, the Central Bank will typically be faced with massive excess demand for imported inputs with virtually no useful information by which it can identify the most efficient uses. Firms have an incentive to inflate their demands for inputs and purchase whatever they are permitted to import, hoarding those inputs which cannot be used until complementary inputs become available. Hence the firm may paradoxically run at an increased level of inputs and yet find its production input-constrained because it has an inappropriate mix of them. Indeed, the behaviour of the manufacturing firm under socialism might be altered more drastically. With input prices artificially low due to overvaluation, output prices artificially low due to price controls, and private agents highly liquid, the firm has an incentive to switch from production to the accumulation of real assets by way of increasing the acquisition of inputs and reducing the disposal of output. Socialist governments penalise hoarding by private agents, but manufacturing firms are in a much better position than traders and households to disguise hoarding. Hence, despite the appearance of production being constrained by shortage of imported inputs, firms may in fact be holding an excessive level of inventories relative to market-clearing conditions.

The Tanzanian experience of the early 1980s demonstrates the importance of these changes in inventory behaviour. The period of intense foreign exchange rationing and price control, the incentive structure which induces inventory accumulation, was quite brief, namely 1979–83. Although these controls were put in place during the early 1970s, prior to 1979 the coffee boom provided sufficient foreign exchange to avoid intense rationing and after 1983 prices were decontrolled. The normal relationship between inventories and output in Tanzania can be inferred by observing changes in inventories and changes in value-added over a long period using National Accounts data. The longest period for which there is consistent data is 1976–88 (for which there are now consistent accounts at constant 1976 prices). During this period GDP grew by Tsh5,900m and inventories by Tsh5,800m, so that an extra shilling of value-added was associated with approximately an extra shilling of inventories. Firms and traders presumably needed to carry this level of stocks since inputs have to be accumulated prior to production and because output must be stored until customers are found. We will suppose this to be the normal relationship between value-added and inventories in Tanzania outside conditions of rationing and price control, since in neither 1976 nor 1988 were these controls very important. During 1979–83, the period of foreign exchange rationing and price controls, GDP declined by Tsh363m. Note that our point here is not to attribute this decline in GDP to the control regime, but simply to infer the consequences for inventories. Had the normal relationship between value-added and inventories applied during this period there would have been a consequential reduction in them of around Tsh350m. Intuitively, the non-economist familiar with the intense shortages experienced in Tanzania in these years would expect that inventories would be depleted by more than this. There was a radical reduction in the need to store output while customers were found, since with endemic shortages goods were purchased as soon as they were made available – the visible evidence being that shelves were bare. Further, the sense of national crisis management imparted by President Nyerere and his government might have been expected to induce parastatal firms to economise on inputs. In fact, inventories increased by Tsh2,151m. Thus, far from shortages inducing firms to economise on inventories, compared with the normal relationship they were increasing them by around Tsh2,500m. This is not a trivial amount: during this brief period of mounting economic crisis the economy devoted 10 per cent of a year's GDP into the unnecessary accumulation of inventories. While such an accumulation can be presumed to have been privately profitable for those involved, the social rate of return on excess inventories is evidently negative since they deteriorate.

Imported Versus Non-tradeable Capital Goods

The socialist economy alters the composition of fixed investment as between imported and non-tradeable capital goods. This is brought about through two distinct effects, excessive regulation and the over-valuation of the exchange rate. In all societies the acquisition of non-tradeable capital goods is more regulated than that of tradeable capital goods. The typical non-tradeable capital investment requires construction activity. This is regulated both as to building standards and design, and as to the location and acquisition of the land which it occupies. Virtually all formal construction activity is subject to some form of planning permission. Thus, per dollar of investment expenditure, the costs of regulation compliance are higher for non-tradeable capital goods than for imported capital goods. In socialist Africa, economic activity has been subject to very intensive regulation, which in economic terms can be expressed as a high cost of regulation compliance per unit of activity. The acquisition of both non-tradeable and imported capital goods has reflected this. However, because non-tradeable capital is more intensive in regulation than imported capital, as the costs of regulation rise so the compliance cost of a dollar of non-tradeable capital rises relative to that of imported capital. As a result, the total cost of a unit of non-tradeable capital rises relative to that of imported capital, inducing substitution towards the latter.

While excessive regulation raises the cost of non-tradeable capital, an over-valued exchange rate lowers both the cost of imported capital, and the cost to importers of those goods which are given privileged access to foreign exchange. Because socialism assigns high status to investment, capital goods are given priority in the rationed allocation of imports. An extreme instance of this was the priority given to the basic industries strategy during the early 1980s in Tanzania. At a time when there was overall severe import compression due to falling export earnings, and despite the fact that existing industrial capacity was heavily under-used because of a shortage of imported inputs, capital equipment retained a high share in the composition of imports. Idle capacity was being augmented instead of existing capacity being more fully utilised. The effect of over-valuation is thus qualitatively similar to that of over-regulation: it induces substitution from non-tradeable into imported capital.

There is a variety of evidence on the failure to accumulate non-tradeable capital during African socialism. We start with the weakest data and work up. In Angola, although National Accounts data are inadequate, the evidence can be seen by any traveller: building virtually came to a halt in the late 1970s. In Ethiopia, the National Accounts for the period are again of little use for investment, but the 1984 Census provides a reasonable measure of the size of the construction sector. Less than 0.2 per cent of the labour force gave the construction sector as its primary activity. Construction would, more typically, be around 4 per cent of GDP and be a relatively labour-intensive sector. In Tanzania, the National Accounts for the period are usable for the analysis of investment. As noted above, the intensive socialist phase was from 1979–83. The incentive to switch into imported capital increased rapidly through this period as the exchange rate became progressively more over-valued. However, in response to the mounting crisis, the entire investment programme was severely curtailed after 1981, and so 1981 is the last year in which the increasing incentive to import capital goods could actually be translated into extra imports. We therefore compare the structure and level of investment in the 'normal' year of 1976 (the earliest year in the National Accounts series) with that in 1981. In 1976, 51 per cent of investment consisted of the acquisition of non-tradeable capital goods and 49 per cent was imported. By 1976 the proportion of investment which was non-tradeable had declined to 41 per cent, with imported capital rising to 59 per cent (in all cases shares have been measured at 1976 relative prices so as to reveal only the quantity shift). Nor was this just a relative change. The quantity of imports of capital goods was 55 per cent higher in 1981 than in 1976, reflecting a substantial investment boom. Yet the volume of non-tradeable capital goods was no higher than in 1976 and the output of the construction sector actually declined relative to GDP. This shift of resources out of the construction sector in conjunction with a pronounced boom in imports of capital goods is the clearest evidence of the change in the composition of investment induced by the socialist incentive structure.

The Sectoral Allocation of Investment

While the previous effect concerned the composition of capital goods according to their source, the final effect concerns their composition by sector of use. To the extent that investment is allocated according to profitability, it will be misallocated because prices are distorted through both exchange rate over-valuation and price controls. Since profitability may not have been the central consideration in the allocation of public investment, the above misallocation may have been either mitigated or worsened by the use of other criteria. Almost invariably investment will have been skewed away from the export sector relative to an efficient allocation. A more detailed consideration of sectoral effects is deferred until Section 3.

Summary

At the start of the transition, the socialist economy will thus tend to be characterised by an asset portfolio in which a large (though concealed) part will be in foreign assets, with a high level of inventories (which is not recognised because firms appear to be input-constrained), with a high proportion of fixed investment in the form of imported capital and little non-tradeable capital, and with a neglect of the export sector.

3. Private Investment Responses during the Transition from Socialism

The transition phase is characterised by a removal of, or reduction in, the distortions which brought about these features. In particular, foreign exchange is allocated by a market process and the regulatory hostility to private sector investment is reduced. However, a new negative element is introduced, namely uncertainty over the course of economic policies.

Financial Assets Versus Investment: Does Liberalisation Induce Repatriation?

Once liberalised, the rate of return on investment in the typical formerly socialist African economy is likely to be high, because opportunities have not been well exploited to date. We have suggested that during the socialist phase there is likely to have been a substantial illegal private capital outflow, and so the repatriation of these resources and their deployment in high-return opportunities offers the prospect of rapid growth. However, this does not imply that liberalisation will necessarily induce repatriation. Upon embarking on liberalisation the government will inevitably face a problem of credibility. The problem is compounded because policy reform is a slow process due to legislative and political obstacles which means that it must be spread over several years. While the government can pre-announce its agenda, some of its promised reforms will inevitably not be fully credible. Doubts will arise as to whether the government will stick to its timing and, more fundamentally, whether some proposed reforms will happen at all, or – even if implemented – be reversed. In the worst scenario, the government may be so little trusted that potential repatriators will not do so until many years after all the reforms have been made.

The main focus of the literature on this problem has been how the government might increase the credibility of its promises to undertake or maintain reforms (Rodrik, 1991; Wijnbergen, 1985). One theme is that to be convincing the government must avoid a 'time-inconsistency' problem. This means that it is no good promising to maintain a policy which, if the repatriator acts on the promise, it then becomes rational for the government to break. For example, a promise of permanent tax exemption on investments financed with repatriated funds initially costs the government nothing, and if believed might indeed be very effective in attracting repatriation. However, no astute asset holder would believe such a promise because once large irreversible investments had been made it would be rational for the government to renege. A second theme is that a government can convince by undertaking reforms which, were it not really committed to completing and sustaining the transition, it would not undertake. For example, suppose that part of the prospective reform package is a trade liberalisation which can be made compatible by a phase of aid followed by devaluation. Even a government which has no intention of maintaining the programme might wish to remove import restrictions temporarily, thereby gaining access to the aid. Only a government genuinely wanting to liberalise trade on a sustainable basis would forego the aid and devalue at the start of the trade liberalisation. Hence the latter will be more credible than the former. Repatriators will consequently be more likely to defer investment in those sectors which benefit from the trade liberalisation if the former course is followed.

An alternative approach (Collier and Gunning, 1993) is to exploit differences in the degree of credibility of different parts of the programme, and to take into account that doubts about some policies are more damaging to repatriation than are others. The idea is that those aspects of proposed policy reform on which repatriators hold the most damaging doubts should be implemented first, and the least damaging deferred. Behind this is the notion that in most circumstances implementation of a policy is probably the most reassuring action that the government can adopt.[3] They distinguish between two types of doubt and two types of policy impact. Doubt can be related to timing – the repatriator suspecting that a promised reform will be implemented later than the government indicates; or be fundamental – the repatriator doubting whether the government will make the reform at all. The policy impact can be on the rate of return on investment, or directly on asset values. They show that while intuition might suggest that the government should always resolve fundamental doubts ahead of timing doubts, in fact repatriation will be most sensitive to those timing doubts in which the impact is on the value of the asset. For example, during the transition from socialism a question inevitably arises as to whether expropriated property will be returned to its previous owners (who are often unknown). The government may choose – as in Uganda – to invite such claims, and return assets in those cases where ownership can be established; or – as in Ethiopia – it can declare such claims invalid *ab initio*, and vest ownership in itself. These choices can imply very different periods of uncertainty concerning property rights. In the former case, the early repatriator risks acquiring an asset whose ownership is subsequently contested.

Hence, even though repatriators are sure that the reform will take place, investment will be deferred until it has actually been completed.

Both approaches to incredibility can be followed by the government during transition. It can avoid time-inconsistent promises; undertake some 'tough' decisions which an uncommitted government would avoid; and sequence those asset reforms, which are bound to be undertaken sooner or later, at an early stage in the reform programme.

The Change in Inventory Behaviour

Recall that during the socialist phase inventories are accumulated to a socially excessive extent. During the transition, inventory behaviour may be altered in three respects. First, although inherited stock levels are excessive in relation to the level of output, output may still be constrained by shortages of particular inputs in particular firms (reflecting the firm, commodity and time-specificity of import licenses). This implies an initial surge in imported inputs as firms gain access to them with very high shadow prices. Second, if firms regard the liberalisation as less than fully credible, perceiving some risk of reversal, then they have an incentive to hoard inputs. Third, in the longer run (once credibility is established and firms have satisfied bottlenecks), firms should reduce their inventories – relative to output – to normal levels. The implication is that inventories are likely first to increase and then to decline.

As discussed above, in Tanzania, during the socialist phase, inventories were accumulated relative to the level of output. During the liberalisation, which began with price decontrol in 1984, these excess inventories were decumulated. Between 1984 and 1988 GDP grew by Tsh4,663m. In the normal relationship previously established, this would have implied a similar accumulation of inventories. In fact, inventory accumulation was only Tsh2,079m (all at 1976 prices). This destocking constituted a windfall of 7 per cent of the level of GDP at the start of the liberalisation. Thus, although the effect seems not to have been noticed by researchers, it may well be on a scale commensurate with programme aid in the early years of transition.

The Switch from Imported to Non-tradeable Capital Goods

Recall that liberalisation reduces the cost of non-tradeable capital relative to imported capital, as a result of the reduction in the cost of regulation in which the former is intensive, and the removal of the implicit subsidy on the latter conferred by overvaluation. Hence the representative agent now regrets the composition of the inherited capital stock: there is too much imported capital and too little non-tradeable capital. We would therefore expect stock adjustments in each case. In neither case can the adjustment be instantaneous, both involve processes. The reduction in the imported capital stock is largely dependent upon depreciation, since – as discussed below – it is difficult to resell second hand equipment. However, the incentive to add to the stock of imported capital is clearly reduced (subject to sectoral effects, discussed below). As a result we would expect a collapse in investment in imported capital, which would be sustained until the imported capital stock had depreciated to its newly optimal level. The increase in the stock of non-tradeable capital also involves a process – namely construction. By definition, non-tradeable capital cannot be imported and so its rate of augmentation depends upon the capacity of the economy to augment it through the output of the construction sector. However, by the same argument, the neglect of the non-tradeable capital stock implies that the construction sector is also initially small. The increase in the non-tradeable capital stock therefore requires substantial expansion in the size of the construction sector.

There are grounds for expecting the short-run change in the size of the construction sector to be proportionately larger than the desired change in the capital stock. In steady state growth, the size of the construction sector relative to GDP is proportional to the sum of the depreciation rate and the growth rate:

(1) $c/y = (g + d).K/y$

where c = construction sector output; y = GDP; g = the steady state growth rate; d = the depreciation rate; and K = the (non-tradeable) capital stock.

Were the economy to reach a new, post-socialist, steady-state in which the growth and depreciation rates were the same as under socialism, but the economy had increased its non-tradeable capital stock relative to GDP, then the construction sector would increase as a share of GDP proportionately to the increase in the non-tradeable capital stock relative to GDP. However, much of the point of the policy change is that the long-run growth rate is likely to be higher than under socialism. Hence, if g rises as well as K/y, then c/y rises more than proportionately to K/y. Further, the move from the socialist phase to the transition phase is not a switch between steady-states. During the socialist phase, K/y was declining because of the switch into importable capital, whereas during the transition, K/y, is rising towards its new steady state level. c/y will have been below its steady state value while K/y was falling and will be above its steady state value while K/y is rising. Thus, not only is the steady state share of the construction sector in GDP higher post-socialism by more than the increase in the non-tradeable capital stock relative to GDP, but the share starts below the old steady state and, during the transition, must be above the new one. The implication is that if the change in the steady state non-tradeable capital stock is substantial, the short-run change in the size of the construction sector will be very large. The magnitude of the change in the capital stock in turn depends upon both the intensity of the incentives to switch the composition of the capital stock during the socialist phase and upon its duration. Thus, in Angola (where the exchange rate was massively over-valued, regulation was intense and the socialist phase lasted for around fifteen years), we would expect the switch in the size of the construction sector to be more pronounced than in Tanzania (where the overvaluation was smaller, regulation less intense, and the duration of socialism shorter).

We now turn to some evidence. Recall that in Tanzania during the socialist phase the composition of investment switched powerfully from non-tradeable to imported capital goods. We now consider whether this was reversed during the liberalisation phase. Although liberalisation began in 1984 with price decontrol, the major depreciation of the exchange rate did not get underway until 1987, and so 1988 – the last year of our consistent data series – is the year which best reflects a liberalised incentive structure for investment. We compare the level and composition of investment in that year with 1981, the peak of the socialist investment structure. The reduction in the subsidy on imported capital had the predicted effect: imports of capital goods fell from 17 per cent of GDP in 1981 to only 8 per cent in 1988 (all measured at 1976 relative prices, so that we are only capturing the quantity changes, which are our focus). More remarkably, despite this apparent investment slump, the construction sector was the fastest growing sector of the economy in the post-1983 period, growing by 55 per cent as compared with overall GDP growth of 20 per cent. Thus, just as during the socialist phase resources had moved out of the construction sector during an apparent investment boom, so they moved into it in the liberalisation phase during an apparent investment slump.

A second example is the Nigerian liberalisation post-1986. Nigeria was never a heavily regulated economy, and so the changes we observe reflect only the removal of the implicit subsidy on imported capital goods through the overvaluation of the exchange rate. However, from the early 1980s, this subsidy built up to around 75 per cent by the time of its removal with the introduction of the foreign exchange auction in September 1986. Between 1986 and 1987 the volume of investment collapsed by 42 per cent, the steepest decline in Nigerian experience to date. Yet output of the construction sector, and hence the volume of investment in non-tradeable capital, increased by 9 per cent. This trend continued over the next two years, with total investment stagnant but non-tradeable investment increasing by a further 15 per cent. As in Tanzania, the construction sector grew more rapidly than GDP overall, so resources were moving into the production of non-tradeable capital goods precisely during what was apparently the worst investment slump in Nigerian history.

Intersectoral Resource Shifts

We have discussed a switch from imported into non-tradeable capital goods induced by changes in their relative costs. This incentive operates at the microeconomic level and hence is intra-sectoral. Additionally, liberalisation changes relative product prices and so induces intersectoral resource shifts. Since sectors have different factor intensities, the intersectoral effects may either reinforce or offset the intrasectoral effects, depending upon which sectors are intensive in which factors.

The resource shifts between sectors induced by liberalisation involve four sectors of the potentially market economy. The non-market, government sector might also change in size but, by definition, this is not induced by changes in relative prices. The net resource shifts are the outcome of three distinct effects. First, trade liberalisation is always a central component of liberalisation and this tends to shift resources out of the protected import substitute sector. Second, trade liberalisation is made compatible with the balance of payments constraint by exchange rate depreciation. This tends to shift resources out of the non-tradeable sectors into both the import substitute and export sectors. Third, as discussed above, there is an increased demand for non-tradeable capital goods, inducing a switch into the construction sector. The likely net effect of these changes is that two sectors expand and two decline. The expanding sectors are exports and construction. As we have seen above, during the years of transition the expansion of the construction sector may be greater than that of exports, while the disequilibrium in the capital stock is corrected – even though in the eventual steady state exports are likely to expand more than construction. Of the two sectors that decline, import substitute production is likely to contract more than consumer non-tradeables production. This is because a compatible liberalisation will leave the relative price of the outputs of the two sectors little altered, but inflict a cost shock on the import substitute sector, which is more intensive in imported inputs. Hence, during the transition phase, we would expect sectoral outputs to respond as:

$$(2) \qquad Gnk > Gx > 0 > Gnc > Gm$$

where G = the rate of change of output; nk = construction sector (non-tradeable capital goods production); x = export sector (and unprotected importables); nc = non-tradeable consumer goods sector; and m = protected import-substitute sector.

In principle, the factor intensities of these four sectors can have any pattern and whether they have a consistent pattern across Africa is not known. Here we use Zambian data from the 1980 Input–output Table to estimate intensities. There is no reason to expect this to be general.

The National Accounts do not aggregate activities by the above categories and so we must build approximations. The export (and unprotected importables) sector in Zambia is approximated by mining plus agriculture. The protected import substitute sector can be well approximated by manufacturing. The construction sector is similarly identified in the National Accounts. Non-tradeable marketed production other than of capital goods is approximated by the sum of non-government services, finance and transport. In each case we compute the inputs of imported capital and non-tradeable capital per unit of value-added. The results have been normalised for the aggregate of all these sectors and are set out in Table 1.

Table 1:
The Intensity of Sectors in Imported and Non-Tradeable Capital

Sector	Km	Kn	Km/Kn
Construction	2.72	0.86	3.12
Export	0.99	0.90	1.10
Total expanding sectors	1.20	0.90	1.33
Consumer non-tradeables	0.78	1.67	0.47
Import substitutes	0.75	0.29	2.59
Total contracting sectors	0.77	1.10	0.70
Total all above sectors	1.00	1.00	1.00

Km = imported capital goods, *Kn* = non-tradeable capital goods

Source: 1980 Input–output Tables, as revised in Adam and Bevan (1993).

As shown in the table, there are considerable differences in both the absolute amount of each type of capital used per unit of value-added and in the use of one type relative to the other. The construction sector is both absolutely and relatively intensive in imported capital goods. Hence, paradoxically, in order to expand the stock of non-tradeable capital it is first necessary to increase the stock of tradeable capital. At the other extreme, the consumer non-tradeables sector is around six times more intensive than the construction sector in non-tradeable capital per unit of imported capital, and twice as intensive per unit of value-added.

Were both types of capital easily mobile between sectors, then it would only be the net effect of expansion and contraction on the demand for the two types of capital which would generate investment. As it happens, although there are large differences in factor intensities between the four sectors, when they are further aggregated into the two which expand and the two which contract the differences are smaller. This is because of the two sectors most intensive (absolutely and relatively) in non-tradeable capital, one expands and the other contracts.[4] The expanding sectors are absolutely less intensive in non-tradeable capital than the contracting sectors, absolutely more intensive in imported capital, and relatively almost twice as intensive in imported capital. Were capital mobile between sectors, then – since the changes in output prices are likely to be substantial – this would produce a powerful switch in the composition of demand for capital goods from non-tradeable to imported capital. Thus, the intersectoral effects would offset and perhaps reverse the intrasectoral effects discussed in the previous section. However, capital is not readily mobile between sectors. For example, the fact that the consumer non-tradeables sector in contracting wishes to shed 67 per cent more non-tradeable capital per unit of value-added than the average for all the sectors, is unlikely to make much extra non-tradeable capital directly available for the export sector. The capital released may be shops and offices in Lusaka; the capital required may be mine shafts in the copperbelt and grain stores in rural areas. Indirectly, the desire of the contracting sectors to shed non-tradeable capital will help by reducing their demand for output of the construction sector, leaving more available for the expanding sectors. This we take up below.

Since capital is not very mobile intersectorally, the extra demand of the expanding sectors cannot be met by shifting it from the contracting sectors. New capital goods must therefore be supplied to the expanding sectors. This is qualitatively offset by the fall in demand for new capital goods by the contracting sectors. However, in analysing this offset, we must again distinguish between imported and non-tradeable capital goods. It is helpful to illustrate with a simple numerical example. Suppose initially that the capital–output ratio throughout the economy is 4:0, made up equally of the two types of capital; that the depreciation rate is 10 per cent for imported capital and 4 per cent for non-tradeable capital; and that each pair of sectors wishes to change output by ten units from a base of 100 at which it has been in steady-state.

First, consider imported capital goods. The expanding sector wishes to add 20 units of imported capital and the contracting sector wishes to shed 20 units. If capital were mobile intersectorally, this resource shift could be achieved instantly with no implications for the net demand for the two types of capital. Because it is not, the

differences in the depreciation rates become important since these
determine the speed of capital-shedding in the contracting sector.
Since the contracting sector was previously just replacing its capital
stock, by dropping its demand for new imported capital goods to
zero it can shed all 20 units of capital within one year. In this case,
over the year as a whole, the total imports of capital would not
change: in the initial steady state each sector was importing 20 units
of capital per year to cover depreciation, now for a year the expanding sector imports 40 units and the contracting sector nothing.
Thereafter, the newly expanded sector imports 22 units and the
newly contracted sector 18. Now consider non-tradeable capital.
Again the expanding sector wishes to add 20 units of non-tradeable
capital and the contracting sector to shed 20 units. The contracting
sector was previously purchasing eight units per year to cover
depreciation and so, even by dropping this demand to zero, the
demand of the expanding sector will take 2.5 years to meet unless
the construction sector expands.

Now allow for differences in capital–output ratios. In the
Zambian example, the expanding sectors are over 50 per cent more
intensive in imported capital than the contracting sectors. Keeping
all other figures the same, the expanding sectors now need three
units of capital per unit of output instead of two and so, if the
sectors make all their adjustment in the first year, imports of capital
in that year will rise from 50 to 60. By contrast, the expanding
sectors are 20 per cent less intensive in non-tradeable capital: they
need only 1.6 units of capital per unit of output. The period of
adjustment shortens from two and a half to two years.

Finally, allow additionally for the fact that the economy is not
starting from steady-state. Let us suppose that the discouragement
to non-tradeable capital has been so severe that only half of depreciation has been met with replacement, whereas the imported capital
stock has been increasing at double the rate of its depreciation due
to the implicit subsidy. The liberalisation removes these effects as
well as changing the relative price of output. The latter effect
induces the same desired change in output as in the previous
example. Now, in addition, the former effect directly alters the
demand for capital goods. This effect is likely to be so large that
even abstracting from the desired changes in output, firms would
wish to switch from imported capital to non-tradeable capital were
they able to do so. However, we illustrate the power of the effect by

the more modest supposition that once the artificial incentives are removed, firms simply wish to keep the capital stocks which they have, rather than changing them to achieve their output objectives. Even with this minimalist position, the effects of not starting from steady-state are dramatic. Right from the first year there is a net slump in imported capital: the expanding sector can meet its demands arising from extra output within the slack created by its reversion to an (otherwise) steady-state. Further, the economy can never satisfy the increased demand for non-tradeable capital unless the construction sector expands. There is, therefore, a prolonged construction boom.

This final variant of the numerical example produces results which accord well with the experience described in the previous section: a slump in imported capital combined with a construction boom. The numbers are merely illustrative, although they have all been chosen on the basis of African data. However, they serve to show the likely relative importance of intrasectoral and intersectoral effects. In the above example the intersectoral effects qualitatively offset the intrasectoral effects but were swamped by them. That the expanding sectors were substantially more intensive in imported capital and less intensive in non-tradeable capital did little to moderate the net outcome.

Constraints on the Expansion of the Non-tradeable Capital Stock

While the above argument suggests that the demand for non-tradeable capital goods will increase sharply during the transition, this demand may be frustrated by supply constraints, or offsetting considerations may prevent demand increasing in the first place.

The expansion of the construction sector is limited by rising unit costs. This could arise both because of the increasing opportunity cost of the resources, which must be attracted from other activities and also (and probably more importantly) because of the organisational difficulties of rapid expansion of any sector when the society has few private firms.

A central part of our subsequent argument is that during the transition the demand for non-tradeable capital goods is likely to be depressed by considerations of risk. We distinguish between two types of risk: that which relates to sectoral performance, and that which relates to the country of location. Both are liable to be significant in socialist transitions. Because the economic policies associated with socialism had some political rationale when introduced and have built up influential constituencies which benefit from them, there is inevitably some doubt as to whether any policy shift will be sustained. For example, in Zambia, the first attempt at transition in 1985 was reversed in 1987. In a number of the socialist transitions in Africa, unlike most of Eastern Europe, there has not been a fundamental change of government and so the forces which were influential under socialism are still present in the government. If there is a significant risk of policy reversal then firms will be wary of sectorally irreversible commitments. Turning to country-level risk, many of the socialist transitions in Africa are occurring in the context of civil war, and there is therefore a significant risk that the government will be violently overthrown. In these circumstances private agents will be wary of investments which are locationally irreversible. Although most attention has been paid to sector-specific risk, firms may be willing to make highly sector-specific investments in the face of such risk as long as their investments are not locationally irreversible. If planned in advance, much machinery and equipment installed by firms which operate multi-nationally can be relocated in a different country should policy change. For example, Mozambique is currently able to attract substantial textile investment despite the fragile and early stage of policy changes. Hence mobility of capital may be an effective antidote to sector specificity. Country risk obviously applies even to capital which is not sector-specific as long as it is immobile.

Now consider the characteristics of imported and non-tradeable capital goods. While the former are often sector-specific, they are to some extent internationally mobile. Indeed, *ex ante*, the extent can be chosen. For example, vehicles are highly mobile internationally – some installed machinery can readily be dismantled, whereas large plants will be much more difficult.[5] The investor who anticipates that he may wish to remove his capital goods will tend to choose those specifications which are more mobile, even if they are otherwise less efficient (such as lap-top instead of desk-top computers). Paradoxically, because of their greater opportunities to relocate and because most sector-specific risks are country-specific, multi-national firms may be better placed to reduce sector-specific risk than domestic firms. Non-tradeable capital goods are sometimes less sector-specific than imported ones – for example, buildings can often have many uses. However, they are by definition locationally immobile. If country risk is severe, this would discourage all forms of non-tradeable private investment. If sector risk is very severe, this would discourage all non-tradeable private investment except that which is not sector-specific (which is probably quite a limited subset). By contrast, imported capital, if planned *ex ante* to be removable, is not prone to discouragement on grounds of either type of risk. Further, because non-tradeable capital usually has much lower depreciation rates than tradeable capital, the horizon over which the investor must be concerned about policy reversal or political disturbance is much longer. To take extreme but important cases, investment in a vehicle requires only a short horizon because under African conditions vehicle life is short, and during its life it is easily internationally mobile even if fairly sector-specific. By contrast, the building of worker accommodation on a tea estate is highly sector-specific, locationally irreversible and requires a long planning horizon.

Thus, as discussed in previous sections, while relative price changes discourage investment in imported capital (unless offset by an unusually large intersectoral effect), the increased risk associated with the transition from socialism discourages investment in non-tradeable capital. The implication is that if both effects are pronounced, investment may collapse and stay low until confidence in the new regime is built up.

The low rate of investment in already small economies tends to make the second-hand markets in all types of capital very thin. The goods themselves may be saleable only at a deep discount upon purchase cost, and there may be virtually no market in enterprises as going concerns. This low degree of marketability itself further reduces private investment since the assets acquired are illiquid. Investments become irreversible and this is disadvantageous on two counts. First, as discussed above, in a high risk environment agents will wish to stay liquid. Second, to the extent that agents save over a life-cycle, they will become reluctant to invest in long-lasting capital if it is not realisable. There is some evidence for these concerns during the Ghanaian transition of the past decade. A study of investment in manufacturing firms (Collier, 1993) found that the rate of investment had been extremely low and was still very low in 1991, eight years after the start of the reform process. Although investment was positively and significantly related to profitability, even at high rates of profitability the investment rate was low. Capital markets appeared to be very thin in two respects. First, only a very small proportion of firms were sold as going concerns, although there was quite a high rate of liquidation. If the owner wished to leave the firm, usually the only option appeared to be to liquidate it. The resale of capital goods appeared to involve a large capital loss. Comparing resale values with replacement values and controlling for depreciation, the discount involved was in excess of 40 per cent. That is, upon making an investment over 40 per cent of its cost is lost. We would expect this to make entrepreneurs wary of investment. Analysis of the determinants of investment found that, controlling for other variables, those entrepreneurs who had previously liquidated another business were much less likely to invest in their present business – perhaps because these entrepreneurs, having had to realise losses, were best aware of the dangers involved. A more extreme instance of the effect of marketability, again from Ghanaian evidence, comes from an analysis of agricultural investment (Besley, 1993). Ghanaian land rights vary: some plots carry inalienable ownership rights (which must be passed on in the family); and others allow the present owner the right to sell the land. Besley found that irreversible investments such as tree planting were significantly higher on the latter plots.

These examples bring out the distinction between systemic and individual risk and their differential impact upon investment. Whether or not cocoa trees are saleable, they are clearly an irreversible investment as far as the economy is concerned. Hence, in the face of a risk of low cocoa prices (whether due to world markets or domestic taxation) saleability does not help. For example, in Ghana during 1991 several manufacturing firms reported that they were holding off from investment because of the impending presidential elections. This is an example of the value of the liquidity premium in the face of policy uncertainty (a system-wide risk). Similarly, if cocoa prices fall, the trees can only be sold at a lower price. However, much risk is at the level of the individual. Household circumstances may change so as to require that assets be realised. Indeed, for asset-owning households who are unlikely to be in a good position to get either public or private transfers in adverse circumstances, asset depletion may be a frequent recourse. Some asset markets, such as livestock, are well developed and used for this purpose. The household must therefore structure its asset choices so as to preserve a high degree of liquidity. As we have seen, investment in Ghanaian manufacturing, while more liquid than inalienable land, is not a good asset in these terms since resale can only be achieved at a large discount.

To summarise, the transition phase is likely to be characterised by excess capacity of imported capital and high risk, which discourages investment in non-tradeable capital. Between them, these imply low levels of investment. The actual investment rate is then likely to be reduced even relative to this low level, since when investment is low capital markets are thin, and so investments become less marketable. This perhaps accounts for the Ghanaian experience of persistent low private investment.

4. The Measurement of Performance during the Transition

Before turning to policy intervention we consider two aspects of policy diagnostics: resource reallocation between sectors and the investment response.

A conventional diagnostic of successful sectoral resource relocation is that the size of the non-tradeable sector should contract while that of the tradeable sector should expand as a result of reform. It is now common practice to disaggregate National Accounts into these two components as memorandum items. However, while it may be desirable for the non-tradeable consumer sector to contract, it is desirable for the non-tradeable capital goods sector to expand rapidly. Indeed, in some fairly successful African transitions the construction sector has been the most rapidly growing sector of the economy. The implication is that the monitoring of resource reallocation must distinguish between the two components of the non-tradeable sector. Similarly, the protected tradeable sector should contract. Thus, as discussed in Section 3, the 'expanding' sector and the 'contracting' sector each contain a tradeable and a non-tradeable activity, so that the tradeables/non-tradeables disaggregation is quite inappropriate.

Several empirical studies of the response to reform have focused upon investment (Harrigan and Mosley, 1991; Faini and de Melo, 1990). A limitation of these studies is that they treat investment in a highly aggregated way. Harrigan and Mosley, for example, consider only aggregate investment, combining fixed investment with inventories. As discussed above, investment in inventories is likely to diminish during a successful transition, and this is a socially desirable response. Conversely, during an unsuccessful transition there is likely to be a speculative accumulation of inventories. Hence the aggregate investment response can be very misleading: an increase in investment may be undesirable, a decrease desirable. For example, during the unsuccessful Zambian transition of 1986 there was enormous inventory accumulation amounting to triple the size of fixed investment. Yet this surge in investment was part of the problem rather than being a sign of recovery. Even when analysis is confined to fixed investment, the dependent variable is usually taken to be its share in GDP. This is again a misleading concept because the structure of relative prices is massively altered pre- and post-reform. For example, in the unlikely event of nothing happening to the volume and composition of either investment or GDP, then the depreciation of the exchange rate will sharply raise the share of investment to GDP (since the share of imported capital goods in investment invariably exceeds the share of exportables in GDP). That is, when nothing happens there appears to be an investment boom. It may seem that the way round this problem is to measure shares at constant prices rather than at current prices. However, National Accounts are invariably based on *ex ante* relative prices, and *ex ante* relative prices are distorted. In particular, in the socialist phase imported capital goods are undervalued relative to non-tradeable capital goods. Hence, if at the correct, *ex post* relative prices, aggregate fixed investment is constant but there is a switch from imported to non-tradeable capital goods, there will appear to be an investment boom.

The most appropriate measure of investment behaviour during the transition is again to disaggregate. Just as the aggregation of fixed investment and inventories can yield uninterpretable results, so can the aggregation of imported and non-tradeable capital goods. Again, not only is the size of the measured aggregate change likely to be spurious, it provides little guide to policy because it is not normatively appropriate. Just as the policy maker should welcome a fall in inventories and a rise in fixed investment, so he should welcome a fall in imported capital goods and a rise in non-tradeable capital goods. Indeed, the rate of growth of the construction sector is probably rather a goods diagnostic of the investment response. If the growth rate is low, this is likely to be a sign either that there are organisational problems in the sector or that private investment is being inhibited by considerations of risk.

5. Policy Implications

We have suggested that private investment in the post-socialist transition may be low for three reasons. First, investment in imported capital goods will be low because the inherited stock is excessive. Second, investment in non-tradeable capital goods (which would otherwise be substantial) may remain low because it is unsuited to the high-risk environment likely to prevail. Third, because these two factors reduce the investment rate, markets in capital goods (and markets in firms which are in effect packages of such goods) will be thin and the consequent low marketability of investment will further reduce it. Confronted by low investment, a common policy response by both donors and governments is to diagnose the cause of the problem as being a shortage of credit. On the above analysis this would be a mistake in two respects. We have suggested that unlike other developing economies, private entrepreneurs in socialist Africa are likely to be highly liquid, and so quite able to finance investment should they choose to do so. The provision of cheap finance would simply be an incentive for entrepreneurs to borrow the money but not use it for domestic investment, since other factors constrain investment.

If private agents are indeed liquid, while private investment is very low, then there is a case for an active policy towards investment promotion but not by means of the provision of financing. Consider the scope for public action.

First, the government can offset low private investment with high public investment. There is an obvious problem with this strategy. During the socialist phase state investment is likely to have been high and often poorly chosen, whereas private investment will have been very low. Thus, a policy of high public investment may simply continue the policy error; the task is to stimulate private activity in those areas which the state wishes to shift back into the private arena.

Second, the government can attempt to tackle the causes of low private investment. There is nothing to be done about the inheritance of an excessive imported capital stock: while this is an explanation for low investment it is not in itself a problem. By contrast, the inadequacy of the non-tradeable capital stock is a problem. We have suggested two constraints upon its expansion: supply problems in the construction sector and the high risk associated with non-tradeable capital. In both areas the government has some scope for action. Logically, prior to problems of construction supply is the reduction in the regulatory burden on investment, both imported and non-tradeable. For example, property rights to urban land need to be well defined and marketable. Until these changes are made the problems are not those of transition but the original constraints implied by socialism. However, even when the regulatory environment for the acquisition and ownership of non-tradeable capital goods has been made less hostile, the transition needs the construction sector to be capable of providing a supply. Since the formal construction sector is likely to have been very small and publicly owned, and therefore to face organisational difficulties in rapid expansion, one option is to permit foreign private companies into the sector. For example, Botswana has been able to expand its non-tradeable capital stock very rapidly (from an amazingly small base) by the use of foreign construction companies and this has also been the strategy in the Middle East oil economies. For the better endowed African socialist economies, such as Angola, this may be the appropriate response.

In addition to augmenting the supply capacity of the construction sector, the government can attempt to increase demand for non-tradeable capital goods by reducing the risks faced by investors. Many of the risks perceived by investors originate from fear of government, and so it might appear that the government should be able to reduce them. To an extent this is correct: government pronouncements and actions can undoubtedly create a more or less reassuring climate for investment. However, there is an irreducible level of fear of government which may be intrinsically high in African transitions for three reasons. First, there may be powerful ideological opposition within the country and indeed with the government, which has agreed to policy change either because of the widespread policy fashion or because of aid rather than out of conviction: 'a man convinced against his will is of the same opinion still' may characterise the government's stance. If the government's intellectual commitment is itself precarious, then it will inevitably face a problem in convincing private agents to make irreversible commitments. Second, even if the government is convinced that policy change is optimal, the change may be time inconsistent. That is, at sometime after the change, if private agents act on the belief that the change is permanent, their own actions alter the balance of advantage for the government in favour of a resumption of socialist policies. For the private sector to be convinced that this will not happen, the government must itself be convinced not just that the transition from socialism is currently the best policy but that the original transition to socialism was mistaken. If the government justification of the transition from socialism is that the policy change is warranted by changed domestic circumstances (i.e. economic decline) this is insufficient to avoid the time-inconsistency block on private investment. Third, even if the government convincingly recants on the original adoption of socialism, there will be uncertainty remaining as to whether the government will survive. Private investment is particularly vulnerable to populist political movements in Africa because if it is to be substantial in the short term a high proportion of it will be undertaken either by foreign firms or ethnic minorities. To give an example, there can be no doubting the solid commitment of the Museveni government to the protection of the property rights of Asians. It has gone to extraordinary public lengths to restore and guarantee such property rights. However, Asian investors even when completely reassured of this commitment, must consider the risk that the Museveni government will be replaced; and the unknown degree to which the attitude of the Museveni government is sufficiently widely held in Ugandan society for any successor government to maintain the commitment. Thus, the government may be unable to reduce private risk to a level at which substantial investment would occur. In this case, if the government places a high social value on private investment, then it must offset the risk discouragement by some compensating incentive.

An indication that in Uganda and Ethiopia risk is discouraging private irreversible investment comes from evidence on its composition. In Uganda the current policy environment for investment is favourable and there is a low level of regulation. Around $1 billion of private investment proposals have been approved by the Investment Authority in the first eighteen months of its establishment since 1991. However, the composition is heavily skewed against agriculture, which – despite being much the largest sector of the economy – is attracting only 3 per cent of investment proposals. By contrast, manufacturing, although a small share of the economy, is attracting a high share of investment. Uganda is unlikely to have much of a long term comparative advantage in manufacturing because of its land-locked location and small market size. It has, however, a considerable advantage in export agriculture, notably in tea plantations. Twenty years ago production was several times its present level; in Kenya over the same period tea exports have tripled, and the Ugandan tea trees are still healthy, needing only rehabilitation. Yet, while the return on investing in plantation rehabilitation may be very high, it is proceeding only slowly in comparison with manufacturing. This is consistent with the above analysis of the risk properties of different investments. Rehabilitating tea estates is intensive in non-tradeable capital which is both sector and country specific. By contrast, investment in manufacturing equipment is footloose and can take advantage of prevailing opportunities determined by changing protection levels in different countries.[6] Ethiopia is currently at an earlier stage in the transition than Uganda, but it has also recently established an Investment Authority. The composition of investment proposals is characterised by the same feature as that in Uganda, with only a tiny share going into the agricultural sector.

So far we have suggested that public action should not compensate for low private investment by high public investment, and that there is only limited scope for removing the causes of low private investment. The remaining interventionist policy option is therefore to induce private investment by compensating private agents, offsetting the negative factors. For this to be appropriate it must be both justified and feasible and neither may be the case. For it to be justified, there must be some divergence between private and public costs and benefits of investment. We have distinguished between three underlying causes of low investment in non-tradeables: bottlenecks in the construction sector; systemic risk; and low marketability. Of these, the first does not constitute a case for public subsidy of private investment. If the unit costs of construction are high because of irreducible organisational problems associated with rapid expansion, then these costs apply to both private and social calculations. Systemic risk is, however, rather different since much of this risk is fear of government. There are good grounds for society as a whole to ignore these fears, which are quite properly taken into account by private agents. To the extent that the government cannot eliminate the fears through reassurance, there is therefore a case for it compensating for them. Low marketability discourages investment because of individual rather than systemic risk: recall that in the face of systemic risk marketability does not help. There is a divergence between social and private returns with respect to individual risk since, in aggregate, individual risks net out. This is a standard argument but it may have particular pertinence in the context of socialist transition because of the unusually low marketability of investment.

During the period of socialism there was a subsidy on investment given by means of the overvaluation of the exchange rate. This was therefore a subsidy on imported capital. Currently, during the transition the investment subsidy has been removed. What may be justified, however, is to introduce a subsidy on non-tradeable capital. In effect, this would subsidise the act of irreversible commitment, compensating for the risk that a future government will confiscate the investment. While a subsidy on irreversible commitment may be analytically justified, it may not be practically feasible. Here we consider various possibilities.

Just as the overvaluation of the exchange rate gave an implicit subsidy to domestic expenditure on imported capital, so an undervalued exchange rate subsidises repatriated expenditure on non-tradeable capital. Since the bulk of private liquid assets in the African socialist transitions are currently held as foreign assets, much of the investment, which it is the objective of policy to induce, would be financed by foreign expenditure and so benefit from an undervalued exchange rate. Undervaluation is not perfectly targeted since it makes two errors. First, it fails to subsidise the purchase of non-tradeable capital goods financed by domestic assets. Second, it subsidises the purchase of non-tradeable consumer goods financed by foreign assets. Neither of these is critical. It is the foreign assets which represent the untapped resource of the economy and which it is therefore most desirable to access: investment financed out of domestic resources has an opportunity cost in terms of consumption foregone; investment financed out of private resources held abroad has, in effect, no opportunity cost of which the domestic economy should take account. By the same reasoning, even the repatriation of resources for the purpose of purchasing non-tradeable consumption is not entirely undesirable as a temporary policy. A repatriation of private foreign assets for the purchase of consumer non-tradeables – which has as its counterpart an accumulation of official reserves – in effect switches ownership of private foreign assets to the government and therefore makes them usable by the economy in the future. In addition to these two errors of targeting, undervaluation attracts resources to activities which at the margin are only profitable because of the mispricing. This would be particularly serious were irreversible investments made in these activities.

Exchange rate undervaluation is, however, manifestly only a temporary policy, since it is achieved by the government accumulating reserves. Smart private agents should recognise that the policy is temporary, and so not commit irreversible investments to activities which are only profitable because of it. Further, knowledge that the policy is temporary will bring forward repatriation for the purchase of non-tradeable capital goods, since delay is expected to reduce the subsidy.

Thus, the strategy of subsidising capital investment by means of the exchange rate – which was a central economic policy of African socialist governments – was not intrinsically wrong, but rather the chosen direction of the deviation from the market-clearing exchange rate was wrong. Whereas an overvalued exchange rate subsidised the purchase of imported capital with domestic resources, the justified intervention is to subsidise the purchase of non-tradeable capital with foreign resources, implying an undervalued exchange rate.

Other than by means of undervaluation, strategies of subsidy can be problematic. The record of 'backing winners' is so poor and the political pressures to misappropriate targeted subsidies are so acute that the subsidising of particular investment projects is not likely to be desirable. There may be occasional exceptions to this. For example, the rehabilitation of tea plantations in Uganda is not highly speculative (other than for political risks) because the plantations used to be profitable. However, even in this case, the design of a system which directs a subsidy to tea rehabilitation without misappropriation by either government or firms, would be difficult. The advantage of working through the exchange rate is that the firm only receives the subsidy if it actually makes the expenditure.

A remaining strategy is for the government itself to make the investment in non-tradeable capital, leasing it to private entrepreneurs on short though renewable tenure. This would shift the risk involved in the irreversible commitment involved in ownership from the private entrepreneur to the government. This gives rise to two problems: the sector-specificity of the non-tradeable capital, and its financing. The more specific the non-tradeable capital purchased by the government, the more severely does the government encounter the problem of 'backing winners': namely that it lacks the knowledge on which to make good choices. Hence, if this strategy is to be followed, the government investment should be limited to those investments which are highly generic. For example, public expenditure on sites and services for industrial activities is generic, whereas the construction of a brewery for leasing is highly activity-specific and would involve many choices of specification for which public sector employees had no particular competence. The leasing strategy shifts the risk from private to public agents but also shifts the burden of financing. In some transitions, such as Ghana and Uganda, public revenue collapsed to such low levels that it is not feasible for the government to make substantial investment expenditures, so that low private investment cannot be compensated by public investment combined with leasing. Finally, the entire policy of leasing is motivated by the need to overcome the problem of the fear of government on the part of private investors. Although leasing avoids an irreversible commitment in non-tradeable capital by the private investor, it does so at the cost of increasing the direct relationship between the private agent and the government: the government becomes the landlord. This actually increases the scope for the government to be predatory, and so may make the entrepreneur wary of other irreversible non-marketable investments such as reputation, without which activity can only remain limited.

6. Conclusion

We have argued that an inheritance from socialism is that the portfolio of assets under the control of private agents (and quasi-private control) is not just different from that which optimising private agents will wish to choose in the post-socialist economic environment, but systematically different. Not all of the inheritance is unfortunate: in particular, the high liquidity of private agents in the form of foreign assets is both an important potential resource for the economy and implies that private agents are likely to be much less subject to financial constraints on investment than is normal in developing countries. The bias, both by sector and by the tradeability of the capital goods, implies that there will be particularly little non-tradeable capital in the export sector relative to that which is now desired. Since non-tradeable capital goods cannot by definition be imported, they must be produced by the economy but the inherited construction sector is not well placed to deliver this extra supply. Further, because non-tradeable capital is, by its nature, highly irreversible, while the irreducible degree of risk is high during the transition phase, private agents may be reluctant to undertake investments which are otherwise highly profitable. Turning to the policy response, first we have suggested that conventional measures of investment become misleading during the transition and that more disaggregated measures are required. Second, we have suggested that it is appropriate to subsidise the irreversible investment commitment, and that the exchange rate is the most appropriate vehicle by which such a subsidy can in practice be delivered. Paradoxically, the exchange rate was used for an investment subsidy under socialism, however, the wrong component of investment was subsidised. Instead of overvaluation, which subsidises the relatively mobile and hence reversible investments in imported capital, the exchange rate should be under-valued. Since, manifestly, this policy can only be temporary, it has the advantage that irreversible commitments are unlikely to be lured into activities which are only profitable while undervaluation persists. Further, the subsidy is only appropriate as a temporary measure: as confidence is restored, private agents will become more willing to enter into irreversible commitments. Undervaluation has a cost, since to achieve it the government must accumulate reserves. The government is therefore deferring some of its expenditures into the future. The argument is therefore akin to 'crowding out' although the mechanism is different. By not spending some of the foreign exchange which it receives, the government induces repatriation of private foreign exchange, thereby substituting from public expenditure into private investment in non-tradeable capital goods. The underlying rationale is that such investment is very scarce in socialist economies, and will otherwise continue to be underprovided during the transition period.

Notes

1. Bevan *et al.* (1990) suggest that an additional reason for the monetary build-up in Tanzania was that extra transactions balances were needed relative to expenditure because of the unpredictable nature of shortages.
2. There is currently little incentive to smuggle exports since they are untaxed and the exchange rate is not overvalued.
3. Although this proposition may seem trivial, it is not invariably correct. For example, Engel and Kletzer (1991) construct a case in which the government must first impose trade restrictions in order to convince private agents that it will eventually adopt free trade.
4. To arrive at a total for each of the expanding and contracting sectors we have simply weighted according to the shares of each sector in output. This implicitly assumes that both the expanding sectors expand at the same rate, and similarly that the other two sectors contract at the same rate. A more sophisticated approach would allow for differing rates of change of output.
5. An example of the high degree of mobility of tradeable capital under difficult circumstances is the relocation of huge quantities of plant from the Ukraine to east of the Urals during the German invasion of 1941.
6. During the socialist period in Uganda, unlike most other African socialist economies, although the exchange rate was heavily overvalued this gave little stimulus to the acquisition of imported capital goods because the collapse of export earnings was very pronounced and the various governments had atypically low commitments to industrialisation.

References

Adam, C.S. and D.L. Bevan (1993) 'Revised Input–Output Table for Zambia, 1980', mimeo, Oxford: CSAE.

Bevan, D.L., P. Collier and J.W. Gunning (1990) *Controlled Open Economies*, Oxford: Clarendon Press.

Besley, T. (1993) 'Investment and Marketability in Ghanaian Cocoa', mimeo, Princeton.

Collier, P. (1993) 'The Determination of Ghanaian Manufacturing Investment', mimeo, Oxford: CSAE.

Collier, P. and J.W. Gunning (1993) 'Policy Uncertainty, Repatriation and Investment', mimeo, Oxford: CSAE.

Engel, C. and K.M. Kletzer (1991) 'Trade Policy under Endogenous Credibility', *Journal of Development Economics*, 36: 213–28.

Faini R., and J. de Melo (1990) 'LDC Adjustment Packages', *Economic Policy*, 491–512.

Harrigan, J.M. and P. Mosley (1991) 'Evaluating the Impact of World Bank Structural Adjustment Lending', *Journal of Development Studies*, 27: 63–94.

Rodrik, D. (1991) 'Policy Uncertainty and Private Investment in Developing Countries', *Journal of Development Economics*, 36: 229–42.

Wijnbergen, S. van (1985) 'Trade Reform, Aggregate Investment and Capital Flight: on Credibility and the Value of Information', *Economic Letters*, 19: 369–72.

Wilson, A. (1993) 'Entrepreneurial Attitudes to Structural Adjustment in Tanzania', mimeo, Department of Sociology, University of Hull.

Part II

Public Enterprises and Privatisation

6 Privatisation in Sub-Saharan Africa: Results, Prospects, and New Approaches

Elliot Berg

P21 *L33* *P31*

1. Introduction

Reform of public enterprise sectors has been a key element in adjustment programmes since the early 1980s, in Sub-Saharan Africa as in the rest of the developing world.[1] The prime objective of most PE reform programmes is to increase efficiency of resource use; reduction of fiscal burdens is a linked objective. These are to be achieved first by making the enterprises that are retained in the public sector more productive and, second, by divestiture – reducing the size of the PE sector through the sale or liquidation of state assets, or through other forms of privatisation.

Various approaches have been pursued to improve performance of retained state-owned enterprises (SOEs). Financial rehabilitation (debt restructuring and provision of new working capital) is a common starting point. The associated reform package usually contains a set of standard items, such as making government oversight at once more effective and less intrusive, notably by a shift to *ex post* from *ex ante* controls over PE management (increased autonomy); strengthening of boards of directors; making managers more accountable and paying them according to performance; depoliticising decisions on prices, employment, wages, and investment; and clarifying objectives and priorities, as well as mutual obligations with government, through such instruments as performance contracts.

The second main avenue of reform is usually called privatisation, but numerous ambiguities of concept and definition surround this term. In common discourse, and in almost all government and aid agency documents, privatisation and divestiture are used as synonyms. But they are of course not synonymous. Divestiture is normally understood to mean change in ownership – the shedding of state-owned assets by sale or liquidation. Privatisation need not involve transfer of ownership from the state to private parties. Management or delivery of goods and services can be privatised

229

through management contracts, leases, and contracting-out, leaving ownership in state hands. Liquidation, moreover, normally means abolition, not privatisation in the sense of transferring state assets into private hands.

In the public enterprise reform programmes of the past decade, privatisation of ownership by divestiture has been the centrepiece, though management privatisation is also included. Since the stated objective of most of these programmes is not ownership transfer for its own sake but rather greater efficiency of resource use, this is appropriate. Although privatisation of all dimensions of an economic activity (asset ownership, operational financing, management) will in most circumstances bring about the greatest efficiency gains, in many cases full privatisation is not feasible. In some cases full privatisation may be undesirable: a poorly considered sale of assets can be worse than no sale. In both instances, other instruments, involving partial privatisation, can bring substantial efficiency benefits.

In the first part of this chapter we concentrate on classic divestiture – the sale or liquidation of state-owned assets. Later in the chapter, we distinguish between this traditional privatisation approach and indirect approaches that involve less than full privatisation of ownership. The distinction is a bit wobbly: some non-divestiture instruments, especially management contracts, are already in wide use, hence part of the traditional privatisation package. But it is an analytically useful distinction nonetheless.

That it is only mildly inaccurate to call divestiture of ownership the traditional approach to privatisation is confirmed by a review of the terms of World Bank adjustment loans, the principal locus of so many privatisation programmes.[2] Two thirds of the privatisation components of these programmes entail preparation for divestiture (studies, classifications, strategies, and action plans); more than 60 per cent involve help with actual transactions; a quarter aim at strengthening the institutional arrangements for managing divestiture; about 20 per cent assist in restructuring enterprises prior to divestiture; 13 per cent create implementation facilities; and 7 per cent support social safety nets.

Divestiture has been the most criticised element in structural adjustment programmes in Africa, and one of the most difficult to implement. Most observers of Africa's privatisation experience lament the modest pace of SOE sales and the large gaps between privatisation rhetoric and actions. This is the general tone in most studies (see Adam and Cavendish, 1990; Stewart *et al.*, 1992; also United Nations/Economic Commission for Africa, 1991; Cook and Kirkpatrick, 1990). Those who are critical of market-orientated reform strategies in general tend to be especially severe in their judgement of privatisation policies. They attack it as ideologically motivated, infeasible, or undesirable, and call instead for efficiency-raising reform of state-owned enterprises. Here's how one recent analysis puts it (Stewart and Wangwe, 1992):

> The weakness of the medium to large indigenous private sector (in Sub-Saharan Africa) presents a major problem for privatisation, both from a political and an economic perspect-ive. The vacuum that would be created by large-scale privatisation might be filled by foreign investment, but recent history and the nature of current technological development suggest that foreign investors are not anxious to expand in most African countries because of the fragile economic climate, poor infrastructure and low skill levels. Moreover, the foreign investment solution would not generally be politically acceptable, nor does the evidence suggest that it would solve all efficiency problems. DFI (direct foreign investment) as a substitute for public enterprises would reduce opportunities for Africans to build up capabilities. Analysis of the minimal privatisation achieved in Malawi and Zimbabwe suggests that there are severe political and economic obstacles to privatisation which will, for the time being, prevent it being of more than marginal significance. The weakness of capital markets ... is also a major impediment ... Privatisation will thus have only a minor role in the near to medium term. What is needed is to increase the efficiency of parastatals. (pp. 24–25)

But if divestiture efforts have yielded only modest progress, the general perception among concerned observers and practitioners, both outside and inside the donor community, is that reform programmes aimed at making enterprises retained in the public sector more autonomous, financially independent, and efficient have also rarely been successful. Despite intensive efforts, improved performance of state-owned enterprises remains an elusive goal. This comes out in a paper by Mary Shirley and John Nellis on the lessons of experience with public enterprise reform (Shirley and Nellis, 1991). Their analysis contains a *pro forma* acknowledgement that there have been some successes in programmes to make PEs operate more efficiently and effectively.[3] But the ensuing discussion focuses on the lack of success in public enterprise reform efforts short of divestiture, especially in low income countries. This failure they attribute to three problems: technical and political difficulties of implementation, the failure to adopt all the linked elements of a reform programme, and persistent backsliding – the enormous difficulty of sustaining reforms once introduced.

In the Kikeri *et al.* (1992) synthesis of privatisation experience, the failure of efforts to make SOEs work better is the starting point of analysis. The turn toward privatisation has taken place, the authors affirm, because the alternative – improving performance of state-owned enterprises without privatisation of ownership or management – has yielded few durable results.

> Disappointed with the high costs and poor performance of SOEs, and faced with the modest and unenduring nature of SOE reforms that do not involve changes in ownership, many governments have turned to privatisation. (p. 21)

An obvious dilemma exists. Each of the two main components of PE reform has so far delivered slender results in Sub-Saharan Africa (and in most other low income areas), compared with progress on most other reforms, or with expectations as reflected in objectives set out in policy loans. Those reformers who have come face to face with the obstacles to making state-owned enterprises work significantly better in these environments tend to throw up their hands and conclude that privatisation has to be a better way to go.

However, many of those who have analysed divestiture efforts and prospects in low income countries, and especially in Africa, conclude that ownership privatisation has unpromising prospects; is in any case not likely to yield more than modest gains in efficiency and growth; and may conflict with long-term development objectives, especially the building of indigenous capabilities. Their conclusion, implicit or open: accept the continued existence of substantial PE sectors and intensify sector reform programmes and the rehabilitation of individual enterprises.

In this chapter we describe the nature of the divestiture side of the dilemma, and suggest ways to reduce constraints to more effective privatisation in African conditions. We examine both traditional or classic divestiture and the indirect forms or lesser degrees of privatisation, which include non-divestiture instruments (management contracts, lease contracts, and contracting-out) and partial divestiture – sales of pieces of SOEs by a process that can be called internal divestiture, fragmentation or spin-offs. We argue that divestiture has to remain at the centre of privatisation efforts, and that prospects for greater effectiveness are good – the economic and ideological environments are more congenial and much has been learned about how to do divestiture better. We argue also that progress in privatisation can be quickened by greater use of indirect instruments, which have considerable privatising power but have been neglected up to now.

The chapter is organised as follows. In the next section, we discuss the uncertain state of knowledge about the extent and impact of divestiture in Sub-Saharan Africa, summarise the information base – which is mainly concerned with numbers of divestitures – and assess progress. In the following section the reasons for the slim record of achievement in divestiture are explored and the lessons of experience are summarised, indicating how divestiture programmes can be made more effective. In the final section we argue that the PE reform arsenal should be enlarged to make greater place for the indirect methods of privatisation, which rely on non-divestiture and piecemeal divestiture approaches. The concluding remarks suggest reasons for the relative neglect of indirect privatisation approaches and indicate how their use can be expanded.

2. How Much Divestiture?

A comprehensive assessment of African privatisation would have to use at least three criteria for evaluating success and failure. The first is simply the magnitude or volume of sales – numbers of SOEs sold, share of government-owned equity divested, share of public sector employment affected. The second is the efficiency and equitableness of the process: were assets transferred to private parties using economically rational and transparent procedures, at fair prices and without distortionary sweeteners? Finally, what have been post-privatisation impacts: at the firm level, in productivity gains; and at the macroeconomic level, in reduced fiscal drain and growth-enhancing changes in prices and quality of goods and services.

The assessment here concentrates on the first criterion, and mainly on numbers of transactions. The reasons are simple: little systematic information is available about other measures of the scale of privatisation efforts; good case studies of divestiture processes are scarce; and information about post-privatisation impacts are scarcer still – except for effects on subsidies to PE sectors.

How much privatisation, in the sense of divestiture of state-owned assets, has taken place in Africa in recent years? Until very recently, it was extremely difficult to answer this basic question with any certainty at all. Numerous attempts have been made to determine the number of sales and liquidations. But these have not been comprehensive, and are full of inconsistencies and ambiguities. Part of the reason is that terms are used loosely and concepts are poorly defined: the entity in question may contain many component units.[4] Unclear or varying use of the term 'liquidation' is another frequent source of confusion; sometimes it is used to mean piecemeal sale of physical assets of a terminated enterprise; sometimes it is merely the road followed to legally transform an operating entity prior to sale.

Confusion springs also from the multiple stages of approval that a transaction must go through in many countries. A sales agreement may be signed between a negotiating team and a buyer, but many layers of approval may be required – by the privatisation agency management, by the cabinet-level committee responsible for privatisation, sometimes by the ministry of finance. Then the buyer must pay the agreed-upon amount. The number of sales depends on the stage of the process chosen.[5]

A related element of confusion is the phenomenon of 'redivestiture'. Enterprises are commonly listed as 'divested' in government reports when an agreement is signed between the privatisation agency and a buyer. But in many cases, it seems, 'buyers' fail to find financing or have second thoughts, and the transfer does not take place or government reclaims the state-owned enterprise. That this can be an important source of statistical noise is indicated by the Ghana experience: of the 21 enterprises listed as privatised in the divestiture agency's 1991 report, no fewer than 11 found their way back into the state's portfolio in 1992 (according to the Director of the Divestiture Implementation Committee).

Although the data remain weak, recent research financed by the World Bank has helped fill some of the information gaps. It confirms, on the basis of more recent and more solid data, the conclusion that not much shrinkage of state enterprise sectors has actually occurred in Sub-Saharan Africa, despite a decade or more of effort in many countries.

Newly assembled macroeconomic data, summarised in Table 1, show that public enterprise sectors were able to ward off the privatisation initiatives undertaken in the 1980s; these efforts seem to have left hardly any macroeconomic traces. In the small sample of African countries with data, the average PE sector-generated share of GDP (14 per cent) was unchanged between the late 1970s and the early 1990s. The average employment share was actually increased. Only in shares of investment and in net financial transfers is shrinkage evident. The table shows that most of these findings apply to developing countries in general.

A second research effort, the output of which will be published in late 1996, undertook detailed inquiry into country-level divestiture statistics. This is the first time that divestiture transactions data have been scrutinised this way – across countries, using careful definitions and with much field-level investigation. The result is the best data set on privatisation transactions that has yet appeared.

Table 2 summarises these data. Over 2,000 completed divestiture transactions were identified through 1995. This is four or five times as many as were identified in previous World Bank tallies. As the annual totals show, there has been a decided acceleration on divestiture in 1994 and 1995. Over 40 per cent of the total have occurred since 1993. But the numbers do not undermine the general conclusion that the reach of privatisation has been very modest in Africa.

This is indicated first of all by the slender macroeconomic impacts observable in the aggregate data on the weight of public enterprise sectors in GDP and in wage employment (Table 1). but there are other indicators. Table 2 shows that privatisation has been concentrated in only a few countries. In terms of numbers of transactions about three quarters of the total has taken place in ten countries, and half in four of these: Angola, Mozambique, Guinea and Ghana. In terms of value of sales, three quarters of the $2.1 billion total was generated in four countries, South Africa, Ghana, Nigeria and Mozambique, and half in South Africa and Ghana alone. Of the 33 countries with sales value information, only 9 have sold more than $50 million in equity. Almost half the countries had total sales values amounting to less than $25 million, and this over more than a decade.

Table 1: *Changes in Economic Weight of PE Sectors, 1978–80 to 1990–91 (unweighted averages)*

	1978–80	1990–91
PE share in GDP (%)		
All developing economies (40)	11.1	11.05
Low income (15)	14.27	14.05
Middle income (25)	8.14	9.3
Africa (14)	13.9	13.8
PE share in non-agricultural GDP		
All developing economies (40)	12.0	13.55
Low income (15)	18.8	18.55
Middle income (25)	9.4	10.6
Africa (14)	17.3	16.8
PE share in gross domestic investment		
All developing economies (55)	22.5	18.6
Low income (18)	30.8	25.1
Middle income (37)	26.9	15.5
Africa (14)	30.5	23.6
PE share in employment		
All developing economies (21)	10.2	10.9
Low income (10)	15.0	16.3
Middle income (11)	5.3	6.0
Africa (9)	19.3	22.1
Net financial flows to PE sector as share of GDP		
All developing economies (37)	0.02	−1.25
Low income (15)	1.5	0.1
Middle income (25)	0.4	−1.9
Africa (12)	1.1	0.1

Source: World Bank (1995), Statistical Tables.

Table 2: *Summary of Divestiture Transactions and Sales Values in Sub-Saharan Africa, end-1995*

	Prior to 1990	1990	1991	1992	1993	1994	1995*	Year n/k	Total no. of Transactions	Total Sales Value US$m	Av. Sales Value US$m
Angola	n/k	n/k	n/k	n/k	n/k	n/k	n/k	269	269	25.1	0.1
Benin	17	3	8	3	5	3	5	2	46	62.1	1.4
Botswana	0	0	0	0	0	0	n/k	1	1	n/k	
Burkina Faso	0	0	2	1	5	5	3		16	9.8	0.5
Burundi	0	0	0	9	5	1	n/k		15	4.6	0.3
Cameroon	10	0	13	3	1	5	5		37	n/k	
Cape Verde	0	0	0	0	1	10	10		21	24.1	1.1
Central African Republic	22	n/k	n/k	0	0	0	0	2	24	n/k	
Chad	0	0	0	0	0	12	12	1	25	n/k	
Comoros	0	0	0	0	4	n/k	n/k		4	0.2	0.1
Congo	9	0	0	0	0	0	0		9	n/k	
Côte d'Ivoire	0	0	3	3	3	8	14		31	37.4	1.2
Djibouti	0	0	0	0	0	0	0	1	1	n/k	
Equatorial Guinea	0	0	0	0	2	n/k	n/k	1	3	0.2	0.1
Eritrea	0	0	0	0	0	0	0		0	0.0	
Ethiopia	0	0	0	0	0	0	0		0	0.0	
Gabon	49	0	0	0	0	0	0		19	n/k	

cont ...

Table 2 cont ...

	Prior to 1990	1990	1991	1992	1993	1994	1995*	Year n/k	Total no. of Transactions	Total Sales Value US$m	Av. Sales Value US$m
Gambia	8	7	4	4	4	3	0		30	8.1	0.3
Ghana	3	29	11	10	7	26	10		96	463.7	4.8
Guinea	77	8	2	5	16	3	4		115	76.0	0.7
Guinea Bissau	2	3	3	8	1	3	11		31	18.4	0.6
Kenya	0	0	1	9	20	15	64		109	58.9	0.5
Lesotho	0	0	0	0	0	0	8		8	n/k	
Liberia	0	0	0	0	0	0	0		0	0.3	
Madagascar	11	11	12	21	1	3	3	1	59	16.4	0.3
Malawi	0	0	2	2	2	1	n/k	28	35	5.3	0.2
Mali	2	3	16	25	n/k	n/k	n/k	2	48	37.8	0.8
Mauritania	6	n/k	n/k	5	n/k	n/k	3	17	31	n/k	
Mauritius	0	0	0	0	0	0	0		0	0.0	
Mozambique	55	40	53	62	43	135	112		510	137.0	0.3
Namibia	0	0	0	0	0	0	n/k	1	1	n/k	
Niger	20	4	2	1	1	1	n/k	1	30	n/k	
Nigeria	15	36	8	14	8	0	0		81	286.9	2.6
Rwanda	n/k	n/k	n/k	n/k	n/k	n/k	n/k		n/k	n/k	

cont ...

Table 2 cont ...

	Prior to 1990	1990	1991	1992	1993	1994	1995*	Year n/k	Total no. of Transactions	Total Sales Value US$m	Av. Sales Value US$m
Sao Tome e Principe	0	1	1	3	3	0	1	1	10	1.8	0.2
Senegal	8	7	11	n/k	n/k	n/k	n/k	9	35	48.6	1.4
Seychelles	0	0	0	0	0	0	n/k	1	1	n/k	
Sierra Leone	0	0	0	0	6	1	1	1	9	n/k	
Somalia	0	0	0	0	0	0	0		0	0.0	
South Africa	2	0	1	0	0	0	0		3	63702	212.4
Sudan	0	0	0	10	12	3	n/k	1	26	n/k	
Swaziland	0	0	0	0	0	0	0		0	0.0	
Tanzania	0	0	0	12	32	22	14		80	39.4	0.5
Togo	12	4	3	2	0	2	1		24	37.1	1.5
Uganda	0	0	0	2	4	10	18		34	72.4	2.1
Zaire	0	0	0	0	0	0	2		2	n/k	
Zambia	0	0	0	0	7	39	47		93	86.6	1.2
Zimbabwe	0	0	0	0	0	3	0		3	6.5	2.2
Total	**308**	**156**	**152**	**214**	**193**	**294**	**348**	**340**	**2005**	**2118.6**	**1.1**

Source: World Bank, Africa Private Sector Division, June 1996. Based on data from Government Privatisation Agencies and Ministries, and World Bank Files.
*the column for 1995 is incomplete.

Box A: Guinea: Many Sales, Poorly Done

Guinea is a relatively successful privatiser, measured by the number and speed of transactions. More than 85 out of the country's 170 PEs were sold or liquidated between 1985 and 1990, more than 20 per cent of the total number of estimated sales or liquidations in Sub-Saharan Africa as of the early 1990s. The sales included 28 of 30 industrial state-owned enterprises targeted for privatisation in 1985. More than 50 state-owned retail shops were liquidated, and five banks, which were reopened as joint ventures. The privatisation effort was done poorly, however:

- Valuation criteria were established but how they were applied was scarcely transparent. It seems that the emphasis was on valuation of physical assets, not on the enterprise as a whole. All the industrial state-owned enterprises were liquidated before sale; most in fact had been closed or were operating at minimal levels. Perhaps for this reason, neither net present values of potential future earnings nor replacement costs seem to have been used as valuation criteria. In some cases, this led to extremely low selling prices. For example, in the case of SOGUIPLAST, a plastics manufacturing plant, the pay-off period for the credit that financed the sale was so long that the net present value of the sales amount was equal to about half the replacement value of the generators installed in the plant. The SANOYA textile mill had incurred pre-privatisation rehabilitation costs of 42 million ECU; it was sold for 1 million ECU.

- Publicity was limited; no formal tender was made. The government received only 56 offers for the 30 industrial state-owned enterprises; 17 of the enterprises received only one offer.

- Lengthy pay-off periods and high inflation rates (around 30 per cent in some years) made real costs to buyers low. Even so, many buyers failed to respect agreed payment schedules. Generous sweeteners were obtained: high levels of protection were freely granted as were duty-free imports of equipment and intermediate inputs. Monopoly rights were granted to the soft drink bottling plant, the cigarette factory, and the match factory; Ciment de Guinée benefited from a *de facto* monopoly. Some enterprises were exempted from sales taxes.

cont ...

Box A cont ...

Despite the very cheap selling prices, most of the privatised enterprises fared badly. Of the 28 industrial PEs that were privatised, 15 never even resumed operations (though 4 of these were only recently privatised). Thirteen did start up, but of these only 5 were still in business in mid-1991, and only 4 were solidly profitable: the brewery, the cement plant, a quarry, and a printing establishment. The tobacco plant was operating but in trouble because of problems that prevail throughout the industrial sector: expensive and unreliable energy supplies, spare part procurement problems, costly and unreliable raw material supplies, lack of qualified workers, ineffective protection (smuggling), lack of working capital, and inexperienced management.

The fiscal and employment benefits of privatisation have been minimal:

- It is not even clear that fiscal burdens were reduced. Accumulated external arrears of the PEs were $140 million, but current, direct pre-privatisation subsidies were undoubtedly small, because most of the enterprises had been shut down prior to privatisation.

- Total selling prices amounted to 21 billion GF, but only 2 billion had been paid by mid-1991. Real net present values are much lower because of long instalment payment periods and high rates of inflation.

- Indirect subsidies in the form of duty and sales tax exemptions probably total 2 billion GF.

- The five operating privatised enterprises employ 600 workers out of the 4,000 on pre-privatisation payrolls.

Guinea provides an extreme example of a poorly executed privatisation programme. It is not typical of African experience. It was more hurried, less structured, more shaped by the special political and economic imperatives of the post-Sékou Touré environment. But one or another of its aspects can be seen in other countries of the region (République de Guinée, 1991).

Moreover, the average value of transactions is extremely small; if the few big privatisations (South Africa and Ghana's Ashanti Goldfields sale), most are a few hundred thousand dollars in value. The numerous sales in Angola and Mozambique and Guinea are accounted for largely by retain shops and similar small scale operations. Very few of the main public services have been touched up to now.

The relative meagreness of results is indicated by a few country-level details, even for countries that are good performers in volume of privatisation transactions. The well-documented Guinea experience is shown separately, in Box A.

- Ghana has had a privatisation programme since 1983. As of March 1991, 38 SOEs had been divested – 22 liquidations, 8 partial sales, 5 sales of full equity, and 3 leases. Only 5 significant, fully concluded sales could be identified. The modest headway made in Ghana is indicated by the fact that total receipts in 1991 and 1992 were only about $15 million, and the total sale value of privatised assets since the mid-1980s is probably not more than $30 million. Acceleration has occurred, however, since 1993, as Table 2 shows.[6]

- In Nigeria, the privatisation effort has been relatively well organised and focused. Some 58 transactions had resulted as of mid-1992. But only a few were of substantial size – the sale of 13 insurance companies, the Federal Palace Hotel, and government holdings in several cement plants. Total receipts were 1.5 billion naira, less than 1 per cent of the book value of state-owned assets.

- Togo was a leading privatiser, and innovative as well in the use of lease contracting. But it appears that many of the privatisations there, including the famous steel mill lease, have not survived the recent political turmoil in that country.

- Niger is sometimes classified as a success among privatising African countries. It is hard to understand why. In that country's public enterprise reform programme undertaken in the mid-1980s, 15 enterprises were targeted for sale – 10 for full and 5 for partial privatisation. By the end of 1991, however, in addition to liquidation of 5 enterprises, the only durable divestiture was of a tiny television maintenance operation.

- Senegal's privatisation programme began in the late 1970s, probably the first in Sub-Saharan Africa. By 1983, 16 enterprises were reported to be in liquidation and 4 had been transferred to private ownership. Over most of the next decade, however, little progress was made. Adjustment loans in the mid-1980s gave major emphasis to divestiture, but despite lengthy dialogue with external partners and much conditionality, few transactions took place. In 1987 there were more PEs than there had been in 1981, the nominal value of government equity invested in them had doubled, and the state's share of total equity in the sector rose from 61 to 71 per cent. As of mid-1990, five enterprises had been sold. Total proceeds were derisory – about $5 million. The number of firms listed as liquidated is longer, but the list includes companies that had been dead for a decade or more.[7] Table 2, however, indicates that 35 transactions had occurred by 1995, with considerably greater sales values.

3. Reasons for Slow Divestiture and Prospects for Acceleration

The academic literature and the analyses of practitioners contain a standard list of obstacles and constraints to privatisation in developing countries. These common explanatory factors are summarised below, grouped into two categories: those that derive from the general socio-political environment or context, and those that are more specifically related to implementation difficulties in low income African countries. Not all the conventionally indicted factors are equally significant, however, and some that are fundamental are not always given due recognition. After the listing of general explanatory factors, therefore, those factors that seem most basic are considered further. In the final part of this section the future prospects for divestiture in Africa are assessed.

Environmental Obstacles: Economic, Political, Intellectual

In several key respects, the economic environment has been un-congenial to divestiture operations.

- The small indigenous private sector has limited capacity to absorb privatisable public entities. Sales to non-African minorities or to foreigners can speed the process but raise risks of slowing indigenous acquisition of entrepreneurial capabilities.

- Most Sub-Saharan Africa economies are small, and single-firm industries are common. Divestiture thus often means turning public monopolies into private ones, because in many cases

authorities are reluctant to allow competition via import liberalisation and because regulatory capacity is limited.

- Often the macroeconomic setting is uncertain and risky; fiscal
and trade imbalances exist or threaten, high inflation rates are
not uncommon, and many key markets remain regulated,
especially for foreign exchange, credit, and labour. Financial
systems have been in deep disarray in much of the region.
Private businessmen fear the remnants of dirigisme and anti-
business bias that they believe run deep in politicians and civil
servants.

- Economic institutions remain unfriendly to private enterprise in
many countries of the region: property rights systems are thinly
developed and judicial and regulatory arrangements weak.
Playing fields are often uneven. Politicised and non-transparent
economic decision making remains frequent.

The political environment is also less than welcoming. Sale of
state-owned enterprises has a small domestic political constituency:
the private sector, a few reformers (mostly technocrats), and some
users or consumers favour it. But the latter have small interest in
such sales. Those against privatisation tend to be more numerous,
more intensely affected, and more influential: workers worried
about losing jobs; officials who see loss of influence and rents; and
students, university professors, and other intellectuals who see dirty
deals everywhere and in any case oppose selling national assets to
rich and powerful people, local or foreign. In the many African
countries with socialist or dirigiste traditions, distrust of
businessmen and of private markets runs deep and is readily
brought to the surface.

Nor was there much intellectual or ideological enthusiasm for
the privatisation idea. Until the beginning of the 1990s at least, the
dominant view in African intellectual circles was that privatisation
in typical African circumstances was infeasible and undesirable. The
indigenous private sector was believed to be too undeveloped to
take over divested activities while foreign investment was seen as
inimical to capacity building. Stewart *et al.*, (1992) is illustrative, as
are criticisms emanating from the Economic Commission for Africa
and the African Development Bank (see Susungi, 1988). This is
perhaps not surprising because up to the end of the 1980s at least,

much of the intellectual community in industrialised countries also remained unconvinced about the economic benefits of divestiture in developing country environments.[8]

Implementation Difficulties

In the least developed countries, implementation of divestiture programmes presents some special difficulties, problems that arise more intensely than is normally the case in middle income and developed country privatisation efforts.

- The problem of defining acceptable buyers often proves to be acute. Government officials, politicians, and other influential persons are frequently opposed to allowing foreign investors to acquire divested enterprises. Often there are also restrictions against Asians and other non-African citizens. And prosperous, economically dynamic ethnic groups are sometimes discriminated against.[9] The problem is exacerbated by weak capital markets, rarity of stock exchanges, and financial system disarray.

- Governments in many African countries are reluctant to sell profitable PEs and the money-losers they were ready to dispose of have rarely been attractive to buyers at terms governments will accept. Few governments accepted the idea that non-viable enterprises should be liquidated straightaway, rather than put up for sale – a source of much delay and wasted effort.

- Asset valuation is a nagging problem almost everywhere. In these economies there is rarely a competitive market that can determine potential earning power of the assets up for sale. Asset valuations tend to be too high because they are based too much on historical cost or book value. The notion that the worth of assets should be close to their book value, an article of faith among politicians and much of the public in many countries, seems to have especially deep roots in the poorest countries.

- Governments resist measures that increase unemployment, which is likely to result from most African cases of divestiture because of the high rate of overmanning typical of these SOEs. Potential buyers worry about residual liabilities, especially severance pay for workers, and about freedom to hire and fire.

- Governments do a poor job of convincing their people that benefits of privatisation outweigh costs. Benefits often seem distant, vague, and uncertain. Costs are clear and immediate.

- The mechanics of selling state equity in state-owned enterprises or operating companies take unanticipated amounts of time and care, and require skills and organisational capacities that have been in very short supply. Preparatory work is therefore slow, and dependent too much on expatriate experts. Stakeholders and the private sector have typically been left out of the process.

Aid, Political Will, and Soft Budget Constraints

Several factors that are at once broader than day-to-day implementation constraints and specific to African experience have also contributed in a major way to the slow pace of divestiture. The first is that privatisation programmes came to Africa mainly as part of World Bank structural and sectoral adjustment lending. It came laden with conditionality.[10] Although this has had positive effects in defining and implementing programmes, it has also entailed inevitable negative impacts on internalisation of the privatisation idea. The fact that privatisation has come to be so widely viewed as imposed by the Bank and Fund, and not truly homegrown, has diluted political will and support.

The second retarding factor of this type is the softness of budget constraints in much of the continent. Africa is a heavily aided region; in most years from the mid-1980s on, more than 20 countries received external assistance amounting to more than 10 per cent of their GDP. Overall, between 1980 and 1989, foreign aid to the region amounted to 11 per cent of GDP, 10 to 20 times more than other developing regions (Lister and Stevens, 1992).

The large donor presence in so many countries of the continent has had unintended negative effects on privatisation. Access to aid resources, combined with donor reluctance to impose sanctions for non-performance on policy loans, has created a 'soft budget' environment. It has reduced the necessity and hence the local political will to undertake painful and potentially destabilising reforms.

The financial sector reforms of the 1980s and parallel programmes to rehabilitate SOEs, which implicitly forgive debt and otherwise restart the sector, have worked in the same direction. They have tended to dissipate what would otherwise have become

irresistible pressures for cost-cutting or revenue-raising improvements and shedding of low-priority activities.

Which Obstacles are the Most Significant?

All of these obstacles and constraints help explain why there have
been so few transfers of state-owned enterprises into private hands
in Africa. Not all constraints are found in each country experience.
They are certainly not all of the same weight. Moreover,
conventional diagnoses understate some crucial factors.

Over-emphasised Factors

Thus, lack of local buyers may be only a weak constraint, given the
existence of flight capital in so many African countries, and the
widespread presence of energetic entrepreneurs. Where these do not
exist, governments can certainly reduce this constraint by deciding
to allow foreign purchasers. Thinness of capital markets, similarly,
is probably not a profound obstacle, given the relatively small scale
of most transactions and the potential use of pension funds and
insurance companies, as well as embryonic stock markets in some
countries. Unwillingness to sell profitable enterprises is not a basic
or generalised factor; its weight seems to have declined over time.

Some of the listed factors are not really inherent obstacles to
privatisation but derive from other policies. Just as the 'no buyers'
constraint can be released by allowing foreign participation, so can
privatised firms be exposed to competitive influences if governments are willing to liberalise import regimes. What is at issue then
is not so much privatisation but fears of de-industrialisation via
import competition, social unrest due to disemployment, and
erosion of national autonomy, as well as doubts about direct foreign
investment as a capacity-building instrument.

Some factors that are frequently mentioned as crucial seem less
so in reality. For example, lack of a guiding strategy is frequently
cited by consultants and donor agency staff to explain lagging
privatisation programmes. These critics usually have in mind the
lack of a comprehensive vision of what the size and structure of the
state sector should become. They deplore, for example, the lack of
clear government statement about which PEs should be retained in
the public sector, which should be privatised fully, which partially,
and which liquidated.

Box B:

Factors Limiting Impact on Efficiency and Growth

Observation and anecdotal evidence suggest that those divestitures that have taken place have had limited impact on efficiency and growth. Given the scarcity of post-privatisation evaluations, any conclusions on the matter of impacts have to be tentative, but there are reasons to believe that they have been small.

- The divestiture programmes typically involved small enterprises, often in manufacturing, that were never employers of more than a tiny proportion of the labour force. The bigger, more strategic state-owned enterprises (railways, urban transport companies, ports, power and water companies, marketing agencies, and so forth), which are usually the main budget-drainers, investment capital wasters, and ineffective input or other service providers – in other words, the major sources of inefficiency and blocked growth – were almost always left untouched by privatisation pro-grammes. In no African case does it appear that more than a small share of government equity in the PE sector been offered for sale.

- Much that was sold consisted of minority holdings in already privatised operations. Or governments retained major shares in the privatised entity. Although positive changes in corporate culture can result in such cases, this is unlikely to occur in African circumstances, where government–business distrust runs deep and retention of shares is often interpreted by private owners as a sign of continued government desire to intervene.

- Many of the liquidations that comprise a large part of privatisation or divestiture programmes were quasi-fictional in that they involved enterprises that have long been closed.

- Severance benefits in a few cases were so large as to require significant reallocation of public resources from other productive uses. This was a major factor in Ghana.

- As mentioned earlier, small market size coupled with continuing protection against imports meant, in numerous cases, that competition did not encourage greater efficiency in the privatised firms. Also, special favours granted to privatised firms (tax holidays and other tax or accounting benefits, duty free imports, priority access to credit or other scarce inputs, or tariff protection) reduced the social benefits of the transactions.

cont ...

Box B cont ...

- Credit sales induced speculative purchases by unqualified buyers, discouraging asset acquisition by competent, experienced managers.

- Governments were often in a weak bargaining position: they faced few buyers, were willing to make many concessions to avoid unemployment, and sometimes were subject to external conditionality requiring action. This may have led them to sell too quickly and too low. More commonly and more importantly, it spurred them to give away distortionary fiscal, credit, and other sweeteners.

- For various reasons (lack of transparency, lack of rules and procedures for asset disposal, lack of arm's-length bargaining – all in a socio-political context where patron–client systems prevail and states are soft), cronyism and corruption have sometimes marked the process.

But this kind of grand design is not essential to privatisation effectiveness or to PE reform programmes in general. More or less *ad hoc* programmes can be effective, and indeed may be preferable. PE classification exercises are long and costly. They have tended to break down anyway, mainly because governments have been unwilling to accept many technical recommendations on enterprise liquidation, preferring instead to go the last mile in seeking buyers.

Key Factors

Lack of political will is the factor that is perhaps the most often cited in explaining slow privatisation in Africa, though what is really at issue is soft budget constraints. Emphasis on lack of political will is an especially popular explanation in donor circles. It is obviously not wrong: if more governments had been truly committed and eager to move forward on privatisation, more substantial results would be evident today.

But lack of will is not by itself an illuminating explanation. It is based on the observation that African governments have not pursued privatisation policies that are clearly conducive to increased efficiency and growth. But by this standard, any government that sacrifices some efficiency objectives for other goals – for example, class, ethnic or regional balance in development opportunities or income distribution, or the search for greater national autonomy and indigenous capability – can be accused of lack of will.

Two interesting questions then arise. What factors determine this kind of choice? Why have so many African governments failed to push forward faster and further with announced privatisation programmes? The first answer is tautological but useful: expected benefits from these programmes were too small or too uncertain to outweigh expected costs, the major cost being disemployment and its political risks. Or, the benefits that looked persuasive on a general level, and in the early stages of negotiation of the policy loans that were the chief vehicles of privatisation programmes, turned out to be less attractive as details were filled in and implications unfolded.

Another possibility is that as the privatisation programmes got under way, a negative shift took place in the outcome of the implicit cost–benefit calculations made by responsible authorities. The costs of implementing the programme rose with time, and the costs of non-implementation (sacrificed benefits of reform impact and sacrificed aid money) fell.

This suggests that one of the most fundamental reasons for slow privatisation is the existence of a soft budget constraint, as noted earlier. It operated in an environment of relatively heavy aid inflows, combined with the absence of sanctions for non-performance on privatisation-linked policy loans. The relatively easy access of many African countries to foreign assistance reduced their need to make hard budgetary choices. Many African governments were able to delay direct confrontation of structural problems by seeking aid resources; they did this quite successfully, as shown by healthy rates of growth of aid flows after 1985 in many cases.

At the same time, donors imposed few sanctions on governments that performed poorly on privatisation conditionalities in adjustment loans. Delays in disbursement were common, but at least until 1990 it does not seem that a single World Bank adjustment loan in Africa went undisbursed for reasons of non-performance on public enterprise reform-related conditionality. Financial sector reforms (mostly externally financed) contributed to this softening of budget constraints. By cleaning up balance sheets, absorbing accumulated debts of loss-making enterprises, rehabilitating poorly managed operations, and generally giving SOEs a fresh start, these reforms sometimes had the unintended effect of removing imperatives for fundamental change – and notably change in the direction of divestiture.

Second in the list of fundamental factors explaining privatisation performance in Sub-Saharan Africa is the combination of elements we earlier called socio-political and intellectual. In the majority of African states, governments have so far failed to convince private actors that the climate for investment and related activity is genuinely receptive. Businessmen continue to worry about the unevenness of playing fields and the apparent reluctance of governments to keep hands off divested enterprises. This derives from dirigiste traditions, from the slow pace of reform of administrative regimes and regulatory systems,[11] and from continuing hesitations among African intellectuals, officials and policy makers about whether the expected benefits from divestiture programmes outweigh their costs and risks.

Third, despite general improvement after 1985, the macroeconomic environment in most countries remained uncongenial for divestiture as for other private sector-orientated programmes. Exchange controls remained pervasive, interest rate controls and administrative allocations of credit were common, and problems of containing budget deficits and inflation remained widespread.

A final major source of slow divestiture has been the many implementation difficulties, taken together, notably: lack of information about the SOEs and the sector, lack of skilled staff to run divestiture agencies, the tendency to hold to book value in valuing assets for sale, and lack of liquidity to finance purchases.

Implications and Prospects

Some observers have concluded from this record that the prospects of privatisation in Sub-Saharan Africa (as in low income regions generally) are so unpromising that divestiture programmes should be abandoned and reform energies focused on the improvement of PE performance. But this is the wrong conclusion to draw. The record of attempts to reform enterprises retained in the public sector is if anything less cheerful, and the prospects of better performance less bright. And, in any event, effective rehabilitation and efficiency-raising improvements of some PEs would not change the basic reality that state sectors remain overextended in Sub-Saharan Africa, at substantial cost in terms of budgetary resources and economic growth; governments continue to do – usually poorly – many activities that can be done – usually better – by private agents. So divestiture has to remain a central element in reform strategies in Sub-Saharan Africa, as in low-income countries generally.

Forces Favouring Divestiture

It is true that many of the obstacles and constraints outlined above still persist, and will continue to present formidable barriers to progress in divestiture. But many forces are working to expand the potential scope and promise of privatisation in Sub-Saharan Africa, and these brighten future prospects.

The urgency of the task of efficient state-shrinkage is more pressing than ever. Public sectors remain burdened with resource-absorbing enterprises and activities that contribute little to growth or equity. The prospects for more effective public sector management in the medium term are poor, because public sector management requires general administrative reforms that are everywhere slow, difficult, and subject to backsliding. (Even the relatively limited objective of rationalising salary policies, a priority of public sector reformers in the 1980s, remains out of reach.) The presence of state-owned enterprises in sectors that can attract private activity blocks the growth of private sectors that have to be the main agents of future growth.

Moreover, important elements in the environment are becoming more friendly to privatisation. Ideas and attitudes have changed substantially in the past decade; certainly the basic point that governments need not and should not do things that private sectors can do has made real headway. The collapse of state planning in Eastern Europe and the former Soviet Union, the revelations of the depths of its inefficiencies, and the free market orientation that has emerged in all formerly socialist countries have had profound effects on intellectual and political attitudes regarding privatisation.

The macroeconomic environment (especially the fiscal and monetary situation in most of the region) has become more favourable to privatisation and to private sector activity in general. Exchange rate policy has become more flexible and appropriate in many countries of the region since the mid-1980s. Fiscal and credit policies have become more prudent in most countries, and inflation rates have slowed. Regulatory systems are gradually becoming more market-friendly and many of the region's economies have become more open.

Moreover, in the post-cold war world, real aid flows to Sub-Saharan Africa can be expected to increase little, if at all. And programme assistance, the most fungible of aid forms, seems to have reached its peak. This means not only continuing or intensified austerity, but harder budget constraints. A tighter budget constraint by itself can be a potent privatising force: forced to make decisions as to who will receive budget support or credit allocations and who will not, decision makers in core economic agencies become powerful agents of divestiture.

Finally, much has been learned in the last decade about the strategy and tactics of privatisation, and this should mean better results in the future. Two particularly useful sets of lessons have been learned. The first is about how to do divestiture better. Assessments of divestiture experience point the way to broader coverage and more intensive effects on efficiency and growth. The second is that the privatisation arsenal should become more diversified; greater attention should be given to additional techniques and approaches, notably those involving non-divestiture and indirect divestiture, which have much privatising potential but have been relatively neglected up to now. Improved divestiture policies are outlined in this section, the less traditional approaches to privatisation in Section Five.

Improved Design and Implementation of Divestiture Programmes

Good prescriptions on how to improve the design and implementation of divestiture programmes are found in recent World Bank syntheses of experience (Kikeri, 1989; Kikeri *et al.*, 1992; and Galal *et al.*, 1992). These papers acknowledge that their analysis is more pertinent for middle income countries than for the least developed. But there is much that is applicable. The following list of prescriptions for more effective African divestiture programmes builds on and adapts those prescriptions.

Put the macroeconomic environment in order and get prices right – especially exchange rates and interest rates. This plus subsidy reduction, sound investment screening, and resistance to cost plus pricing will encourage competition, evenness of playing fields, and hardening of budget constraints.

Harden budget constraints. Most recent analyses give this great emphasis, and properly so. The key role of external donors in Sub-Saharan Africa creates special problems of implementation in much of the region. Donors finance much public expenditure, and many had – at least until recently – lukewarm attitudes toward the suitability of privatisation programmes. In some cases they have been willing to bail out sinking state-owned enterprises, even where justification is uncertain. Greater donor care in prioritising their assistance, inter-donor dialogue, and better co-ordination can help to reduce this problem.

Whatever the readiness of governments to launch divestiture operations, a great deal of essential preparatory work can and should be done even in advance of any actual privatisation operations, or very early in their evolution. Universally necessary pieces of the general regulatory framework can be introduced and gaps in company law and other elements of the legal and judicial systems filled, such as rules on contract disputes and on handling of residual liabilities of liquidated state-owned enterprises. The PE sector can be made more 'commercialisable' by transforming SOEs to joint stock companies whenever feasible. Because better PE sector management will in any circumstance require better information, it is always worthwhile to complete accounts and audits and to begin the process of building long-term capacity in information management. Important or troubled enterprises can usually benefit from management audits, even when no formal reform programme exists.

Everybody nowadays agrees that governments should start out with viable winners as first targets for privatisation, and also with firms working in competitive markets. These tend to be non-manufacturing operations – banks, real estate, airlines, for example. Confidence building and climate changing are the most important objectives at the outset, outweighing other significant objectives such as giving attention to the economically most significant public enterprises.

Pay much more attention to general public opinion and to dialogue with major stakeholders – workers, management, creditors, legislators, and politicians. Public lectures and seminars, press briefings, television and radio debates, preparation of written publications about the programme – all are useful. This implies painstaking attention to openness, to transparency all along the way, from opening up company accounts of state-owned enterprises up for divestiture, to use of unambiguous criteria for selection of offers, and full public exposure of these criteria and of prices offered and obtained. It also suggests the importance of careful and credible studies showing costs and benefits of existing situations and proposed privatisation. In the public debate, more stress has to be given to the costs of not divesting and to the hoped-for benefits of divestiture.

Economic as well as financial costs and benefits have to be taken into account. This underlies the 'avoid sweeteners' dictum, but also signals the fact that financial analysts responsible for managing divestiture processes too often concentrate on the financial rather than the economic aspects of divestiture transactions. It also encompasses the much-emphasised point that the name of the divestiture game should be economic efficiency and faster growth.

An *ad hoc*, case-by-case approach is a better way to begin in African circumstances than global classification exercises that sort SOEs into those that should be sold, those that should be liquidated, and those to keep. It is faster, cheaper, less likely to generate endless conflicts about what should be sold and what should be liquidated. This approach allows a policy of letting sleeping dogs lie, instead of pushing for formal liquidation of moribund enterprises. Benign neglect, along with general budgetary austerity and the existence of market-based interest rates, often forces gradual closure of non-viable state-owned enterprises. Letting them alone makes it possible to postpone confrontation on intractable issues such as heavy severance pay claims. One major related point: avoid the strong pressures to put up for sale enterprises that should be liquidated, except at appropriately low prices and with full information on the status and prospects of the enterprises in question. This risks becoming a prime source of delay and demoralisation.

It is usually better to avoid incurring rehabilitation and restructuring costs before sale, other than cleaning up liabilities and giving assurances about residual claims. Let the buyer restructure. Let the market determine selling price, using formal asset evaluation only as a benchmark. And sell for cash wherever possible.

On organisational nuts and bolts, most observers and practitioners agree that the best set-up for administering a divestiture programme is a two-tier structure – a political committee for policy and a technical committee for implementation, these together making up the single responsible entity ('focal point'). Also, to minimise *ad hoc*, politicised decisions, it is best to create single-channel procedures and work hard to avoid end runs around them.

These points are directed at African decision makers. But donors have much input into the formulation and implementation of privatisation policies. Two recommendations are therefore aimed their way. Firstly, in technical assistance projects with a privatisation focus, donors should give far higher priority than in the past to capacity building. The privatisation technical assistance of the 1980s left behind too little local capacity to manage privatisation programmes and policies. It is possible to do much better now. Strengthening of indigenous management capacity in the private sector should also be given special and explicit consideration in privatisation strategies.

Secondly, donors should sharply reduce – if possible abandon – linking of divestiture actions to conditioned lending. This is not a consensus view: many practitioners believe that conditionality on divestiture should, rather, be reinforced. They argue that it should be made more effective by relying more on prior actions and by clearer specification of conditions (specifying divestiture of a share of PE sector assets rather than specific enterprises, for example) and by raising its credibility – stopping disbursements if there is non-compliance, for example.

But moving away from conditionality is not an entirely new idea either. Kikeri *et al.*, (1992), in their review of lessons of experience, make the recommendation that public enterprise reform conditionality be dropped from structural adjustment loans. They put the argument in terms of different time paths; macro reforms can be implemented quickly, while the institutional changes that are entailed in PE reform take much longer. But it would be no less desirable to drop the conditionality from PE sector loans. Explicit conditionality obstructs the growth of local proprietorship and complicates political acceptability, thus creating the impression of outside pressures and tainting the idea as foreign and imposed. Explicit conditionality is too often counterproductive: it inevitably dilutes local commitment and tends to substitute game playing for true problem-solving dialogue. And its effectiveness is limited, as the record suggests (Berg, 1990).

4. Supplementing Divestiture with Indirect Privatisation Approaches

Divestiture programmes and policies in Sub-Saharan Africa can be expected to yield better results in the future than they have in the past, for reasons outlined above. But divestiture should be supplemented by approaches that do not entail ownership privatisation or do so only partially and indirectly.

This is so for several reasons. The obstacles noted above will continue to constrain the pace of divestiture in many countries, even though faster movement can be expected in the future than in the past. Moreover, there is as yet little evidence that African governments are willing to entertain divestiture of the core public enterprises – in rail and road transport, power, water, telecommunications, and related sectors. If more of these are to be made private, and more efficient, avenues other than full divestiture have to be explored. And finally, these supplementary privatisation approaches have considerable promise as load-shedding devices for central and local governments, as well as gateways to full divestiture in the public enterprise sector.

Indirect Approaches Defined

Although continuing to move forward with divestiture programmes that aim at ownership transfer, therefore, greater emphasis should be given to indirect privatisation instruments, supplements to 'classic' divestiture. The principal types are shown in Box C. Most are well known. Some, like management contracts and lease arrangements, are already common features of present privatisation programmes. They are indirect in the sense that they do not entail the sale of publicly held equity shares or of entire companies. Management contracts aside, they have received only marginal attention in privatisation strategies.

A further word on terminology. The traditional privatisation technique or approach is used here to mean classic ownership divestiture – sale of partial or full government equity holdings, ortrade sales (sales of going concerns), or liquidation. Indirect privatisation techniques encompass three categories: 1) internal divestiture or fragmentation, whereby specific activities, functions

Box C:
Indirect Privatisation Instruments

Management contracts represent minimalist approaches to private management of publicly owned assets. Private contractors are given responsibility for day-to-day operation and maintenance of a publicly owned facility. These arrangements are widely used, in developed as in developing countries, and are common in water supply, mining, hotels, hospitals, manufacturing, agricultural enterprises, and telephone services. Some involve straight fees for services, with remuneration not linked to performance; at the extreme these resemble technical assistance arrangements. But many have incentive features (for example, profit-sharing) that bring them closer to lease contracts of the kind described below.

Lease contracts are of several different types, varying principally by who is responsible for financing investment.

- Under straightforward leasing – sometimes called *affermage* – the contractor (or lessee) pays the public owner a fee for the right to operate a public facility, and bears the financial risks of its operation. It has been used in power, ports, urban transport and railways, water and sewage, and solid waste collection and disposal. It has also been used in industry: the leasing of part of a steel mill in Togo is a famous example. The private firm finances working capital and replaces nondurable capital assets. The contract is usually 5–10 years, with contractors collecting tariff revenues directly and paying over a share to government. Regulatory burdens for bidding, contracting, and monitoring can be considerable.

- Concessions involve greater contractor responsibility, notably for investment to replace or extend fixed assets. They cover longer periods – usually 15–30 years. France has pioneered this approach, which is used widely in its water system, as well as in Spain and in some Latin American and African countries. Concession arrangements also exist in other sectors – solid waste disposal, urban metro systems, toll roads, among others. Concessions are the essence of 'landlord port' arrangements, whereby private operators are given concessions to run specialised port facilities (grain, oil, or minerals).

Fragmentation is a form of divestiture that looks for the parts of a function or government agency that are most quickly and easily divested, and which promise efficiency gains. It is called 'peripheral privatisation' in some places, 'spinning-off' or 'internal divestiture' in others. Examples are the sale of hotels and restaurants owned by railway companies, the spinning-off of feed mills and rice mills owned by ministries of agriculture in Asia, Latin America, and Africa, and the sale of so-called 'social assets' or 'ancillary assets' (schools, rest homes, resort facilities, and municipal heating plants) in formerly socialist countries.   cont ...

Box C cont ...

Contracting-out, often called 'out-sourcing' or 'subcontracting' in manufacturing, mining, and construction, is widespread in public sector service
provision. It is an extremely diverse and highly versatile form of privatisation.
Examples include security and janitorial services, maintenance of office
equipment, data processing, food services, and road maintenance.

De-monopolisation – removal of an outright ban on private service
delivery – is often a necessary first step before the private sector can provide
an historically public service. Deregulation in its de-confinement aspect is the
removal of regulatory obstacles to private participation in a market.
Deregulation is more than simply lifting prohibitions. There is also the hard
work of establishing a regulatory framework that is at once private sector-
friendly, focused on the need to maintain competition, and sensitive to the
need to expand and improve service standards while giving careful attention
to environmental and other criteria. Regulatory frameworks of this kind are
lacking in most Sub-Saharan Africa countries, and their absence constrains
mobilisation of the private sector for public service provision. Effective
privatisation demands early and intensive attention to the detailed
requirements for workable regulation of private activity in service delivery.

---

or bureaux are spun off to private actors (including present
employees); 2) non-divestiture instruments that leave ownership in
the public sector and transfer responsibility for asset management
or service delivery to private hands: management contracts, leases,
and contracting-out of specific services or functions; and 3)
de-monopolisation or de-confinement, which allows private
producers or service providers to compete with public sector
agents.[12]

The Scope for Indirect Privatisation

What kinds of goods and services are appropriate targets for
privatisation by indirect methods? Economic theorists and specialists
in organisational behaviour have turned their attention to some
aspects of this question in recent years. However, analytic guidance
for determining privatisability is still embryonic, even for classic
divestiture (see Donahue, 1991 and Kessides, 1993).

One line of argument, drawn from the theory of public goods,
is that the answer depends on the nature of the good or service at
issue. This kind of analysis, however, is of little help in determining
privatisability. Many so-called public services – infrastructure serv-

ices for example – blend public and private goods characteristics and are usually closer to private than to public goods (Kessides, 1993; see also Cointreau-Levine, 1992). And even if they are not, management or service delivery may still be privatisable.

Another approach is to look at the conditions of production and delivery of goods and services – the presence or absence of large economies of scale, heavy sunk costs, and the extent of need for coordination of inputs. By these criteria, also, most public services lend themselves in large degree to privatisation or 'marketisation'.

In practice, there are two ways to see the scope and potential of indirect privatisation: firstly, look around the world at current usage of these instruments; and, secondly, examine public sector activities and functions in a disaggregated fashion, to see how many might be transferred to private agents. Looking at actual examples gives plenty of ideas about how to use indirect privatisation instruments. Their scope – particularly for contracting out and fragmentation or internal divestiture – can be widened by creative privatisers who discover new possibilities for disaggregating SOE (or central government) functions and activities, and thereby invent new privatisation opportunities. In the analysis of scope and potential that follows, management contracts and leasing are considered together, and separately from contracting-out and fragmentation.

Management Contracts and Leasing

Management contracts are far from problem-free, as will be noted later. But there is a wide body of information on experience and pitfalls. Countries new to management contracting can find guidance on where it seems to work best sectorally, and what to look out for (see Brooke, 1985; Centre on Transnational Corporations, 1983; Hegstad and Newport, 1987). It has proved a flexible instrument, capable of injecting skills otherwise unavailable into the PE sector. Sometimes these skills are local, but in low income countries they are usually expatriate.

A wide range of public–private mixes is conceivable. At one extreme is a 'pure' management contract, with no incentive features or any provision for purchase or for capital investment. Such arrangements closely resemble traditional technical assistance projects. Normally, however, the contracts include incentive elements that link reward to performance. Further along the spectrum are provisions for investment by the management partner, which makes the arrangement closer to a joint venture.

Leasing contracts are also common and run a similar gamut, though most tend to involve straightforward rental of assets for a fixed fee. As with management contracts, common practice provides a good rough and ready indicator of privatisability. Vuylsteke's 1988 survey shows lease contract transactions in 20 of the 59 countries covered, and in many different sectors of economic activity.

Lease contracting is a highly versatile instrument. Examples include the leasing of part of a steel mill in Togo. It is widely used in transitional economies, for example, to privatise management of agricultural land and small service enterprises. Equipment leasing is a common device for transferring publicly owned and badly managed farm and construction equipment into private management (Seager and Fieldson, 1984). Hotels are frequently leased, worldwide. Leasing has been used creatively to facilitate self-employment of professionals.[13] It is also used for privatising management of core public utilities such as power companies and water supply operations – especially the latter. Lease contracting is indeed the instrument of choice in these sectors; it is much more common than management contracts or the contracting-out of specific activities. France is the leading user of leasing in water and other services.[14]

Contracting-Out and Fragmentation

Every public sector organisation – SOE, government ministry, municipal agency – houses a multiplicity of sub-units engaged in a vast array of functions. Both experience – current usage somewhere in the world – and *a priori* analysis suggest that most of these functions consist of activities that can be and in some places are being done outside the public sector, by private agents.

The decomposition of public sector functions, their disaggregation into privatisable elements, gives enormous potential reach to piecemeal divestiture, contracting out and leasing. Viewed this way, there is nothing that governments do that cannot be privatised to some degree. Privatisability in these dimensions is therefore not a matter of general principles or *a priori* speculation but of analysis of conditions in particular industries and particular economies. What is feasible and desirable to contract out or spin off (or lease) to private agents depends on a large number of situation-specific circumstances, such as: the suitability of the political and regulatory environment; the centrality of the activity to the agency's operations, and the degree of inefficiency of in-house operations; the actual and potential supply of competitive providers and the feasibility of competition-enhancing interventions by the state – e.g. competitive bidding for single subcontracts, use of multiple franchising in such areas as urban transport and solid waste collection and disposal, and maintenance of some force account in-house capacity as a yardstick in road construction and maintenance; the risks run by the subcontracting agency if performance of the contractor falls short, and means to minimise such risks; and the weight given to stimulation of entrepreneurship as a policy objective.

Every general 'public' function, then, such as port management, power supply, telecommunications, or road transport can be regarded as a collection of activities and sub-activities each of which is a potential target for an imaginative privatiser.

Take ports, for example. Many activities make up the global operation of a port: dredging, pilotage, towage, unballasting and bunkerage, stevedoring, cargo clearing and forwarding, cargo storage, training, security, and rat control – to mention only a few. Each is a possible target for privatisation (Scurfield, 1992). Or one can conceive of privatisation (including investment in infrastructure) for specialised ports. Hong Kong and more recently Malaysia (Port Kelang) have in place private ports exclusively for container operations. The use of leasing contracts is spreading; 'Landlord Ports' that lease publicly owned facilities to private operators exist in Colombia, Venezuela, Ghana, Gambia and probably elsewhere.

In telecommunications, feasible privatisation targets might include not only new value added services such as cellular systems or teleports, but such traditional activities as branching of new lines, billing, data processing, maintenance, repair of telephones, or preparation of phone books.

The railway sector is rich with possibilities.

- Railways can sell off or lease remnants of history – businesses that have little to do with railway operations such as printing plants, brickworks, furniture production, and station hotels and restaurants.

- Railways have sometimes created subsidiary joint ventures with private partners, contracting an activity to the subsidiary.

- In many countries, labour-intensive activities such as undergrowth clearance and ditch cleaning are contracted to local subcontractors or villagers.

- Subcontracting of heavy mechanical tamping (right of way maintenance) is not uncommon. Some railroads farm out all track maintenance to private contractors under competitive bidding. It should be easy to subcontract maintenance of telecommunications equipment – telephone exchanges, radio equipment, transmission lines, and some signalling equipment.

- Many other services are being subcontracted or sold: on-board catering and sleeping car services; ancillary freight handling and storage services (parcels, for example); and administrative support services such as printing, data processing, office cleaning, office equipment, and maintenance. Medical services and social services are also commonly subcontracted or leased.

- Quarries producing ballast for track maintenance are targets for sale or concessions or subcontracting.

Although contracting-out of individual services seems to have made little headway in the water and power sectors, the potential is there for such services as operation of standpipes, meter reading, billing and collection, and maintenance of private connections. And some examples do exist. In Santiago, Chile, the public water company took this path, encouraging its employees to leave the utility and form private firms that would bid for contracts to provide these kinds of services. Results are said to be extremely positive.[15]

According to one recent review of private sector roles in solid waste collection and disposal: 'Among the various private sector participation options, contracting for solid waste service holds the greatest promise to developing countries as a way of lowering costs'.[16] Private contracting exists in many cities in Asia and Latin America: Caracas, Santiago, Buenos Aires, Sao Paolo and Rio de Janeiro, Bogota, Bangkok and Jakarta, among others. Some 80 per cent of Malaysia's cities contract out waste collection services.

Internal divestiture and contracting-out (along with demonopolisation) have been particularly significant in road transport. Many countries are considering selling or contracting-out maintenance workshops. Over-the-road freight services were effectively privatised this way in Hungary and Poland, and recent Russian truck auctions were similar. Urban transport worldwide benefits from the competitive presence of private mini-vans, taxis, pedicabs, and other 'traditional' or 'informal' providers. Deregulation in the 1980s allowed such transport operators to take over large market shares in urban transit systems formerly dominated by monopoly public bus companies.

Contracting-out of road maintenance – periodic and routine – is particularly widespread. It is found, for example, in Colombia, Brazil, Kenya, and Ghana. Studies in Brazil, Colombia, and the United States suggest that cost savings of 25–50 per cent commonly result from contracting-out compared with force account maintenance. Innovation is encouraged.[17]

Consider, finally, municipal services in industrial countries. About two thirds of the cities in the US and some 30 per cent of those in France contract out for solid waste disposal and garbage collection. Two thirds of France's larger cities are provided with water by private concessionaires or contractors. In the United States, in about a third of the cities, traffic signal maintenance, legal services, payroll services, and data processing are contracted out to private firms. A vast array of other services is also contracted out, though less commonly: street light operation, fire prevention, ambulance services, operation of hospitals, prisons for juvenile offenders, tree trimming and planting, and many others (see Morley, 1989). Contracting-out of these kinds of services is growing in other industrial countries, and in many developing countries.

These cases illustrate the range of possibilities of contracting-out approaches. The prevalence of these examples does not mean they are easily exportable. But they do show that models exist and that for contracting-out, as for other types of non-traditional divestiture, experimentation does not mean a leap in the dark. For most kinds of contracting-out, for example, much importable institutional material exists such as how to draw up bidding documents, establish and monitor norms of performance, and administer contracts in general.

No comprehensive inventories of indirect privatisation experience exist. Recent World Bank research has produced, however, a systematic survey of leases, service contracts (the equivalent of contracting-out), and management contracts in the main infrastructure sectors worldwide (Table 3) (Kessides, 1993). The list excludes agriculture and industry, hence does not count fairly numerous leases in manufacturing (as in Togo). There is also reason to believe that the extent of indirect privatisation is understated, especially contracting-out, since these are not monitored.

Objections and Doubts about Indirect Approaches

Two objections can be raised to this call for greater use of non divestiture and indirect divestiture techniques: that it would distort reform priorities; that most of the same obstacles that constrain classic divestiture exist also for indirect instruments; and that the successful use of indirect methods requires institutional and regulatory capacities that are rare in Sub-Saharan Africa – or, put differently, these non-traditional methods have yet to prove themselves in low income country environments.

Distortion of Reform Priorities?

The notion here is that privatisation of ownership is the surest method to bring about improvements in efficiency and durable institutional change and full divestiture should therefore remain the quasi-exclusive focus of privatisation strategies. Management contracts and leases are included in these strategies, as their wide-spread prevalence indicates. But they are clearly second-best options. To give them and other non-traditional instruments greater emphasis, as is proposed, will deflect reform energies from the principal target, which is ownership change.

This objection is based on the view that full divestiture and indirect privatisation approaches are substitutes not complements. But the proposal here is not to replace divestiture programmes with non-traditional efforts. It is rather to complement present strategies – to inject additional dimensions into privatisation operations. Normally, divestiture programmes would be carried on side-by-side with indirect actions. There are times where temporary shifts in focus will be appropriate. For example, when divestiture pro-grammes are stalled, it may make sense to seek indirect privatisation opportunities as a way to get off dead centre.

Table 3: *Prevalence of Indirect Privatisation in Infrastructure Activities*

Sector and Country (and Region)	Leases	Contracting-Out	Management Contracts
Infrastructure: power			
Côte d'Ivoire	O		
Gambia	P		
Guinea-Bissau			O
Sierra Leone			P
India	O		P
Indonesia			P
Hong Kong	O		
Philippines	O		
Argentina	O		
Barbados	O		
Bolivia			
Ecuador	O		
Honduras		P	
Venezuela		O	
Infrastructure: transport			
Benin	I	O	
Burkina Faso	O	O	
Burundi	P	O	
Infrastructure: transport (cont ...)			
Cameroon	P	P	P
CAR	I	I	I
Cape Verde		P	
Chad	P	I	P
Congo B.		P	
Ethiopia			O
Gambia		I	
Ghana	O	O	P
Guinea	P	O	P
Guinea-Bissau		O	
Kenya		O	
Lesotho		O	
Madagascar		O	
Malawi		I	
Mali	P	P	P
Mauritius	P	P	P
Mozambique	P	O	
Niger		O	
Senegal		O	

cont ...

Table 3 cont ...

Infrastructure: transport (cont ...)

Sector and Country (and Region)	Leases	Contracting-Out	Management Contracts
Tanzania	I		I
Togo		I	
Uganda		I	
Zaire	O	O	O
Bangladesh		P	
China		I	
India	O	O	
Indonesia		P	
Malaysia	O	O	O
Nepal		O	
Pakistan		O	
Papua NG		P	
Philippines		P	O
Thailand	O		
Argentina	O		
Chile		O	

Infrastructure: water and sewage

Sector and Country (and Region)	Leases	Contracting Out	Management Contracts
Côte d'Ivoire	O		
Guinea	O		
Guinea-Bissau			O
Lesotho			O
Rwanda			P
Gambia	P		
Bangladesh	O		
China	O		
Hong Kong	O		
Malaysia	O		
Egypt	O		
Jordan	O	O	
Morocco	O		
Argentina	P		
Bolivia	O		
Chile	O	O	
Colombia		O	
Mexico	I		
Venezuela	I		

Source: Adapted from Kessides, 1993.

Notes: O = operational; P = planned; I = implemented but not yet fully operational.

It is not unrealistic, in fact, to expect positive synergy effects and true complementarity. As sometimes happens now, management contracts or leases can be a first step, an opening of the privatisation door, leading the way to full privatisation of ownership at a later stage. And the disaggregation perspective that indirect privatisation would bring to privatisation agencies should lead to the identification of many new targets – through internal divestiture for example.

Problems as Constraining as for Divestiture?

It can be argued that the obstacles to indirect privatisation are as formidable as those constraining full divestiture. There are even some additional problems. One is the need to greatly expand capacity in contract negotiation and administration. More important is the need for supporting institutions and capacities. Separation of ownership and management is likely to create new demands for legal and financial expertise, auditing capacity, regulatory arrangements, and legal procedures in which all parties have confidence. Transaction costs are likely to be higher with the disaggregation of management or contracting-out of specific functions and activities. Many SOEs will, therefore, prefer to continue to keep management and all activities in-house. Also, to the extent that enterprise rehabilitation requires new investment, full divestiture may be the method of choice.

Not all of these objections have the same weight. Management contracting and leasing can, and often do, involve new investment; changes in ownership come about by dilution rather than direct divestiture. The transaction cost argument is serious. But indirect privatisation has significant 'macro' advantages over divestiture. It is more attractive to reforming governments. And some constraints are less formidable than for full divestiture of ownership.

Consider first management contracts and leases. Their indirect, partial, and tentative character makes them more acceptable politically and ideologically than full divestiture. Because assets remain in public ownership, the urgency and the transparency of valuation problems are reduced. (With respect to leases, it is probably true that low rental values are easier to swallow psychologically and politically than deep discounts from book value.) It is certainly politically easier to arrange a temporary transfer of asset management than the kind of permanent alienation of state property that is associated with divestiture transactions. Also, management contracting and leasing allow for joint learning and familiarisation, creating new possibilities for greater private participation – moving, for example, from lease contracts without private responsibility for investment to concessions, where the private partner takes on such responsibility.

The problems with management contracts and leases are substantial and, in their general lines, well known.

- They are most effective when remuneration is tied to performance. But many management contracts are on a fixed fee basis. And where fees are performance-based, the contracted management has to have true autonomy, which governments are often reluctant to grant. Even when they grant it in the contract, most have great difficulty in avoiding intervention over such issues as expatriate hiring policies, redundancy, procurement, and company adherence to government's social policies.

- Budgetary deficiencies and weak adherence to contracted obligations for investment or other financing often compromise the integrity of the contract.

- Management contracts are often expensive, since they involve import of expatriates. They have tended, in the past at least, to neglect training and capacity building.

These problems can be overcome. Recent reviews of experience with management contacts confirm their widespread use and conclude that they have performed satisfactorily in most cases.

The factors outlined above, and the fact that management contracts and leases are so widely used, indicate that these instruments suffer less from some of the constraints that have held back divestiture, and that they have considerable privatising potential. African governments, like other latecomers, can benefit from the extensive experience with such contracts in many industries and in countries at all stages of development. The international market for management contracting or leasing firms is reasonably competitive in most sectors, and models exist for contract negotiation and monitoring. The 'testing the waters' advantage is especially valuable in newly liberalising environments and where governments are unwilling to go very far in privatising.

Expandability is easy; when the experience goes smoothly, the private party can increase its participation. This is the way it has worked in water supply operations in France, and there are some similar experiences in Africa, to be discussed below. And finally, even in situations where dirigisme persists, management autonomy is likely to be more protected against an interventionist-minded government where there is a management contract than in an unalloyed public enterprise.

Contracting-out (and internal spin-offs) also have fewer constraints than classic divestiture, and some special advantages in efficiency enhancement and institutional development. Like management contracting, contracting-out is likely to be more acceptable than outright divestiture. Its efficiency impacts are likely to be more consistently positive for several reasons, not least because it is easier to assure privatisation into competitive markets. And it has the very important long-term advantage of stimulating entrepreneurship and the development of small enterprises.

The greater political acceptability of contracting-out derives from its basic characteristics. It tends to be small in scale: the typical contract is for routine road maintenance, for vehicle repair, for data processing, for training. Many of the markets in question are competitive; most are contestable. Creation of rents is therefore less likely, and in any case smaller in scale and removable. It tends also to be labour-intensive, so capital requirements are relatively small. Like management contracting, it is inherently tentative and experimental, with room for learning and later revision of contractual obligations; it is therefore less perilous politically, or indeed for the economy. It tends to draw on indigenous skills and capital. It can in some cases override labour resistance by marrying contracting-out with the privatisation of agencies responsible for the function being contracted for – a sort of worker buy-out.

In sum, the political cost–benefit calculus looks rather better for contracting-out than for divestiture, though the two are of course not full substitutes. Risks are reduced by the small, partial, and tentative nature of the arrangement, and in some cases, by the muting of labour protest. No crown jewels are in sight. Rent generation is less likely. Contracting-out transactions tend to transfer activities into the hands of actors who depend more on skill and competence than on access to money and power, and who are moreover often exposed to competition. Popular fears of rip-offs are less likely than in the case of asset sales. Benefits are enhanced by the wider involvement of local entrepreneurs and the consequently greater capacity-building effects. The dramatic change in management environments and the competitive nature of the markets usually involved create the possibility of quick generation of benefits in more and better services.

Moreover, contracting-out has some efficiency-raising advantages that are of special value in low income country environments. It allows SOEs (or central governments) to employ specialised skills they cannot otherwise afford to recruit or retain, because of unattractive salary levels in the civil service. It allows use of specialised skills that are not required full time, and also greater flexibility in responding to changes in demand or funding. It raises efficiency by increasing specialisation and by permitting greater exploitation of economies of scale and scope for specific activities or processes. It creates yardsticks for cost comparisons with in-house operations. And it allows the nurturing of entrepreneurship in settings where few opportunities to do so exist, thereby favouring private sector development.

These indirect approaches to privatisation have the additional advantage of being applicable in the core public enterprises – railroads, urban transport companies, power, water, telecommunications enterprises – which are as yet unwilling in most of Africa to consider full privatisation. It is also relevant for central and local government. Ministry activities that are not part of priority mandates can be contracted out or spun off, as can those functions for which efficiency objects would be served by out-sourcing – research, data processing, catering, cleaning, medical and educational services, and so forth. Similarly, they have the advantage of bringing efficiency-raising private agents and competitive markets into situations where competition on the enterprise level is not possible due to natural monopoly or government unwillingness to tolerate import competition.

It is worth emphasising that contracting-out tends to encourage use of less capital-intensive methods of service delivery and production: it encourages taxis instead of big bus companies, corner traders rather than state trading emporia, the growth of small professional groups. It encourages use of local energies and skills, and decentralised solutions.[19] There is no better way to stimulate budding private sectors to invent creative responses to new opportunities and old challenges.

Three major problems have to be addressed if leasing contracts, contracting-out of individual services, and internal spin-offs are to become widespread and truly effective instruments. The first is administrative and financial, and applies mainly to contracting-out. To have acceptably functioning systems of contracting-out requires substantial capacity in bid preparation, specification of norms for contracted services, payments systems that are prompt, and so forth. At present, small and medium-scale enterprises lack experience in bidding and managing contracts, and government staff themselves are often only marginally more skilled. Small firms are invariably strapped for working capital and hence unable to support the long delays that normally characterise government payments. New forms of contracting mechanisms, special technical assistance in early stages for bid preparation, provision or guarantee of bid bonds – all can help the transition and these innovations are being introduced in some African countries.

The second problem in related: corruption. Contract-letting in all countries is exposed to risks of bribery and unfair competition in bidding. Current conditions in much of Sub-Saharan Africa – lack of experience with contracting, ambiguous ownership rights, thin regulatory systems, and soft judicial arrangements, and the fact that government contracts are often the only source of work for embryonic contractors, create special vulnerabilities to corruption. They demand unremitting attention to transparency and adherence to well-defined procedures for award of contracts, and constant monitoring.

Finally there are vested interests. Labour resistance is likely because of overmanning. As with all privatisation instruments, transactions should be accompanied by much greater public education, with emphasis on likely benefits and on the costs of inaction. Affected in-house labour should be encouraged to itself take on out-sourced services, and severance and retraining arrangements can dilute the resistance to change from this direction.

Workable in Africa?

One variant of the objection to the wider use of indirect privatisation because of institutional weaknesses is that it has not been genuinely tested in African conditions. But, as the preceding analysis suggests, indirect instruments are particularly attractive in Sub-Saharan Africa because they allow, even encourage, marginal or incremental privatisation actions that build on existing strengths and nurture entrepreneurship and small-scale African enterprises.

Private sector strengths and potentials can also be under-estimated. In every African city there are computer specialists, small transport enterprises, small building contractors, traders, mechanics, carpenters and other artisans, professionals, and small businessmen who are potential entrants into the market for privatised activities if the scale were right. One reason local entrepreneurial capacity and management abilities have not grown faster is the range of opportunities for small- and medium-size enterprises is small. As for being untested, that is changing as new departures in contracting emerge all over the continent.

Table 3 shows that much is already being done and that many new initiatives are planned, in Sub-Saharan Africa and elsewhere. A few illustrative examples of new departures are given below.

Water supply privatisation has spread in Sub-Saharan Africa. The main instrument has been lease contracting in the form of concessions. (See Box C for definition.) Among the many African countries that have adopted this model are Guinea, Guinea-Bissau, Gambia, Ghana, Rwanda, and Sierra Leone.

The Guinea (Conakry) example has been most studied. In 1989 two companies were formed to handle urban water supply. One, a state enterprise called SONEG, owns the physical facilities and is responsible for sectoral planning and investment. The second, SEEG, is an operating company responsible for running and maintaining the system. SEEG is 51 per cent owned by a foreign private consortium. SEEG's lease is for 10 years. Its remuneration is based on rates of collection from consumers and on new connections. SONEG is responsible for tariff-setting and for investments. Early results were extremely positive: the collection ratio increased from 20 to 70 per cent and other performance improvements are evident. Tariffs are sharply up and the plan is to reach full cost recovery levels before the end of the 1990s.[20]

In Côte d'Ivoire, urban water supply has been provided privately under lease arrangements since 1960, and sewage services under maintenance and management contracts since 1973. The first contract was in the form of a concession agreement making

SODECI, a mixed private–public company, responsible for Abidjan's water supply, including general operations, maintenance, and new boreholes. In the 1970s, SODECI undertook water supply operations in other urban areas, and a maintenance contract for Abidjan sewage and drainage.[21]

The water supply operation was extremely efficient, by all accounts, though also high cost. Until the 1980s financial performance was good. But government policies created problems: over-investment in production and the imposition of high tariffs created revenue shortfalls from which the operator was shielded by the terms of the contract.

Under a revised contract in 1987, SODECI, the mixed public–private company, took over all urban water supply services in the country. (SODECI also won a contract to manage all sewage services.) Fees were reduced in 1987 and at the same time all new investment in water supply was to be self-financed. Costs remain high, but not out of line with neighbouring countries, and service is excellent. The results of long-term capacity building efforts have begun to show up. The number of expatriates working for SODECI fell from 40 to 12 during a 25 year period of expanding operations. The general manager and all regional managers are Ivorian, and private Ivorians now own a majority of SODECI's shares (Triche, 1992).

In Kaduna State (Nigeria) the Water Board does some contracting-out. Outside repair shops are used for some vehicle repairs and machinery maintenance. The providers range from independents to private enterprises with excess capacity in their machine shops or garages. The Water Board also leases a computer from a local data services company for billing and collection operations in Kaduna City. The leasing firm does the maintenance also (Triche, 1992).

In the power sector the most striking results of non-traditional privatisation are visible in the Côte d'Ivoire. In response to a deterioration of performance, the power parastatal, EECI, was restructured in 1990. A new joint venture (the Compagnie Ivoirienne d'Electricité, or CIE) took over operating responsibility for generation, transmission, and distribution under a lease agreement. Ownership remains with EECI, as does responsibility for investments and sectoral policies. After only 18 months, efficiency improved dramatically: CIE's collection ratio was 90 per cent compared with 60 per cent previously; power outages were fewer; and maintenance was increased, computerisation spread, and subsidies were eliminated (Electricité de France International, 1992).

Solid waste disposal in many African cities is privately organised, but information is scarce. Dakar and Abidjan (and undoubtedly other cities) have contracted with private companies. In many other cities, private households arrange their own contracting, as in the Kinshasa example cited earlier. A World Bank project in Lagos had some provision for private sector collection of industrial waste. Contractors had to demonstrate sound operating practices and the potential for expansion.[22]

The railways have also been the scene of considerable experimentation in leasing and contracting-out (see Budin, 1992; and Moyer and Thompson, 1992). Cameroon Railways combined its rationalisation programme (requiring cutbacks in employment) with fragmentation and contracting-out. Railway management agreed with staff represented by the railway union to finance the creation of new enterprises employing laid-off staff. The parcel service was spun off in this way; 120 of the former staff of some 165 were employed in the new company, which was operating profitably in 1992. Various activities were contracted out to ex-employees: maintenance of rolling stock, some freight car and track line maintenance, cleaning in workshops, some track lines, and grass cutting along the right of way; some tamping equipment (used for maintenance of ballast on the right of way) was also leased. A similar arrangement exists in Senegal.

The Régie Abidjan–Niger, which links Côte d'Ivoire and Burkina Faso, was broken into two national railways in 1989 following long discord over tariffs and cross-debt. Later, the two governments decided to reunify the two lines and to privatise. Ownership of the rail properties would be passed to two 'Sociétés de Patrimoine', holding companies that each is creating. They will then create a single private operating company that will lease the railway from the holding companies and run it.

Other new departures in indirect railway privatisation in Sub-Saharan Africa include the following:

- In 1980 the consulting wing of the Indian Railways (RITES) signed a management contract with the Government of Nigeria to manage the Nigerian Railway Corporation. (Despite initial successes, contract disputes led to an early termination of this promising initiative (Thompson, undated).)

- Senegal, Burkina Faso, Mali, and Côte d'Ivoire have spun off buffets and hotels.

- In Côte d'Ivoire, the RAN, Abidjan, created in the 1970s a service company to maintain rolling stock.[23] Locomotive maintenance in Senegal is contracted out. Also in Senegal, a semi-private company (SEFICS) was created to manage rail service to a new industrial location.

Ports are another area of considerable new privatising activity. The Port of Cotonou has contracted out for numerous services: general sweeping and cleaning of the port; gardening; security; and certain industrial activities (foundry, tailor shop, machine shop, carpentry and masonry operations). It has also leased the port's cold storage facilities. Mauritania has contracted out for warehousing services. Gambia has signed a management contract with Maersk Lines for overall management of the Port of Banjul.

Contracting-out of road maintenance has been one of the most active areas of innovation, as indicated in Table 3: most of the numerous service contracts in African countries noted there under Transport refer to road maintenance. For routine maintenance and minor emergency and rehabilitation work on gravel and dirt roads, Kenya contracts with 'lengthmen', usually former construction workers.[24]

In Ghana, laid-off civil servants can become contractors for routine maintenance jobs under what is known as the Single Man Contractor System. The SMC is usually a farmer. He is paid on a task basis for cutting grass and clearing ditches on a specified length of road (about 5 kilometres). In Tanzania contractors have built short sections of roads for urban and agricultural projects, and in Burundi several firms undertook equipment-based road construction for the military. In both cases the national highway authorities did not know such domestic capacity existed (examples from Lantran, 1990).

Equipment belonging to Public Works Ministries or parastatals is being auctioned off to private contractors in several countries, or, more frequently now, 'plant pools' are being created or planned. These are essentially equipment leasing agencies, sometimes private, sometimes mixed. Both moves aim at reducing one of the chief constraints on contractor capacity – access to equipment for capital-strapped new enterprises. Projects to set up regional plant pools are under way In Tanzania and in Burkina Faso. In the Burkina case an effort will be made to assist in the setting up of small private garages in the workshops that the plant pool will not take over, to be run by discharged mechanics of the public works department (examples from Lantran and Lebussy, 1991).

Innovations in contracting arrangements are facilitating the spread of contracting-out in construction activities in roads and in general. The AGETIP model of contract management (Agence Pour l'Exécution des Travaux d'Intérêt Public) has spread throughout the continent. AGETIP is a private, not-for-profit organisation (a non-governmental organisation) that handles general contracting assignments, so far mainly from public works agencies and donors. It hires consultants to prepare designs, prepares bidding documents, issues calls for bids, signs contracts, and monitors performance. It also pays contractors promptly.

The Roads Office in Zaire provides a rare story of forward movement in that country. Despite general political disarray and other negative circumstances, the ODR (Office des Routes) transferred in the late 1980s some 80 per cent of its activities to private contractors. A dozen maintenance brigades are still directly managed by the ODR, but these compete for bids with private contractors on even terms. In 1991, maintenance performance was strong – better than it had been in many years (Office des Routes).

Despite the many obstacles to their use in Sub-Saharan Africa – the small size and inexperience of indigenous private sectors, weak legal and regulatory systems, financial sector disarray and lack of access to credit and others noted earlier – it is evident that many new experiments in indirect privatisation are under way. Although these are too new and too little studied to be able to allow firm judgements on their durability and impact, the record worldwide and the good beginnings of many of these indirect privatisations – combined with the *a priori* analysis outlined earlier, suggest that they have very substantial potential in Africa.

Why has Indirect Privatisation been Neglected?

Given the evident privatising potential of these indirect techniques the question arises: why are they not used more widely, not only in Africa but elsewhere in the developing world? Three answers seem most pertinent.

The first is historical and organisational. Modern privatisation began in Margaret Thatcher's Britain, where it was defined as sales of state assets, via share sales or buy-outs of whole companies. Privatisation became identified with ownership transfer. Later in the 1980s, when other governments geared up for privatisation, they set up administrative agencies and hired people with the objective of selling assets. The non-divestiture approaches, except for management contracts and leasing, were neglected. So it is rare even now to find in any privatisation agency in the world anybody who is seriously concerned with non-divestiture and other indirect approaches to privatisation, especially contracting-out and fragmentation or internal divestiture. Everybody worries about identifying state-owned enterprises for sale, about valuation, about bidding procedures, and so forth. Until recently, at least, there was little disposition to search out the more subtle opportunities outlined here.

The second reason for neglect of the indirect techniques is that they are difficult to translate into operating reality. There is little sensitivity to them among officials, even in governments committed to privatisation. Aid agencies have done little in these areas, because they also have been absorbed with asset sales of the classic kind. Hands on experience with introduction of most of these techniques is limited, and the discovery of opportunities requires programme orientations that are new, and innovation in project designs. Even the kind of training most suitable for designers of such projects is not clear. Sectoral competence is needed more than investment banking skills, and sensitivity to the potentials of disaggregation in economic activity more than marketing experience.

The third reason is related, but emerges from the broader historical context: the dominance of donor agency ideas and money in the formulation of policy, with consequent passivity of African policy makers. In the past decade few African governments had the time, the inclination, or the capacity to invent alternative approaches to the policy packages put on the table by their external partners.

The policy agenda on privatisation was externally determined, to a large degree. Because indirect privatisation methods were not much emphasised by donors in policy dialogues, they were not much considered by African officials.

This suggests three requirements for success in any effort to expand use of these non-traditional techniques. The first is general and is already happening: African governments have to exercise greater independence in policy making, and must acquire stronger capacity to do it. Secondly, political authorities and civil servants have to internalise more fully the privatisation idea – that is, believe in it. They have to become convinced more generally that privatisation in its various forms and degrees makes sense and is appropriate to their circumstances. This is already happening, but would be speeded up if policy makers had available more information and analysis on privatisation experiences and options.

Finally, the setting out of promising general ideas, or even specific ones, is not enough. The ideas have to be translated into operational reality. This demands experimental and innovative approaches to project design and closer attention to implementation. These are primarily African government responsibilities, but donors, who play such important roles in project formulation and implementation also should participate.

Experience in road maintenance provides examples of the kinds of innovation that is needed. To stimulate contracting of road maintenance donors and governments have had to: develop appropriate designs – in other words, simple and small scale; work out 'slice and package' systems that allow bigger contractors to bid and subcontract, allowing exploitation of economies of scale; set up equipment pools and other arrangements to facilitate access to capital goods; identify activities that are stable and predictable, hence easier to subcontract; and set up facilities to make credit available to contractors – 'mobilisation advances', modest contract bonds or guarantees, and use of contracting arrangements that make quick payment possible.

A renovated privatisation strategy for Africa and for low income or least developed countries in general, then, should be two-pronged. It should have, first of all, an improved divestiture component, whose tactics, strategy, and processes incorporate the lessons of experience as outlined earlier and elaborated more fully in other recent papers. There is little dispute about most of the specifics of this improved approach to divestiture. It is quite clear what implementing governments have to do. But on some key points opinions vary, especially about what policy stance is optimal for donor agencies. Some believe donors should intensify conditionality and enforce sanctions for non-compliance. Others (including the author) believe reform would be better served by resort to a lower profile, conditionality-free, longer-term approach, with emphasis on policy research and its dissemination, and on dialogue that will increase local commitment by persuading sceptics about the virtues of divestiture. Most observers and participants, whatever their other differences in perspective, recognise the critical importance of harder budget constraints if privatisation of any kind is to move ahead faster.

The second prong of a revitalised privatisation strategy should consist of a significantly greater application of indirect approaches. These changes imply a slight shift in organisational focus and in staffing needs of privatisation agencies – a move away from near-exclusive preoccupation with preparing and supervising the sales of state-owned enterprises, for example – to a more sectorally based, micro approach that requires different kinds of skills and different orientations in strategic thinking. Accompanying this effort there should be research and dialogue aimed at demonstrating that large benefits flow from the private provision of 'public' services and indirect privatisation in general.

Notes

1. For example, as of September 1991, almost two-thirds of the World Bank's 245 adjustment operations worldwide had public enterprise (PE) reform components. They were especially prevalent in Sub-Saharan Africa, where all but three of the 49 structural adjustment loans in that region had PE reform components as did two thirds of the 63 sectoral operations (World Bank, 1992).
2. Between June 1981 and December 1991, 182 Bank operations supported divestiture in 67 countries, half of them in Africa. Divestiture components exist in 70 per cent of all structural adjustment loans and in 40 per cent of all sectoral adjustment operations. There are also 60 technical assistance projects in

support of privatisation efforts, mostly in Sub-Saharan Africa and almost all of these aim at strengthening capacities to divest (see Kikeri *et al.*, 1992).

3. They say (pp. 16–17), 'Recent assessments of SOE reforms reveal that some improvements in performance have indeed taken place'. But the references they footnote for this assertion do not really contain much evidence in support. See also Ahmed Galal, 1991.

4. Thus in Ghana, for example, a 1985 study found 235 public enterprises, 181 of them wholly or majority-owned. But this count took the Ghana Industrial Holding Company, which had 20 component enterprises, as one state-owned enterprise. It also counted the State Hotels Company as one state-owned enterprise, though it had 10–12 hotels under its control. The National Industrial Company, composed of 20 operating units, was also counted as one enterprise.

5. In Zambia in October 1993, for example, the number of privatisations that had taken place was six, if the completed transaction is defined as approval by the privatisation committee, but only two if the handing over of payment is taken to mark completion of the sale.

6. See Sherif, 1993, and the consultant report by Davis on which it draws; and Government of Ghana, 1991. After 1993, divestiture activity picked up mainly as a result of the sale of the Ashanti Goldfields.

7. See World Bank, 1988; and Berg and Associates, 1990. Since 1992 the pace of divestiture has quickened.

8. The May 1989, *World Development* 'Special Issue on Privatisation' is illustrative. Very few of the articles in that volume manifest an enthusiastic analytic embrace of divestiture. Most beat on the point that efficiency of resource use should be the objective and that what matters for efficiency is competitive markets, not ownership. That was the dominant theme in the literature until very recently. The recent Bank-financed study on welfare impacts of 12 privatisation may begin to tilt the analytic balance toward recognition of the importance of ownership (see Galal, *et al.*, 1992; the Kikeri *et al.*, 1992, paper on privatisation lessons also is clearer on this point than earlier World Bank statements). But the tendency to downgrade ownership relations probably remains the dominant theme in thinking about privatisation.

9. The issue has arisen with Kikuyu in Kenya and Bamileke in Cameroon. In the latter case, government recently pulled back from a near sale of aircraft because of the ethnic origin of the potential buyer.
10. As of approximately the end of 1991, the World Bank's adjustment loans to Sub-Saharan Africa contained 864 public enterprise reform conditionalities, of which almost 20 per cent related to divestiture. (World Bank, 1992, p. 90).
11. A representative of the Cargill Corporation, an American agri-business firm, made some interesting remarks on this score at a recent conference.

> We've looked into the cotton ginning business [in Tanzania], [and] were offered the opportunity to bid on one cotton ginnery ... out of a total of 21 or 22. Now, we did not want to own 21 or 22 ... We'd be happy with one (or) two. But the real basis is it's the rules by which we're allowed to operate that one ginnery ... If we're told that we can only buy in a certain region because it belongs to certain co-operative society, and we're not allowed to buy across borders, or we're not allowed to pay the farmer the price that cotton is worth on the world market, then it does not matter whether we own one ginnery, or 22 ginneries. The privatisation of the groundnut processing marketing board in Gambia is (another) example. If we were to become involved in processing groundnuts, we would not necessarily want to run up-country stores. We would not necessarily want to run research stations. We would not necessarily want to run the Gambia River Transport Company. But ... there seems to be a reluctance to set aside what should be available to the private sector and what should be the responsibility of government or parastatals ...
>
> In Africa we tend to feel that the rules may change tomorrow or the day after and that we're not part of that process of discussion ... I think a good example (of the level playing field problem) ... is in Zimbabwe. I question whether Zimbabwe needs five official maize mills. A country of Zimbabwe's size probably need one, but if you've got five friends and you don't want to upset four

of them, then I suspect you support five of them and assume that you're not going to become friendly with number six or number seven. So a level playing field just means being part of a decision-making process. If we're committing ourselves to becoming involved in a business sector, an industry, a commodity, then our point of view should be as important as the other people involved. Not more so and not less so, but certainly equally so. And in lots of the ... countries in Africa that just is not the case. (Maynard, 1992)

12. Another set of privatisation instruments, not discussed here, consists of policies, programmes, or techniques to induce new private financing and production of goods or delivery of services now exclusively or mainly in the public sector. These are numerous and varied. They include the many varieties of Build-Own-Operate (BOO) schemes for inducing private investment in infrastructure; and self-help, volunteerism, and locally financed investment (see Berg and McDermott, 1990). These fall outside the mandate of the present study, which focuses on privatisation of existing state assets or activities.

13. In Singapore in 1984 government dental clinics were leased to young dental officers, to prepare them for running their own practices, see Low, 1988.

14. France is the leading user of leasing in water and other services; concession and *affermage* variants provide a substantial share of these and other municipal services in that country. A study of 220 French cities with more than 30,000 inhabitants found that, in 1988, the following percentages of the indicated services were privately operated, mainly under concession or *affermage* contracts that transferred risk to the operator and tied remuneration to performance: water supply, 66 per cent; water treatment, 29 per cent; solid waste collection, 45 per cent; solid waste treatment, 77 per cent; and urban transport, 53 per cent (Lecat, 1991).

15. The public water company in Santiago began this policy in 1977. Meter reading, billing, maintenance, vehicle leasing, and other services are contracted out after competitive bids and on short-term contracts (1–2 years). The Santiago water supply

operations are said to be among the most efficient in Latin America (Triche, 1992).

16. See Cointreau-Levine, 1992. The sources of greater efficiency are said to be smaller and younger crews, lower absenteeism, lower wages, lower benefits, more flexible scheduling, efficient vehicle routing, better designed vehicles, managerial incentives, faster repairs, vehicle standardisation, and competition.

17. In Colombia, for example, groups of 10–14 men carry out routine manual maintenance on 50 kilometre stretches of rural road. They are organised as co-operatives, contract with the Ministry of Public Works for a year at a time, and provide their own tools, relying on the ministry to provide on-site materials and equipment. There were 28 such organisations in 1984. In 1990 they numbered 362, with 4,500 associates maintaining 20,000 kilometres of road at costs estimated to be half those of force account equivalents (Gyamfi and Guillermo, 1992).

18. See Shaik and Minovi (1994) and World Bank (1995). These studies inventoried some 200 management contracts in development countries. Most were in Africa. Two thirds of the contracts were found to have been 'successful', measured by changes in profitability and productivity.

19. In Kinshasa, at least until the late 1980s, a private company collected trash in garbage trucks and brought it to the landfill. High income areas were served this way, at high cost. Poorer areas of the city were served differently. Scores of independent trash collectors took solid waste to a dump, using small capacity carts that were rented from their owners. The quality of service obviously differed, but costs of the low technology solution were a tiny fraction of those required by the 'modern' solution (World Bank, 1988).

20. See Triche, 1990 and Kessides, 1993. Triche notes in a later paper than some problems have arisen. Delay in purchase of urgently needed equipment, a SONEG responsibility, has impaired the financial performance of SEEG (Triche, 1992).

In Guinea Bissau, Electricité de France worked for two years under a technical assistance contract with the power and water company (EAGB), which was then revised to give EDF operating responsibility under a performance incentive scheme. The arrangement is too recent to assess. (Triche, 1992).

21. This is an interesting example of economies of scope in management contracting. The contractor's experience in managing the water supply operation facilitated its entry into the related activities in drainage and sewage.

22. See Bartone, *et al.*, 1990. Cointreau-Levine notes that in Lagos there are some 100 private contractors, less than 10 of whom have more than five vehicles. After five years of open competition among private collectors, the Lagos State Waste Disposal Board divided the city into sones and gave contracts to selected contractors to collect industrial waste from large generators in these sones. The system was abandoned in 1991. Corruption seems to have brought it down. The LSWB operated its own trucks in the same areas to collect waste from small generators and government agencies. Apparently, some contractors bribed LSWB crews to serve their (private) customers. Also, some contractors reportedly obtained spare parts illicitly, from the LSWB warehouses. Complaints of unlawful dumping also were heard. (Cointreau-Levine, pp. 31–32).

   These papers and others cite studies that demonstrate the much greater efficiency of private waste collection and disposal in cities of the industrialised world. Experience in Brazil and Turkey is said to confirm this finding (see Savas, 1987 and Leite, 1989). Also cited is Schertenleib and Triche, 1989.

23. The experiment apparently failed. Details are sketchy. It seems that the General Manager of the railway and the head of the service company conspired to fix prices at high levels. Also, no effort was made to reduce the pre-existing work force, so economies could not have been realised in any case.

24. Each maintains 1.3 to 1.5 kilometres of road, using simple tools. Some 7,000 such lengthmen now maintain 10,000 kilometres of rural access road in 28 of the country's 46 districts. They work under 'unit price' contracts of 3 to 12 months for specified maintenance activities. They work on roads close to their home, usually 3 to 5 days a week, are provided with hand tools, and supervised regularly (Miquel and Condron, 1991).

References

Adam, C.S. and W.P. Cavendish (1990) 'Can Privatisation Succeed? Economic Structure and Programme Design in Eight Commonwealth Countries', draft paper, Queen Elizabeth House, Oxford University, July.

Bartone, C., J. Bernstein and F. Wright (1990) 'Investments in Solid Waste Management. Opportunities for Environmental Improvement', INUD, WPS No. 405, Washington DC: World Bank.

Berg, E. (1990) 'Comment on W. McCleary, 'The Design and Implementation of Conditionality in Adjustment Programmes'', in V. Thomas (ed.) *The Experience of Adjustment Lending*, Washington DC: World Bank.

Berg, E. and Associates (1990) 'Adjustment Postponed: Economic Policy Reform in Senegal in the 1980s', prepared for USAID.

Berg, E. and A. McDermott (1990) 'Financing New Investment in Infrastructure in Developing Countries', prepared for the World Bank Infrastructure Department, Development Alternatives, Inc..

Berg, E. and M. Shirley (1987) 'Divestiture in Developing Countries', Discussion Paper, Washington DC: World Bank.

Bergeron, I. (1991) 'Privatisation Through Leasing: the Togo Steel Case', in R. Ramamurti and R. Vernon (eds) *Privatisation and Control of State-Owned Enterprises*, Economic Development Institute of the World Bank.

Brooke, M. (1985) *Selling Management Services Contracts in International Business*, London.

Budin, K.-J. (1992) 'Opportunities for and Role and Modalities of Private-Sector Participation in Railway Operations in Sub-Saharan Africa', Sub-Saharan Africa Transportation Programme, Railway Management Component, Washington DC: World Bank.

Centre on Transnational Corporations (1983) *Management Contracts in Developing Countries: an Analysis of their Substantive Provisions*, New York: United Nations.

Cointreau-Levine, S. (1992) 'Private Sector Participation in Municipal Solid Waste Services in Developing Countries', paper prepared for INURD, World Bank.

Cook, P. and C. Kirkpatrick (1990) 'Privatisation in Less Developed Countries: an Overview', in P. Cook and C. Kirkpatrick (eds) *Privatisation in Less Developed Countries*, London.

Donahue, J. (1991) *The Privatisation Decision*.

Electricité de France International (1992) 'Power Utility Management by Performance Contracting', prepared for World Bank Seminar.

Galal, A. (1991) 'Public Enterprise Reform', World Bank Discussion Paper No. 119, Washington DC: World Bank.

Galal, A., L. Jones, P. Tandon, and I. Vogelsang (1992) 'The Welfare Consequences of Selling Public Enterprises, Summary Volume', Washington DC: World Bank.

Government of Ghana (1991) 'Public Enterprise Sector Review', Vol. I, Main Report.

— (1992) 'Report for 1992', Divestiture Implementation Committee, Appendix A.

Gyamfi, R. and R. Guillermo (1992) 'Infrastructure Maintenance in LAC: the Costs of Neglect and Options for Improvement, Routine Maintenance by Contract', Vol. 5, Annex 5, LAC Technical Department, Washington DC: World Bank.

Kessides, C. (1993) 'Institutional Arrangements for the Provision of Infrastructure: a Framework for Analysis and Decision-Making', INUTD, Washington DC: World Bank.

Kikeri, S. (1989) 'Bank Lending for Divestiture: a Review of Experience', prepared for the World Bank's Conference on Institutional Development, December 14–15, Washington DC.

Kikeri, S., J. Nellis and M. Shirley (1992) *Privatisation: the Lessons of Experience*, Washington DC: World Bank.

Lantran, J.M. and R. Lebussy (1991) 'Setting Up a Plant Pool. Contracting Out Road Maintenance Activities', Volume III, Sub-Saharan Africa Transport Policy Programme, Africa Region, Washington DC: World Bank.

Lantran, J.M. (1990) 'Developing Domestic Contractors for Road Maintenance in Africa', Washington DC: World Bank and ECA.

Lecat, J.J. (1991) 'An Overview of the French Concession System: a Mechanism for Private Sector Provision of Public Works and Services', draft paper prepared for the World Bank.

Leite, L.C. (1989) 'Private and Public Services: Different Approaches to Solid Waste Management in Sao Paolo and Rio de Janeiro', unpublished INURD paper.

Lister, S. and M. Stevens (1992) 'Aid Coordination and Management', draft paper, World Bank.

Maynard, M. (1992) Comments in EPAT/Winrock International, *Agricultural Transformation in Africa*, proceedings of a Round Table Discussion, Baltimore, pp. 110–12.

Miquel, S. and J. Condron (1991) 'Assessment of Road Maintenance by Contract', Report INU 91, Washington DC: World Bank.

Moyer, N.E. and L.S. Thompson (1992) 'Options for Reshaping the Railway', WPS 926, Infrastructure and Urban Development Department, Washington DC: World Bank.

Operations Evaluation Department (1992) 'World Bank Structural and Sectoral Adjustment Operations: the Second OED Overview', Washington DC: World Bank.

République de Guinée (1991) *Etude de la Politique de Désengagement de l'Etat*, Ministère du Plan et de la Coopération Internationale, September.

République de Zaire, Office des Routes, *Rapport Annuel 1991*.

Savas, E.S. (1987) *Privatisation*, Chatham House.

Schertenleib, R. and T. Triche (1989) 'Non-Government Delivery of Urban Solid Waste Services', draft INUWS paper.

Scurfield, R. (1992) INUTD, 'Port Privatisation', draft paper.

Seager, P. and R. Fieldson (1984) 'Public Tractor Hire Schemes in Developing Countries', Agriculture and Rural Development Department, Discussion Paper No. 30, Washington DC: World Bank.

Shaik, A.H. and M. Minovi (1994) 'Management Contracts: a Review of International Experience', Background Paper, Policy Research Department, Washington DC: World Bank,.

Sherif, K.F. (1993) 'Regional Study on Public Enterprise Reform and Privatisation in Africa', draft, World Bank.

Shirley, M. and J. Nellis (1991) *Public Enterprise Reform: the Lessons of Experience*, Economic Development Institute, Washington DC: World Bank.

Stewart, F. S. Lal and S. Wangwe (1992) 'Alternative Development Strategies: an Overview', in F. Stewart, S. Lal and S. Wangwe (eds) *Alternative Development Strategies in Africa*, London.

Susungi, N.N. (1988) 'The Caveats on Privatisation as an Instrument of Structural Adjustment in Africa', a research paper of the African Development Bank Group.

Teplits-Semblitsky, W. (1990) 'Regulation, Deregulation, or Reregulation – What is Needed in the LDCs Power Sector?', Energy Division, Washington DC: World Bank.

Thompson, L. (undated) 'Increasing the Role of the Private Sector in Railway Transport'.

Triche, T. (1992) 'Experience with Private Sector Participation in Urban Water Supply and Sewage', draft paper, World Bank.

— (1992) 'Nigeria: PSP in Infrastructure; Urban Water Supply Subsector Report', draft.

— (1990) 'Private Participation in the Delivery of Guinea's Water Supply Services', WPS No. 477, Washington DC: World Bank.

Umali, D.L. *et al.* (1992) 'The Balance between Public and Private Sector Activities in the Delivery of Livestock Services', Discussion Paper No. 163, Washington DC: World Bank.

United Nations/Economic Commission for Africa (1991) *African Alternative Framework to Structural Adjustment for Socio-Economic Recovery and Transformation, a Popular Version*, Addis Ababa.

Vuylsteke, C., H. Nankani, R. Candoy-Sekse and A. Ruis-Palmer (1988) *Techniques of Privatisation of State-Owned Enterprises*, Washington DC: World Bank.

World Bank (1995) *Bureaucrats in Business: the Economics and Politics of Government Ownership*, Washington DC: World Bank.

— (1992) 'World Bank Structural and Sectoral Adjustment Operations: the Second OED Review', Operations Evaluation Department, Report No. 10870.

— (1988) 'Zaire. Urban Sector Mission Report', Vol. 5 Annex 5, Report # 6390–SR.

— (1988) 'Senegal: Parapublic Sector Review', Washington DC: World Bank.

World Development (1989) Special Issue on Privatisation.

7 Privatisation in Sub-Saharan Africa: Issues in Regulation and the Macroeconomics of Transition

Christopher S. Adam

1. Introduction

More than a decade after first appearing on the agenda, privatisation in Sub-Saharan Africa remains an elusive goal. Despite compelling evidence from other developed and developing countries that privatisation is viable and capable of injecting dynamism into previously *dirigiste* economies, most surveys reveal African privatisation programmes to be narrow in scope, subject to reversal and delay, and extremely limited in their impact as measured by almost any criteria (for example World Bank, 1988; Adam, *et al.* 1992; and Kikeri, *et al.* 1992). Estimates of the number of successful sales vary widely by virtue of the definitions used,[1] but even the most comprehensive studies find that less than 15 per cent of African state-owned enterprises (SOEs) have been privatised in the last decade (Berg, 1996, p. 6), while the proceeds from privatisation have been negligible when measured as a proportion of national income or government revenue. Even in Guinea, which has carried out one of the most extensive programme in Sub-Saharan Africa, total proceeds from privatisation have constituted only 5 per cent of GDP (Kikeri, *et al.* 1992). This slow progress is all the more alarming in the light of considerable donor support for privatisation. Moreover, this lack of progress is also conspicuous relative to other developing economies in Latin America, the Caribbean, South East Asia and, in particular, China and the former communist bloc. In many cases the initial conditions faced by these economies – such as the large and inefficient SOE sector, underdeveloped capital markets, distorted macroeconomic prices and political hostility to privatisation – were common. Yet while in other regions these conditions had only a transitory effect on privatisation,[2] in Africa the same initial conditions seem to have had represented a greater constraint to privatisation. The African continent remains dominated by public sector ownership and operation, and has yet to see any marked growth in new private sector operations either through new investment or through privatisation.[3]

Any analysis of privatisation in Sub-Saharan Africa must address the following question: what is unique about the African environment that can explain the slow rate of progress? Three types of explanation are typically advanced. The first concentrates on the political economy of privatisation and the conflict between privatisation and the role of SOEs as instruments of patronage. This argument is particularly relevant in the case of many Sub-Saharan African countries where the political elite have often not emerged from the ranks of economically powerful groups and therefore have relied heavily on state enterprises to buttress political with economic power and to spread the gains from the control of economic resources to their political constituency. Privatisation, often externally promoted, thus represented a challenge to this approach and in doing so rallied these powerful political groups to form blocking coalitions, often with the support of the unions representing the employees of SOEs.

While this argument seems to explain events in some countries,[4] a larger body of evidence suggests that political opposition to privatisation is not overwhelming. On the contrary, when the SOE sector ceases to provide an efficient mechanism for patronage, there tends to be strong support for privatisation from amongst the political elite, not least when it may be expected to benefit from control over the process of asset sales. The evolution of the privatisation programme in Malaysia provides a good example of this kind of transition. There the SOE sector grew rapidly as the centrepiece of the New Economic Programme and became the principal mechanism for employment and patronage throughout the 1970s. By the mid-1980s, however, the sector had become sclerotic and inefficient, and far from representing an abandonment of its commitment to positive discrimination, privatisation offered the government a mechanism for rehabilitating its distributional objectives. Through a programme of public asset sales in which shares were issued on the primary market at a heavy discount to Bumiputera[5] individuals and companies, combined with high secondary market demand, substantial capital gains were realised by these groups, thereby perpetuating the government's objectives. Similar mechanisms have been used in the privatisation programmes in Jamaica and Sri Lanka, for example, while in Africa the programmes in both Malawi and Zambia have enjoyed high-level political support (see Adam, *et al.* 1992, for details).

The second set of arguments, which may be referred to as structuralist, derive from the premise that since African economies are so small and narrowly based, market size alone limits the scope for a competitive private sector. For example, even in a fully liberalised regime, the presence of high transport costs will render large sections of the economy immune to external competition and thus to the pressures of price competition which privatisation is often expected to promote. Faced with market imperfections of this kind, it is argued, public ownership supported by regulation in defence of welfare objectives is a superior mode of operation to private monopoly.

Again, however, these arguments seem incomplete. While cases do exist where non-competitive market characteristics prevail, the extent of pure natural monopoly is relatively narrow and is narrowing. As Kessides (1993) argues, technological developments have played an important role not only in altering the structure of production, and thereby reducing minimum efficient size, but communications technology has also reduced transport costs and thereby increased opportunities for market penetration.

The third set of arguments emphasise transitional issues and are well reflected in the paper by Elliot Berg. He acknowledges the basic structuralist argument, but suggests that such constraints are weakening over time. Consequently, he argues, although privatisation has been very slow, the causes of the slowness are understood and, moreover, are readily addressed. Berg's assessment of the history of privatisation in Sub-Saharan Africa identifies four factors which have retarded progress, but which, due to successful macroeconomic reforms elsewhere in the economy, and through improved programme design and management, are rapidly disappearing. First, structural constraints to privatisation, such as the small size of the indigenous private sector and low levels of aggregate savings, are being eased as programmes of stabilisation and liberalisation establish new relative prices which sustain macroeconomic balance and promote competition, principally in the financial sector. Therefore as income levels and savings start to recover, privatisation programmes in Africa may be expected to pick up speed.

The second factor likely to lead to more rapid privatisation in the future is a side-effect of slow macroeconomic progress, namely the benefits accruing from lessons and experiences of a decade of privatisation elsewhere in world. These lessons are now well documented and can be readily synthesised to improve programme management. Contributing to this is the fact that the 1980s have also witnessed a 'silent revolution' in the perceptions of policy makers regarding the role of the state which has resulted in the almost complete evaporation of ideological opposition to privatisation. In this environment, the lessons from experience are likely to be rapidly assimilated.

Third, Berg identifies the problems of soft budget constraints as 'one of the most fundamental reasons for slow privatisation' (p. 20). He argues that, due to weaknesses in donor enforcement, aid flows in support of SOE reform in the past meant that structural reform to the industrial sector was often delayed rather than promoted. This was particularly true when aid was used to recapitalise financial institutions, whose own soft budget constraints removed the incentive to demand financial reform of ailing SOEs. Poor aid management therefore discouraged privatisation. However, there is an assumption in Berg's paper that the switch in emphasis towards programme aid supported by macroeconomic conditionality has helped to ease the problem of ineffective aid administration.

Finally, an important element of Berg's argument is that, given the lack of developed asset markets, privatisation programmes in Sub-Saharan Africa have been held back by the unduly heavy reliance on full divestiture as the principal instrument of privatisation. Given the structural weaknesses of African economies and their capital markets, public share issues are most likely to be subject to problems and delay. Berg therefore urges wider use of non-traditional privatisation methods including deregulation, management contracting, asset leasing, and franchising of monopoly rights.[6]

This final observation would command support from all quarters, as it is clear that large-scale divestiture will certainly not provide the solution to the privatisation *impasse* in Africa, while evidence is beginning to emerge that the use of non-traditional instruments is beginning to generate positive results (pp. 19–34).

The thrust of the Berg analysis is, therefore, that while many of the constraints to privatisation are currently binding, they can be expected to ease over time. In the case of structural constraints, through the process of macroeconomic liberalisation; in terms of incentives to reform, through external sanctions enforced by tighter donor conditionality; and in terms of efficiency and speed of reform, through the re-orientation of programme design from full-blown divestiture towards greater use of non-traditional means of divestiture.

Elliot Berg's recommendations address many of the key constraints facing African economies, but they tend to downplay two important issues that I shall address in this paper. First, there is an implicit assumption that the structural constraints to privatisation reflect macroeconomic policy failures arising from state control. As a consequence, with continuing macroeconomic reform, these constraints are expected to diminish and therefore the focus of Berg's analysis is avowedly microeconomic, concerned only with issues of internal efficiency. However, one of the legacies of three decades of state control is that macroeconomic policy failures have created the conditions through which many markets are now susceptible to strategic entry-deterring behaviour by large incumbent enterprises, which in many cases are the state-owned enterprises. Too rapid privatisation, especially in the face of weak regulatory capacity of government, may entrench the monopolistic behaviour of SOEs. The second issue concerns the macroeconomics of transition, and in particular the consequences for privatisation of the structure of the inherited capital stock and the effect of financial liberalisation on asset accumulation.[7] The former issue therefore questions the wisdom of rapid privatisation when viewed from a welfare perspective; the latter considers why privatisation may not even be feasible during the process of macroeconomic transition. Sections 2 and 3 of the paper will develop these theoretical ideas while Section 4 reviews the (limited) evidence – principally from Zambia – to illustrate the scope of the problem. Section 5 concludes with some policy implications.

2. Microeconomic Issues: Markets and Regulation

In this section I shall discuss why SOE-dominated sectors in transitional economies may be unusually prone to welfare-reducing market imperfections. The extent to which private market solutions provide for efficient resource allocation in any market will depend on the nature of the good in question, the conditions of production, and the nature of demand. Pure private goods are most efficiently allocated by market mechanisms, but non-market allocation may be more relevant for pure public goods, common resource goods and toll goods where consumption is non-rivalrous and exclusion from the market is difficult. In addition, if production is characterised by natural monopoly, then free-market allocations will not necessarily be efficient. Allied to this, if the provision of services (such as telecommunications) requires high levels of co-ordination, public or quasi-public control and regulation may be required. Third, the efficiency of the market will depend on the nature of demand. In particular, the absence of substitutes or high costs of substitution will generate low price elasticities over the relevant consumption range and thereby increase opportunities for monopoly pricing. Finally, the elasticity of demand will also be a function of the volume and cost of information available to the consumer.

Kessides (1993) suggests that

> for a large number of countries the realm of economic activity in which public intervention is required is narrower than once believed and that where it is warranted, the public role can often be exerted through less distorting policy instruments than those traditionally used. (p. 3)

The relevant question here is whether this conclusion holds for African economies in transition and, if not, what implications does this have for the scope and form of privatisation? At one level it is factually correct that in many African economies a greater proportion of activity is state-controlled than elsewhere. For example, the utility sector is invariably dominated by SOEs operating under conditions of natural monopoly and that SOEs have always been the sole provider of public or common-pool goods. Floyd *et al.* (1984), for example, claim that in the 1970s, while 60 per cent of utility provision in Asia and Latin America was by the public sector, the comparable figure for Africa was 86 per cent. In addition, since African income levels are comparatively low, substitute sources of supply tend to be fewer, information is relatively costly, and central co-ordination capacity more limited than elsewhere in the developing world. Options for (co-ordinated) private provision of traditionally public goods may therefore be more limited, at least in the medium term.

This conclusion is not particularly controversial. Of greater interest, however, is the wide range of activities currently undertaken by the SOE sector which, in general, could be expected to be more efficiently undertaken under private ownership and where privatisation would consequently be expected to be welfare-enhancing. This would include SOEs involved in agriculture, agro-processing, textiles, manufacturing, finance and other services. These sectors offer the greatest scope for efficiency gains as the combined effects of trade liberalisation and the deregulation of domestic markets may be expected to promote welfare-enhancing competition. The role of trade liberalisation is particularly important in Sub-Saharan Africa where high tariffs and quantitative restrictions used as instruments to support the balance of payments created high and severely distorted systems of protection. For example, average effective protection in the manufacturing sector during the 1980s was 40 per cent in Kenya, and 140 per cent in Malawi (Adam, *et al.*, 1992 Chapters 12 and 13), while in Zambia, by the mid-1980s, effective protection in manufacturing averaged around 160 per cent with average nominal protection of 35 per cent (World Bank, 1984). Against such a background of high protection, trade liberalisation may be expected to increase the potential for import penetration and thus competition.

Trade liberalisation on its own is, however, neither necessary nor sufficient for competition to emerge. On the one hand, other domestic producers can provide competition even if market penetration by imports is low. On the other, the advantages accruing to incumbent firms in a market may still deny competition even if explicit barriers to entry and competition are removed. The argument I wish to develop here is that even in markets that are, in principle, competitive and open to imports, the legacy of state ownership places SOEs in a uniquely powerful position to thwart the emergence of competition, at least during the period of transition. Although monopoly power was created in the past through the use of legislative instruments, the removal of legislative barriers will not necessarily eliminate the capacity of the SOE (or former SOEs) to prevent competition because of the firms' ability to make use of instruments and advantages acquired during the control period. Consequently, for many sectors in which SOEs have a significant presence, strategic entry deterring behaviour on the part of incumbent firms may be widespread. The most obvious instruments available to incumbent SOEs to limit competition and maintain their monopolistic position include: preferential location and access to transport linkages which will lower their c.i.f. costs relative to potential competitors; access to spare productive capacity which may be rapidly utilised to flood the market in response to new entrants; access to subsidised credit to allow them to underprice potential market entrants; the maintenance of capital intensive production to blockade small-scale entrants; and the control over supply and distribution networks.[8] If combined with new private-sector management, and generous debt write-offs and financial restructuring carried out prior to sale, the strategic dominance of privatised SOEs may be accentuated.

Imperfect Markets, Regulation and Co-ordination

Therefore, while trade liberalisation and other competition enhancing reforms will extend the domain of marketability within the economy, for a large component of the former SOE sector market dominance is likely to remain (even given considerable technological change in the production possibilities for public and natural monopoly goods). Obviously this problem is most likely to materialise if SOEs dominate their markets. Again, the evidence from Kenya and Malawi, where respectively 65 per cent and 89 per cent of the manufacturing sector is classified as oligopolistic or monopolistic and where the dominant firm or firms are state-owned, is indicative of the problem (World Bank, 1989). In such circumstances, market-based outcomes will not necessarily be optimal and thus an important public policy issue emerges: what are the costs and benefits of limiting the scope for market dominance? To address this problem, the government must confront the choice between two second-best outcomes both of which have welfare losses associated with their agency characteristics.[9] It can either sell the monopolistic enterprise and attempt to regulate the private firm, or it can maintain the enterprise in public ownership and accept along with this the incentive problems associated with public sector management. The solution to the problem depends principally on the information flow concerning market conditions; the regulatory capacity of government; and the capacity of the private sector owners to indulge in strategic behaviour. Clearly, when the government has good information on the structure of the market (so that it can identify strategic behaviour on the part of the firm), and when it has adequate regulatory capacity, then private ownership in association with an anti-monopoly regulatory regime is the preferred option. In general, given the poor performance of SOEs in most economies and the standard litany of problems about public management, it would be expected that the efficiency losses due to public ownership are comparatively large, so that private ownership with the risk of partial regulatory capture is still preferable to public ownership. However, in circumstances where government's regulatory capacity is limited, and where information flows are weak, the costs of regulatory capture by the private sector may be significant and may even outweigh the costs of the agency problems associated with public ownership.[10] While evidence cannot be readily adduced on this issue, since in many cases the absence of privatisation means we cannot observe strategic behaviour in action, the more important consideration is a dynamic one. It seems reasonable to argue that, while in the medium term private sector operation with efficient regulation will produce the most efficient outcome, long-run post-privatisation performance will depend heavily on the manner in which the transition to regulated private enterprise is executed. Rapid privatisation in the presence of regulatory deficiencies increases the likelihood that the monopoly advantages of the incumbent firm are locked in, thereby reducing the gains to privatisation.

Do African economies have a regulatory deficiency? At first sight it may be argued that the practice of control and regulation are common features of African economies – indeed in some sense it is their defining characteristic. In Zambia, for example, the latter years of the Second Republic coincided with the apogee of regulation: controls existed over consumer prices for a wide range of goods, over import prices (and quantities), over credit and factor prices. These were implemented and monitored by institutions such as the Prices and Incomes Commission, and the Foreign Exchange Management Committee which developed considerable expertise in administering controls. However, the unifying characteristic in these types of control was that they were operated by fiat under a general anti-competition approach to regulation. The challenge facing governments considering privatisation is to switch from this anticompetitive stance to a regulatory regime based on competition-promoting regulation operated at arms length through market-based instruments. There is evidence that countries with traditions of non-market control are capable of achieving this transition. For example, in the late 1980s the governments of both Kenya and Jamaica introduced instruments of competition policy designed to check predatory pricing and other forms of strategic behaviour and to provide for a non-interventionist regulatory framework.[11] Despite these few exceptions, however, competition policy and the development of a regulatory framework has been accorded a relatively low priority, both by governments and the donor community, compared to the process of asset sales and the removal of the existing institutions of the control structure. We shall return to this issue in section 5.

This section has suggested why privatisation under conditions of transition and underdeveloped regulatory capacity may at best reduce, and at worst jeopardise, the potential welfare gains from privatisation. It does not however explain why sales of SOEs in transitional economies are occurring at such a slow rate. This is particularly surprising, not least because it may be expected that regulatory weaknesses mean that rich pickings are on offer to investors who acquire assets before a sound regulatory framework is established. Elliot Berg, amongst others, argues that the low level of domestic savings constitutes the major constraint, but I wish to argue that in addition to the savings constraint there is a more pervasive problem related to the nature of the embodied capital stock of economies moving away from 'African socialism'.

3. Macroeconomic Issues:
Investment, Uncertainty and Liberalisation

Privatisation is the sale to the private sector of the profit stream accruing from the assets that comprise the SOE. Using the cost-benefit framework of Jones *et al.* (1991), the decision facing a welfare-maximising government considering the sale of an asset can be described as follows. The change in welfare from the sale of an asset is given as:

(1) $\Delta W = V_{sp} - V_{sg} + Z(1 + \lambda_g - \lambda_p),$

where Z is the price at which the asset is sold, V_{sg} is the
(discounted) social value of the asset under continued government
operation, V_{sp} the (discounted) social value of the asset under
private ownership. The social valuations under public and private
ownership will incorporate all aspects of the operation of the asset
under the two ownership structures including the welfare costs and
benefits arising from the different principal-agent problems
discussed above. The valuations are thus the sum of the change in
consumer surplus, profits, the wage bill, competitive gains or losses,
and deadweight losses under the two forms of ownership. The
coefficients λ_g and λ_p are the shadow prices of liquidity in the hands
of government and the private sector respectively.[12] A welfare-
maximising government will sell the asset only if $\Delta W \geq 0$, in other
words when the right hand side of (1) is positive. Rearranging we
get the following condition for sale:

(2) $Z \geq \dfrac{(V_{sg} - V_{sp})}{(1 + \lambda_g - \lambda_p)} = Z_g.$

A welfare-maximising government will sell the asset if (2) holds,
which means that Z_g can be interpreted as the government supply
price for the asset. Notice that when the welfare consequences of the
cash transfer are neutral (ie, $\lambda_g = \lambda_p$) then $Z_g = V_{sg} - V_{sp}$ which is likely
to be negative. When liquidity has a relative premium in the hands
of government the supply price is lower and *vice versa* when
liquidity is more valuable in the hands of the private sector. The
private sector's purchase price is Z_p which is simply the discounted
private value of future profit streams.

   In general Z_p will be greater than Z_g and therefore a market will
exist for the sale, even though the eventual price cannot be
determined precisely as this will reflect the relative bargaining
strength of buyer and seller. Consequently, Jones *et al.* (1991) argue
that 'given the likelihood of a negative supply price (ie, $Z_g < 0$) a
considerable economic range for bargaining is likely' (p. 39). In
other words, if governments genuinely sell assets according to their
perceived economic supply price, then privatisation should occur.

Obviously, assets will not be sold if Z_g exceeds Z_p which will occur if the government sets too high a supply price by underestimating $V_{sp} - V_{sg}$ or overestimating $(\lambda_g - \lambda_p)$, or if the private sector's valuation of the asset is lower than the government's supply price. We consider each in turn, starting with the government supply price. The most obvious reason for too high a supply price is if government overvalues assets. As Berg notes 'asset valuations tend to be too high, too much dependent on historical cost or book value' (p. 11). In addition, however, governments often seek to sell assets prior to restructuring in the expectation that the private sector will restructure the asset more efficiently, but in adopting this strategy the government often underestimates the costs of restructuring by the private sector. Thirdly, even if governments can value assets according to their true economic costs, it may not be possible, for political reasons, to set the appropriate negative supply price for fears that charges of cronyism may be raised. For example, while it may be acceptable for debt write-offs to be considered prior to the sale of assets, it may not be politically acceptable for governments to sell assets at an explicit price of zero (or less). Thus Z_g may be a constrained supply price.

If the binding constraint to privatisation is that the supply price is too high, we would expect to observe either bids being rejected by the seller or, in the case of a government committed to privatisation, we would see governments actively lowering the supply price. *De facto*, the latter occurs with the adoption of auction-based or bidder-driven programmes, but even then it is common to find that there are no genuine bids whatsoever.[13] This would suggest that the constraint is a low demand price rather than too high a supply price. The issue that I wish to address in this section is why in fact the private sector demand price, Z_p, may itself be so low during the transition that no sale will be viable (even given the negative supply price). Before doing so it should be stressed that in this context Z_p is 'the price at which the buyer is indifferent between buying the enterprise and retaining their existing asset portfolio' (Jones, *et al.* p. 39). Z_p therefore needs to be viewed relative to the expected return on alternative assets available to the investor at the time of the privatisation.

The fundamental reason why Z_p may be low as a result of the transition from African socialism concerns the value of the inherited capital stock as the economy moves from a controlled to a liberalised regime. The capital stock embodied in the SOE sector reflects not only the relative price structure supported by the control regime of the socialist economy but also the preferential status of the SOEs under that regime. Quantitative rationing and preferential access to foreign exchange at official exchange rates represented a subsidy on imported capital equipment, while trade barriers and regulated market access dampened incentives to innovate or increase internal efficiency. Under the control regime, then, the SOE sector faced a preferential relative price vector for its inputs and a protected market for its output. Private sector involvement in the market, without removal of these macroeconomic distortions, would ensure that the asset composition of the former SOEs would remain optimal, but the monopoly rents accruing to preferential access under the control regime would be subject to competition by prospective private sector purchasers. In this context we would expect $Z_p > Z_g$, and privatisation would be 'feasible' if not socially desirable. In practice, however, the transition from African socialism involves the removal of protection through trade and exchange rate liberalisation, the elimination of debt underwriting facilities available to the SOEs, and the removal of legislative and other anti-competition measures. Consequently privatisation is typically accompanied by a broader dismantling of the control regime, in which case the removal of the implicit subsidy on imported capital will render the composition of the SOE capital stock sub-optimal. Without the previous capital stock subsidy, the stock of assets cannot be as profitable as before, given the new relative prices. The value of the SOE to the private buyer will thus fall, both in absolute terms and also relative to the rate of return on other assets in the economy which, following liberalisation, may include foreign assets and also, as we shall discuss below, high-yielding domestic financial assets. If distortions are large, and newly liberalised financial assets attractive, then Z_p may fall below Z_g so that no sale will occur.[14]

To summarise this argument, the process of transition may be expected to alter the macroeconomic environment to such an extent that the private sector's valuation of privatisation assets falls below the government supply price, even when the latter is negative. Trade liberalisation will involve alterations in relative prices against production of import-substitutes and in favour of the exportable sector. Since SOEs in general were the principal beneficiaries of the control regime and were concentrated in sheltered import-substituting sectors, the adverse effects of the resource shifts will fall disproportionately on SOEs. Profitability will decline and, at the margin, enterprises will no longer be viable. For such enterprises, Z_p will obviously fall dramatically. In addition, the removal of legislative and other controls on domestic competition, and the reform of the financial sector will eliminate the soft budget constraint which has traditionally allowed SOEs to operate beyond the point that they can use domestic resources efficiently. As a consequence it may be harder, paradoxically, to sell the SOEs in a liberalised environment than in a controlled environment.

There are two conditions under which sales may continue. The first is where the purchaser can, for whatever reason, negotiate explicit subsidies or other benefits which replicate the old effective relative prices and thereby return the asset to profitability at *current* relative prices. The second condition is when the asset stock can be changed rapidly and at low cost so as to take advantage of the new relative prices. The policy question then centres on the management of privatisation when SOEs may be viable under private ownership in the medium term, but where the short run effects of macroeconomic transition ensure that bids are not forthcoming.

It is this latter set of issues on which I wish to focus, with particular reference to the process of financial liberalisation, the role of aid, and finally the issues of the time-inconsistency, government reputation and policy credibility. Before doing so, it is important to note one issue concerning capital adjustment and employment. As we have seen, following liberalisation, the capital stock is inappropriate in terms of its composition and, in declining sectors, in terms of its level. Total factor demand, in the latter case, will fall and labour will necessarily be retrenched. In other sectors, though total factor demand may be constant or even growing, the absence of markets which provide tradeability of capital means that the costs of adjustment faced by enterprises to new demand conditions will fall disproportionately on labour, even though under new relative prices production may be expected to be relatively more labour intensive. If there is real wage stickiness (which is most likely to be present in the former SOE sectors which enjoyed high levels of staffing at relatively high real wages) this adjustment will occur predominantly through retrenchment even though it is the composition of the capital stock that is 'wrong'. If retrenchment is politically costly Z_p will obviously fall further.

Privatisation and Financial Liberalisation

Many programmes of privatisation in Africa are occurring in the
context of financial liberalisations, involving the liberalisation of
domestic interest rates, the abolition of capital controls, and the
development of local equity markets. Equity market development
is obviously an essential long-run counterpart to privatisation since
only with tradeability of property rights in the form of equity can
the corporate control function of equity be exercised. However,
possibly with the exception of Nigeria and Zimbabwe, Sub-Saharan
Africa does not have markets capable of handling large equity sales,
and the development of such markets is likely to be slow. In
extreme cases, equity market developments may even be retarded
by the sale of SOEs.[15] More importantly, other aspects of financial
liberalisation efforts may run counter to this medium term objective
and create a number of problems for privatisation. As Collier (this
volume) notes:

> the challenge for financial policy during transition, far from
> being to put in place reforms which contribute to growth, is
> to avoid the generation of shocks which dislocate it.

One potential dislocation arises from the high level of liquidity
preference on the part of the lending institutions. By comparative
standards, even during periods of high inflation, African financial
institutions have been comparatively liquid. Frequently this liquidity
is viewed as a symptom of policies of financial repression and it is
felt that interest rate liberalisation would allow excess funds to be
directed to lending to the private sector at higher interest rates,
raising the volume of real credit to the non-bank sector. In Africa
there is as yet little evidence of excess liquidity being converted into
term credit to the private sector. In many cases the reverse occurs
as the assets of the banking sector are becoming more liquid and are
increasingly dominated by government securities (see for example
Zimbabwe in 1992 and 1993 and Zambia from 1991 to 1993).
'Voluntary' credit rationing on the part of the financial institutions,
reflecting uncertainty about both the profitability of their borrowers
during the liberalisation phase and also about the future stance of
macroeconomic policy, is widespread. In these circumstances,
despite the freedom to set interest rates, banks' expected profits will
be maximised by holding lower-interest but capital-certain liquid

assets, such as government liabilities, rather than high-risk loans and advances to enterprises operating in new and unfamiliar circumstances. In this environment credit for SOE asset acquisition and/or asset restructuring is a particularly unattractive option relative to other forms of investment available to the banks. Moreover, due to the widespread use of government guarantees and other means of supporting SOE debt servicing, the SOEs will often have questionable credit ratings and no independent financial track-record. Thus the willingness of the financial sector to finance the asset restructuring required to support privatisation may be seriously undermined in the early stages of a financial liberalisation. The process of asset transformation therefore encounters a 'missing market' or information constraint: potential purchasers of SOEs require credit to finance restructuring because the capital structure is 'wrong', but banking institutions will not lend, precisely because the asset structure of the firm is wrong. Faced with these constraints, the demand price of the private sector for SOEs will be reduced even though the (restructured) enterprise may be viable.

Suppose, however, banks do lend to private investors to finance restructuring. Are there any sectoral differences in the type of enterprise able to secure credit? Collier (this volume) addresses this question in the context of the general issue of investment and financial liberalisation, but it can be applied as well to the question of privatisation. He argues that in the absence of a track record with which to assess creditworthiness, banking institutions will base their lending decisions of the break-up value of the already installed capital assets. In the context of SOEs this means basing a forward-looking lending policy on the current capital structure, i.e. that established under the pre-liberalisation control regime, even though this capital structure will be sub-optimal given post-liberalisation relative prices. Consequently, the enterprises with the highest likelihood of acquiring credit will be those which are intensive in imported capital, which are in fact those enterprises that, given the new relative prices, have the least efficient (i.e. most distorted) capital stock. By comparison, those enterprises most able to achieve efficient resource use at prevailing world prices are those with a lower imported capital–labour ratio. However, for the reasons just cited, these are the enterprises least likely to receive credit from the financial system.[16] If the same mechanism also applies to working capital, the problem is exacerbated since those firms for whom the marginal productivity of working capital is highest will be those most likely to be rationed in the credit market.

These concerns apply principally to firms in the domestic private sector relying on formal sector finance. Purchasers whose credit-worthiness and reputation are established in different markets will not face this form of rationing. There are two classes of potential investors here: the first are foreign investors, and the second are those residents who accumulated savings offshore by evading controls on foreign asset acquisition. As a consequence the privatisation process becomes biased towards sales to offshore investors or to domestic entrepreneurs who have access to accumulated earnings. From a macroeconomic perspective, asset sales to foreign investors, and in particular to domestic residents drawing down offshore balances may constitute an important capital account inflow, albeit with significant political costs.[17]

External Shocks, Uncertainty and Aid

So far we have argued that the inherited capital stock, the absence of equity markets, and voluntary credit rationing are important explanations for slow progress with privatisation. However a more general concern to the private sector is not just the current composition of capital, but the ease with which the composition of capital can change in response to external shocks. In shock-prone economies, the sector-specific capital (and human) assets typically embodied in SOEs may not provide attractive asset combinations to the private sector. In controlled regimes, the impact of external shocks is often mitigated by offsetting changes in trade or other policy instruments. Following liberalisation, however, the industrial sector will be more exposed to the full effect of external shocks.

The previous argument suggests that the SOE capital stock reflects not just a previously overvalued real exchange rate but also an environment where public policy has acted to shield the sector from the full effect of external shocks. When this implicit insurance falls away and the sector is exposed to shocks, the capital stock may be too sector-specific and illiquid.

One interesting aspect of this problems concerns the interaction of foreign aid and the process of transition. Elliot Berg has already indicated two possible channels through which aid can adversely affect privatisation. The first is the fiscal effect whereby aid postpones necessary fiscal adjustments, and the second is through the delay in meeting necessary financial portfolio corrections on the part of the financial institutions. These relate to the microeconomics of privatisation. An alternative effect may be through the macro-economics of aid. If aid were expected to be permanent the demand for non-tradeable goods and services would rise, appreciating the real exchange rate and causing a contraction in the non-boom tradeable sector. Depending on the distribution of SOEs between non-tradeable and the non-boom tradeable sector (ie the import substituting sector) the effects of a permanent aid boom may support or discourage privatisation. Most observers, including the potential purchasers, do not, however, expect aid flows to be permanent. If aid is expected to be temporary the initial relative price effects will be reversed when the aid flow returns to more normal levels (Collier and Gunning, 1992). If the SOE sector's output consisted principally of non-tradeables then the temporary real exchange rate effects of aid would temporarily produce favourable conditions for sale of SOEs. In reality, however, though SOEs dominate some non-tradeable sectors such as the utilities, they tend to be concentrated in tradeable sectors and therefore, short-run real exchange appreciations will have adverse effects on the sector by lowering the relative profitability of SOEs during the period of aid-financed transition. Thus aid flows which are perceived as temporary may then induce waiting behaviour by the private sector.

Country Specific Risk, Government Reputation and Policy Credibility

Acquisition of assets requires investors to take a view on the future direction of demand, supply and government policy. Faced with high levels of uncertainty, and the intrinsic time-inconsistency of privatisation,[18] the ability of investors to reverse their investment will be important: such are the functions of equity markets. In the absence of developed equity markets, non-marketable, sector-specific, assets will therefore carry a penalty reflecting uncertainty over the government's credibility, thereby reducing their value. Arguments concerning policy credibility were advanced by Adam, *et al.* (1992) in describing the very favourable terms gained by foreign firms in the Jamaican privatisation programme where guaranteed monopoly profits represented an insurance against future policy reversals by the Government of Jamaica (which at the time was burdened with a very poor reputation as a pro-private sector government). Similar problems of credibility exist in Sub-Saharan Africa, with the case of Zambia being apposite. Trade and exchange liberalisation commenced in 1985 but was dramatically reversed with the collapse of the foreign exchange auction in 1987 and the cancellation of the IMF programme. The programme was restarted in 1989 but again was subject to uncertainty in the run up to the elections in 1991. Even under the present regime, where the likelihood of wholesale policy reversal on privatisation *per se* is diminished, the SOE sector, particularly the utility/non-tradeable sector, remains susceptible to broader policy reversals and thus implicit taxation. For example, the erosion of the seigniorage capacity in recent years has forced excise and sales tax rate to levels higher than originally anticipated in policy statements.

It is important, however, to stress that this risk of policy reversal need not be malign but may simply arise from the government's response to external shocks (including changes in aid flows), from breakdowns in regulatory capacity, or to imperfect information on the impact of policy measures. A good example of the latter concerns the Zambia Investment Promotion Act which was promulgated in 1991 but was subsequently adjudged to be fiscally imprudent. Previous commitments to providing duty free imports on capital goods for new investment were therefore reversed. Investment decisions based on the expectation that the Act would remain in force were therefore now less profitable than they would otherwise have been. Similar concerns arise in the area of infrastructure where, as Kessides (1993) stressed, the key to successful market-based operation is the ability to combine the break-up of monopoly service provision into competitive units with the co-ordination of these now separate operations (linking individual generators to a grid or regulating access to public trunk facilities of down-stream operations etc). As with market regulation and competition policy, co-ordination of this type is non-trivial and, for many governments, an activity in which it has only limited experience. Faced with uncertainty as to the government's capacity to provide these co-ordination facilities, and given the cost to the operator of imperfect co-ordination, there must necessarily be a discount on the demand for SOEs subject to this kind of co-ordination.

By the same token, African economies in transition are prone to uncertainty about the emerging government's capacity to conduct effective arm's-length regulation. There are three components of a regulatory relationship: the regulator, the purchaser, and the market. Even setting aside the relationship between the regulatory authority and the government, in Africa the cards are stacked against efficient regulation. First, when markets are inherently imperfect, information flows concerning market conditions will be absent. Designing efficient regulatory contracts in such circumstances is notoriously hard, yet it is these type of market structures which prevail in transition economies.[19] Second, for the reasons noted above, the former SOE sector may be dominated by foreign investors whose human capital and financial resources relative to those of the government confer bargaining power on the private sector operator. Moreover, when asset sales proceeds only with the transfer of monopoly guarantees, the regulatory playing field will be far from level and inherently biased against the regulator. Third, governments tend to lack inherited regulatory capacity. It is true that such economies generally have a tradition of control and that significant public sector resources have been employed in operating controls, but arm's-length or market-based regulation capacity is underdeveloped. The mixed evidence on the success of developing efficient regulatory structures in economies where market information is good indicates the complexity of good regulatory design; where information is poor, and when economies are shock-prone (so that the public policy issues in regulation become significantly more complex), the design of efficient regulation is even more challenging. One consequence of this is that there may be only limited savings to government in terms of its SOE oversight function. More generally, however, it is in such conditions that markets are most vulnerable not just to regulatory capture but also to the threat of 'irrational' and 'incredible' policy response by the regulator.[20] Faced with such uncertainty, private sector investment choices will be biased away from assets most vulnerable to regulatory intervention, in other words the former SOE sector.

4. Zambia: an Illustration of Privatisation in Transition

We now turn to some evidence that may serve to support these
arguments, although, almost by definition, the evidence will be
limited and impressionistic. What is clear, however, is that the
issues discussed in connection with Zambia are echoed elsewhere
in Sub-Saharan Africa.[21] For most African economies, the post
Independence era was dominated by the rapid growth of public
intervention, and SOEs were important instruments in that intervention. SOEs were created (or acquired) for a variety of reasons,
but mostly in a relatively *ad hoc* fashion. Thus they owed their
existence to perceived failures in goods or factor markets; to
protectionist and nationalistic concerns; in response to concerns
about control of the 'commanding heights' of the economy; as a
means of employment generation; and, frequently, as a result of
rescue operations in which government acted as residual legatee to
failing private sector operations (whose failure was often due to the
structure of the macroeconomic control regime in the first place).
Finally, there was a class of enterprises for which governments
(through their venture capital agencies) provided credit at a time
when private credit was not forthcoming but which were never
fully weaned off the State. The SOE sector was therefore highly
heterogeneous and operated across a variety of market conditions.
Not only was it the dominant mode of production in the utilities
sector, in transport and the capital-intensive industrial sectors
(Floyd, *et al.*, 1984), but in the naturally more competitive sectors
such as manufacturing, SOEs enjoyed the protection of high tariff
and non-tariff barriers and preferential access to credit.

Many of these features were to be found in Zambia. The SOE
sector inherited in 1991 by the current MMD government was
amongst the largest in Sub-Saharan Africa. The sector traced its
origins to the early post-Independence period of the late 1960s
when, following the ideological commitment for state intervention
as outlined in President Kaunda's Mulungushi Declaration, the State
embarked on a programme of nationalisation of existing private
sector firms, including the major mining sector enterprises, and of
heavy public investment in new SOEs. By the mid-1980s the sector
accounted for 35 per cent of GDP, 13 per cent of total external debt,
almost 60 per cent of total investment, and 45 per cent of formal
sector employment, while net transfers to the sector totalled almost

10 per cent of total budget expenditure (World Bank, 1984). The sector (including companies where government did not have full equity) consisted of 145 enterprises, of which 130 fell under the control of the Zambia Industrial and Mining Corporation (ZIMCO), the parastatal holding company (Zambia Privatisation Agency Progress Report, 1992). Of the 20 or so non-ZIMCO SOEs the largest were Zambia Consolidated Copper Company (ZCCM) which was 60 per cent government owned, the oil sector SOEs (Indeni Petroleum Refineries, Tazama Pipelines and ZIMOIL), Zambia Airways, Zambia Railways, Zambia Electricity Supply Corporation and the Posts and Telecommunications Corporation. The ZIMCO companies were generally smaller, consisting of enterprises across the entire economy, but operating in sectors which were, at least in principle, tradeable. Thus ZIMCO had a presence in agriculture and agro-industry (10 per cent by number), manufacturing and non-copper mining (35 per cent) energy and transport (25 per cent) and services, real estate and finance (30 per cent). The distribution of SOEs by size and sector is given in Table 1. The majority of enterprises were established or were developed during a period of extremely high trade protection (explicit tariff levels averaged between 50 per cent and 150 per cent during the 1970s and early 1980s), and were predominantly import-substituting. As the beneficiaries of the foreign exchange allocation system, however, SOE production technologies were heavily import dependent.

The size classification in Table 1 is that used by the Zambian Privatisation Agency and relates mainly to asset and employment levels rather than by market share. However there is a close correlation between size and market concentration so that SOEs classified as medium or large often dominate their industrial sub-sections and in many cases enjoy monopoly positions (see McBrady, 1993). Though the majority of SOEs were small, averaging less that 50 employees, there was a sizeable number of large SOEs, accounting for the overwhelming proportion of the contribution of the SOE sector to the economy as a whole and dominating their sectors either by dint of legislative fiat, by natural monopoly, or through simple incumbent firm advantages. Thus SOEs were the dominant market participant in fertiliser production, sugar milling, brewing, maize milling, heavy manufacturing, cement production, tourism and finance as well as the utility sectors of transport, electricity, oil importing and refining and telecommunications.

Table 1:
Zambia SOEs by Size and Sector

Sector	Small	Medium	Large	Total
Agriculture	4	1	3	8
Agro-Industry	10	16	3	29
Mining	10	0	5	15
Manufacturing	17	3	3	23
Construction	4	2	1	7
Retail Services	12	1	5	18
Finance	11	1	3	15
Transport	11	2	6	19
Energy	2	1	5	8
Communications	0	1	1	2
Total	81	28	35	145

Source: Zambia Privatisation Agency (1992).

The SOE sector in Zambia consisted of three groups: the first was ZCCM which accounted for an average of 90 per cent of total Zambian export earnings. ZCCM is a significant net contributor to the budget (see Aron, 1992). The second group consisted of the major parastatal enterprises such as Zambia Airways whose losses were explicitly financed through the central government budget. Finally, the remainder of the sector which was only marginally financed by direct transfers from the government budget. For this sector fiscal transfers occurred in three other ways: through the preferential access to foreign exchange at the official exchange rate which for net purchasers of foreign exchange (virtually all SOEs except ZCCM) represented a significant fiscal transfer; through preferential access to domestic credit through the Zambia National Commercial Bank; and by enjoying protected monopoly positions in markets where government price control was widespread.

Table 2 summarises the limited data that exist for the industrial SOE sector: all data are based on the World Bank's *Industrial Policy and Performance* report, 1984. However the period from 1984 until the beginning of the current macroeconomic transition in 1989 did not witness any significant change in industrial structure. If anything, the events of that half decade probably increased the dominance of the SOE sector.

The public sector was particularly dominant in the manufacturing sector. Food processing was highly protected but relatively efficient, while manufacturing was less heavily protected but dramatically less efficient. Moreover the capital intensity of the manufacturing sector was increasing very dramatically. This growth rate is remarkable given that not only is it certainly higher than the rate of growth of output, but was occurring at a time when SOE employment levels were high and also rising. Although we do not have evidence of the composition of the capital stock this does seem to reflect the importance of the high level of implicit subsidy enjoyed on imported capital investment, a subsidy which was supported by low nominal and effective protection on imported capital goods, which were 8 per cent and 35 per cent respectively for the period covered in Table 2.

Table 2:
Zambian Manufacturing Sector:
SOE Market Share, Protection and Efficiency 1984

Sector	SOE Market Share	ERP	DRC	K/L Growth pa (1980–84)
Food processing	72%	166%	0.47	2%
Light manufacturing	55%	114%	1.60	15%
Heavy manufacturing	64%	44%	3.00	18%

Note: ERP = effective rate of protection; DRC = domestic resource cost; K/L = capital–labour ratio. Values of DRC greater than 1.00 imply inefficient use of resources.

Source: World Bank (1984).

Although not definitive, this evidence indicates substantial market dominance by SOEs in well-protected import-substituting sectors, with enterprises operating with an excessively high capital stock. The agro-industrial sector, which is the main non-copper export sector in Zambia, is the exception, being more efficient, less capital-intensive and less concentrated than other SOE dominated sectors.

The Zambian Privatisation

The Zambian privatisation programme was launched against the background of concerted stabilisation efforts designed to eliminate chronic macroeconomic incompatibility. In addition to exchange rate unification, the government embarked on programmes of trade liberalisation, tax harmonisation, fiscal reform, and financial liberalisation, a component of which was the establishment of a local equity market. The stabilisation effort was protracted and subject to frequent reversals: inflation remained high throughout the stabilisation period, reaching over 200 per cent year-on-year in 1991 and 1992. By the end of 1993, however, the primary budget deficit had been eliminated and domestic inflation had been dramatically reduced, but this was at the cost of a severe fiscal and credit squeeze. Real incomes were compressed and private savings were estimated to be around 12 per cent of GDP in 1993. Despite the liberalisation of lending rates, the financial sector has responded to the change in the control regime by increasing their liquidity so that by mid-1993 liquid assets of the banking sector (cash and government securities) averaged approximately 85 per cent of total deposits and evidence of voluntary credit rationing was widespread (Bank of Zambia).

In 1992, before stabilisation had been achieved, the government embarked on an ambitious programme of privatisation of all 145 SOEs (see also Due, 1994). The lateness of the reform programme in Zambia, which only began in earnest in 1991, meant that the programme of privatisation was established against a favourable domestic political environment: the incoming MMD government identified itself with the objective of reversing the *dirigisme* of the UNIP-led state control, and as a government it embraced the objectives of private enterprise and wider shareholder democracy. Thus, unlike countries such as Kenya, there has been significant (although not universal) support for privatisation. Under the auspices of the newly created Zambian Privatisation Agency (ZPA), an eleven-tranche sale programme was promulgated with the intention that all SOEs would be divested over a period of 5 years to 1998. An important feature of the programme was that although the ZPA carried out extensive valuation exercises, the policy for privatisation was based on a bidder-led approach with the Agency accepting any offers from the private sector. By mid-1993, however, only two of the first 19 (Tranche 1) companies had been sold. Even by the middle of 1994, only marginal progress hade been registered with the sale programme. Running parallel to the 11 tranche sale process independent negotiations are being conducted for the sale of ZCCM probably to the majority shareholder) and the sale and/or closure of Zambia Airways.[22]

One important aspect of the programme was that the sequencing anticipated a concentration of agricultural and agro-industrial sales in the earlier phases of the programme. This emphasis on the export-orientated sector was accompanied by the planned sale of a number of low capital intensity service sector enterprises. In the light of the foregoing discussion, this sequencing seems correct. Nonetheless, the asset stocks embodied in the SOE sector are, to a large extent, fixed, and the newly created equity market is extremely small and – as witnessed from elsewhere the region – is unlikely to have more than a marginal impact on the tradeability of assets in the short to medium term. Moreover, credit for asset financing and restructuring has not been forthcoming from the private banking sector, while at the same time the government established a clear policy that restructuring should not be carried out prior to sale. The attractiveness of the SOEs was therefore severely curtailed, and it is not surprising that the divestiture programme made slow progress with prospects for accelerating asset sales relying on the partic- ipation of foreign investors. In terms of the arguments advanced in Section 3 this seems to be *prima facie* evidence of low values for Z_p rather than high values for Z_g. Although the initial sales in Tranche 1 have been to domestic purchasers, these are of extremely small enterprises with very low capital intensity (the first two sales were a travel agency and a car valet service). The first medium sized sale (Chilanga Cement company) was to the minority shareholder (a foreign investor), while the sale of the majority government stake in ZCCM, the single most important company in the portfolio, is being negotiated with Anglo-American Mining of South Africa, the current minority (40 per cent) shareholder and former owner of the company.

5. Implications for Privatisation in African Economies

This chapter has outlined some possible reasons why, in addition to traditional concerns about the government's capacity to provide effective competition policy and regulatory functions, the privatisation programmes developed in Sub-Saharan Africa may not yield fruit for some time, and why the analysis by Elliot Berg may provide only a partial explanation of the problems of promoting privatisation in economies in transition. These concerns centre around the questions of asset liquidity, and the limitation of the inherited regulatory capacity limitations in the public sector. In this concluding section I shall summarise the arguments developed in the chapter and shall draw some policy implications.

The starting point is that while it is clear that the processes of economic liberalisation will eventually remove many of the structural constraints to privatisation, the inheritance from the previous period of controls and the macroeconomic transition will reduce the attractiveness of the capital stock embodied in the SOE sector. Since this medium term phase may be quite long, the implication is that far from stimulating privatisation, liberalisation may create a 'hole' in the market for SOEs by depressing the private valuation of the SOE below the government's supply price (even when the latter is low). The low private valuation will be exacerbated by the lack of efficient capital markets, the presence of voluntary rationing in the credit market, risk and uncertainty due to concerns over government policy and regulatory capacity, and by uncertainty concerning the duration of aid flows.

Given these concerns, what is an appropriate policy response to accelerate privatisation? An obvious first response is to seek ways in which to lower the government supply price further or increasing the private valuation such as by providing write-offs, underpricing, or tax-breaks to the purchaser, for example. However, since the government's supply price is derived from the welfare calculus mentioned above where the social value of the asset in private hands is inclusive of such factors, this option is by definition welfare-reducing, in that government is prepared to sell an asset at a price which will more than offset the gains from the change in asset ownership. While this may not present a problem to a government committed to privatisation at all costs, there may be limits on how low the supply price can go, particularly when the potential purchasers of state-owned assets are foreign investors and when there are expectations that privatisation will involve widespread retrenchment. In these circumstances even an explicit supply price of zero may be unacceptable. Moreover, from an efficiency perspective, this option must be handled cautiously, since it can act in an identical manner as aid-financing of SOEs by softening budget constraints faced by potential purchasers of the asset, retarding the adjustment of the capital stock, and raising concerns about future policy reversal. As a general response to slow privatisation, attempts to accelerate sales in this manner are thus undesirable. More importantly from a policy perspective is the need to focus on the causes of the slow progress rather than the symptoms. The principal problems are clearly tradeability and credibility.

First, concerning tradeability it may be feasible to lay greater emphasis (as Berg argues) on the development of leasing and other partial sale mechanisms which allow private sector purchasers to alter the capital stock rapidly in accordance with relative prices, with the public sector continuing to accept the liability of the lessor. An emphasis on 'full divestiture' may therefore not be warranted.

Second, this policy direction should be accompanied by an *ad hoc* programme of divestiture of small enterprises – particularly those where minority shareholders have pre-emptive purchase rights. Here the sale process should be low profile and consume limited resources. A number of countries have experimented with different procedures for the sale of small enterprises and amongst the least resource intensive seems to be the Malaysian 'first-come-first-served' model which placed the resource costs of preparing privatisation transactions on the purchaser rather than the seller.

The third main policy implication is that the inevitable delay produced by the macroeconomic transition should be treated not as a problem in the process of privatisation but as an opportunity to implement effective commercialisation of SOEs prior to eventual privatisation. I have argued above that the poor performance of the SOE sector derives from a combination of environmental factors and weak or inappropriate control and regulation capacity. One of the persistent concerns of proponents of privatisation is that commercialisation is a poor substitute for privatisation since, without the discipline of the market, attempts to generate reforms cannot be long-lasting. This was probably true in the early 1980s when markets were heavily protected, but when commercialisation occurs in markets that are being opened through macroeconomic adjustment and trade and fiscal liberalisation the impact may be expected to be much more significant. Commercialisation in an environment of macroeconomic liberalisation is a more credible policy than when it occurs in a controlled regime. For the broadly non-marketable component of the SOE sector (which may be large) public sector ownership and management is likely to persist for some time. This provides the obvious opportunity for implementing measures to enhance the social value of future asset sales through commercialisation of the enterprises (as discussed by Kessides, 1993, and Berg, this volume).

Fourth, and for the same reasons, the period of delay induced by the macroeconomic transition provides the opportunity to develop a public sector regulatory capacity. One of the lessons of privatisation elsewhere is that by proceeding on the assumption that markets will be self-regulating, issues in regulatory capacity have been overlooked and have been introduced only after asset sales have been finalised and often after anti-competition privileges have been entrenched through the sale process and are therefore difficult to remove (see Vickers and Yarrow, 1988, and Adam, *et al.* 1992). In this sense, there may be clear gains to delay. Moreover, the delay provides governments in transition the opportunity to develop appropriate regulatory mechanism while enterprises remain within the public sector. The advantage of this form of 'experimental' design of regulatory mechanisms is that vulnerability to regulatory capture can be more readily identified and avoided without the required changes to, and refinements of, regulatory rules which may undermine the credibility of government.[23] This entails the transformation of pre-existing rules-based regulatory bodies into ones based around explicit performance contracts. The commercialisation of the regulatory function will therefore run parallel to the commercialisation of enterprises themselves so that by extending autonomy to SOEs and therefore creating conditions that mimic the information flows that will exist in a regulated imperfect market, appropriate incentive contracts can be designed.

Finally, we may note two important externalities of commercialisation for human capital and management. The first is that it provides opportunities for SOE management to begin to create its own 'track record' with the financial sector, thereby reducing the unobservability of managerial quality that generates voluntary credit rationing and creates undesirable links between credit and the break-up value of installed capital. Confronted by a hard budget constraint and a liberalised market, the performance of the SOE then provides the regulator with a better (but not necessarily perfect) observation of managerial capacity and effort, and hence their creditworthiness. The second, related, effect is that to the extent that commercialisation allows markets to function for scarce managerial capital, the process can also reduce the sector-specificity of management.

In the absence of developed asset markets, and given two decades of often severe macroeconomic distortions, slow progress with privatisation is likely to remain a feature of African economies in transition so that although many small-value sales will have occurred even by the end of the century, the SOE sector will still be a dominant player in many African economies. However, the ineffectiveness and frequent reversals of SOE reform measures experienced during the 1980s is much less likely given the comprehensive macroeconomic reforms that are already occurring. The period of adjustment provides governments with an opportunity to develop efficient regulatory mechanisms and a body of competition policy, which will ensure that as and when privatisation occurs it will be welfare enhancing.

Acknowledgements

I wish to thank William Cavendish, with whom I worked on *Adjusting Privatisation*, for extensive discussions on a number of the topics covered in this paper. I also wish to thank David Bevan, Jo Ann Paulson, and three anonymous referees for valuable comments on earlier drafts of this paper.

Notes

1.   For example, whether asset sales by development finance institutions are included, whether management contracting is classified as privatisation etc.
2.   The most dramatic results (measured in terms of enterprises sold) have been seen in the former East Germany and other

Eastern European economies, although rapid progress has also been recorded in Latin America.

3.	In one respect, however, the rhetoric of privatisation has not gone unheeded. Even in the most trenchantly interventionist regimes, the 1980s saw the role of the SOE radically redefined even though no actual asset sales took place. The growth in the sector as measured in terms of the number of enterprises or of employment was completely halted while there was a dramatic reduction in the net claim of the sector on national resources (see Adam and Cavendish, 1991).

4.	The experience of Kenya is a case in point (see Adam, *et al.*, 1992).

5.	Indigenous Malay citizens of Malaysia, as opposed to those of Indian or Chinese origin.

6.	This represents the core of the thesis, although it should be noted that much of what is referred to as 'non-traditional' divestiture by Berg is classed as 'SOE reform' by those writers Berg refers to as being particularly critical of market-orientated reform measures (such as Adam, *et al.*, 1992; Killick and Commander, 1988; Cook and Kirkpatrick, 1988; and Stewart, *et al.*, 1992). Much of this confusion arises from the definitions used. The recommendation of this latter group that resources should be directed more towards greater reform of the SOEs including increased exposure to private sector operations rather than towards privatisation (in the sense of transfer of ownership narrowly defined) is thus no different to the claim by Berg that the emphasis should be redirected from 'full divestiture' towards non-traditional privatisation.

7.	Much of the discussion of the macroeconomics of privatisation draws on the ideas developed in Collier (this volume) and Collier and Gunning (1992).

8.	One well-known example of this is the frequent claims against British Airways by its UK competitors, British Midland and Virgin Atlantic, that competition was 'unfair' because British Airways received significant research and development support from government in the past for the development of Concorde, and enjoyed preferential route allocations under public ownership.

9.	By this we mean the problem of one party (the principal) inducing another party (the agent) to act in accordance with the interests of the principal but in circumstance when the objectives of the two parties differ and where the agent has superior information concerning the conditions in the market. Thus, if we think of the principal as the government and the agent as the management of the SOE, the government cannot easily tell whether poor profitability of the enterprise is due to low managerial efficiency or to poor market conditions. The same problem arises when the principal is a regulator and the agent the private enterprise, where again the latter has superior market knowledge.

10. See Adam and Cavendish 'What Price Privatisation? Government Reputation and Asset Sales' (mimeo 1992) for a discussion of regulatory capture in the Caribbean telecommunications sector.

11. The Restrictive Trade Practices, Monopolies and Price Control Act (Kenya 1989) and the Competition Act (Jamaica 1991).

12. The interpretation of λ_g and λ_p is best described by an example. If the transfer of liquidity from the private to the public sector as a result of the sale of equity allows government to reduce distortionary taxation elsewhere in the economy then the transfer is welfare enhancing and $\lambda_g > 0$.

13. One example of this is the famous case of the Malaysian state railway system which was offered for sale as a going concern in 1986 for M$1.00 (approximately US$0.75). As of 1992, no bids were forthcoming. An example from Africa is the Mulindi Paper Mill in Tanzania which has been advertised for sale internationally, with the assistance of IFC, and again no bids whatsoever have been received.

14. One point that is worth noting here is that theory would suggest that, with free disposal of assets and some salvage value, there should be a price at which the sale occurs. However in the context of privatisation disposal of assets is not free, particularly if the costs of retrenchment of labour are included.

15. For example kick-starting capital markets often requires that equity issues generate high yield and low risk returns. To achieve this through the issue of SOE equity may require heavy underpricing of share or by selling equity in enterprises whose monopoly position is secured. Excessive recourse to

these methods clearly cannot promote mature risk-taking markets.

16. Evidence from Jaramillio *et al.* (1993), which examined credit allocation following financial liberalisation in Ecuador, also finds that credit tended to flow to large established and more capital intensive firms following liberalisation.

17. The origin of potential purchasers has emerged as an important factor in the politics of virtually all privatisation programmes. In some cases (for example Kenya) the issue effectively halted the programme throughout most of the 1980s, while in other countries (Sri Lanka and Malaysia are two examples) the question of ethnicity has heavily compromised the pursuit of efficiency objectives of privatisation (see Adam *et al.*, 1992).

18. The value of an SOE in the hands of the private sector, Z_p, is conditional on the 'terms and conditions' of the sale and the expected policy stance of government. Once the sale has been finalised, government will always have an incentive to alter policy. Hence the policy is time-inconsistent.

19. The use of franchise methods to create competition over monopoly rights is often advanced as a solution to this dearth of information, through which bidders for the franchise reveal market conditions by their competition for the right to operate the monopoly. This may succeed as a first-round strategy, but does not resolve dynamic problems associated with re-negotiation of the franchise where the incumbent firm has advantages in terms of information (see Vickers and Yarrow, 1988).

20. A single example of this problem appeared in Zambia in mid 1993 with respect to maize financing. By the end of 1992 government had removed all control on maize pricing, distribution and financing. However, faced with political concerns about rising real consumer prices for maize, certain ministers attempted to re-impose by fiat controls on farm-gate maize prices. While this attempt did not succeed, it did highlight the problems faced by this type of system.

21. Extensive surveys and discussion can be found in, for example, Nellis (1986), Nellis and Kikeri (1989), Galal (1990), and Mosely, Harrigan and Toye (1991).

22. Zambia Airways was eventually closed in November 1994 and it was anticipated that ZCCM would be privatised by mid-1996.

23. A good example of this is the Swaziland Public Enterprise Monitoring Unit which fills the role of regulator as well as co-ordinating monitoring activities on behalf of the legislature. A key feature of the Unit is the provision of technical assistance to enterprises undergoing commercialisation. Unlike other such units (the Zambia privatisation unit for example), the emphasis is primarily on commercialisation than on privatisation, although the Unit maintains an open, bidder-driven policy on privatisation.

References

Adam, C.S. and W.P. Cavendish (1991) 'Can Privatisation Succeed? Economic Structure and Programme Design in Eight Commonwealth Countries', Queen Elizabeth House Discussion Papers (34), Oxford.

Adam, C.S. and W.P. Cavendish (1992) 'What Price Privatisation? Government Reputation and Asset Sales', mimeo, Queen Elizabeth House, Oxford.

Adam, C.S., W.P. Cavendish and P.S. Mistry (1992) *Adjusting Privatisation: Case Studies from Developing Countries*, London: James Currey.

Aron, J. (1992) 'Political Mismanagement of a Mining Parastatal: the Case of ZCCM', mimeo, Centre for the Study of African Economies, Oxford.

Bank of Zambia (various years) *Main Economic Indicators*, Lusaka: Bank of Zambia.

Bates, R.H. and P. Collier (1993) 'The Politics and Economics of Policy Reform in Zambia', in R.H. Bates and A.O. Krueger (eds) *Political and Economic Reactions to Policy Reform*, Oxford: Blackwell.

Berg, E. (1996) 'Privatisation in Sub-Saharan Africa: Results, Prospects and New Approaches', this volume.

Bevan, D.L., P. Collier, and J.W. Gunning (1991) *Controlled Open Economies: a Neo-Classical Critique of Structuralism*, Oxford: Clarendon Press.

Collier, P. (1996) 'Trade, Price and Financial Reform in the Transition from African Socialism', this volume.

Collier, P. and J.W. Gunning (1992) 'Aid and Exchange Rate Adjustment in African Trade Liberalisations', *Economic Journal*, 102 (413).

Cook, P and C. Kirkpatrick (1988) *Privatisation in Less Developed Countries*, London: Wheatsheaf.

Due, J.M. (1994) 'Liberalisation and Privatisation in Tanzania and Zambia', *World Development*, 21 (12).

Floyd, R.H, C.S. Gray and R.P. Short (1984) *Public Enterprises in Mixed Economies: Some Macroeconomic Aspects*, Washington DC: IMF.

Fye, L (1991) 'Divestiture, Privatisation and Rationalisation in the Gambia', mimeo.

Galal, A. (1990) 'Public Enterprise Reform: a Challenge for the World Bank', Policy Research Paper 400, Washington DC: World Bank.

Grosh, B. (1991) *Public Enterprise in Kenya: What Works, What Doesn't and Why*, Boulder, Co: Lynne Rienner.

Jaramillo, A., F. Schiantarelli, and A. Weiss (1993) 'The Effect of Financial Liberalisation on the Allocation of Credit: Panel Data Evidence from Ecuador', World Bank Policy Paper No. 1123, Washington DC: World Bank.

Jones, L., P. Tandon and I. Vogelsang (1991) *Selling Public Enterprises: a Cost Benefit Methodology*, Cambridge, MA: MIT Press.

Kessides, C. (1993) 'Institutional Arrangements for Provision of Infrastructure: a Framework for Analysis and Decision Making', mimeo, World Bank.

Killick, T. and S. Commander (1988) 'State Divestiture as a Policy Instrument in Developing Countries', *World Development*, 16.

Kikeri, S., J. Nellis, and M. Shirley (1992) *Privatisation: the Lessons of Experience*, Washington DC: World Bank

McBrady, M. (1993) 'Privatisation in Zambia', MSc Dissertation, University of Oxford.

Mosely, P., J. Harrigan, and J. Toye (1991) *Aid and Power: the World Bank and Policy Based Lending*, London: Routledge.

Nellis, J. (1986) 'Public Enterprises in Sub-Saharan Africa', World Bank Discussion Papers 1, Washington DC: World Bank.

Nellis, J. and S. Kikeri (1989) 'Public Enterprise Reform: Privatisation and the World Bank', *World Development*, 16.

Stewart, F., S. Lal, and S. Wangwe (1992) *Alternative Development Strategies in Africa*, London: Macmillan.

World Bank (1984) *Zambia Industrial Policy and Performance*, [4436–ZA], Washington DC: World Bank.

— (1988) 'Techniques of Privatisation of State Owned Enterprises' Technical Paper 88, Washington DC: World Bank.

— (1989) 'Malawi Industrial Sector Memorandum', [402-MAI], Washington DC: World Bank.

— (1993) 'Draft Report for Zambia CG Meeting' unpublished.

Vickers, J.S. and G. Yarrow (1988) *Privatisation: an Economic Analysis* Cambridge, MA: MIT Press.

Zambia Privatisation Agency (1992) 'Progress Report 1992', Lusaka: Zambia Privatisation Agency.

Index

NB Page references to tables are shown in *italic*.